FROM THE AUTHOR

I AM HONORED TO SHARE WITH YOU Lead Them Home's *Guiding Families of LGBT+ Loved Ones*. This resource is designed to **increase family acceptance** and **enhance church inclusion** in order to **nourish faith identity** in LGBT+ hearts. Pastors and church leaders, parents and families, seminarians and college administrators, counselors and social workers, student and campus missionaries, youth and justice workers, and ministries assisting families of LGBT+ individuals — all who care will find *Guiding Families* to be a helpful resource.

This edition includes reflection questions for use in leadership training, adult learning classes, parent groups, and personal reflection.

FOR EVERY PASTOR

Why every pastor? It's simple. We reach many people. You, as pastors, reach countless more! Many of you have experienced Posture Shift, which equips pastoral leaders to effectively care for and share Christ with LGBT+ people. *Guiding Families* incorporates key Posture Shift teaching points to help you encourage parents and families to generously love and care for LGBT+ loved ones.

Our hope is that *Guiding Families* will eliminate the "outsourcing" of care that LGBT+ loved ones and their families often experience. Our resource offers you an easy framework to quickly educate yourself on caring directly for LGBT+ people and wisely walking with their families.

To train your team, visit **postureshift.com** *and request a Posture Shift proposal.*

FOR EVERY PARENT

Whether your loved one just came out or did so years ago, our hope is that *Guiding Families* will equip and encourage you. It starts with what Lead Them Home refers to as a **posture shift.** Against the backdrop of decades of mistreatment of LGBT+ people, we must shift our posture to ensure that our actions, attitudes, and words look more like Jesus.

Many years ago, it often took months of interaction to positively shape how families would respond to LGBT+ loved ones. I wrote *Guiding Families* because teaching the content in this resource allows parents and families to start relating more effectively in just a few hours.

For additional support, contact us at **info@leadthemhome.org**.

FOR ALL WHO CARE

Teaching love and compassion for LGBT+ people can sometimes trigger concerns about biblical compromise. **Nothing in *Guiding Families* will dishonor God's Word. We encourage you to maintain your biblical *position* to honor God and adjust your *posture* to love like God has loved you.** We all fall short of the glory of God. Those who have encountered Jesus have been saved by an *amazing* grace. We did not earn it. We do not deserve it. We have not achieved it. God saved us precisely because we are sinners in need of grace. People saved by grace do not mistreat — or place roadblocks in the paths of — others. We are called to clear roadblocks and authentically reveal Jesus living in us to people where they are.

We pray that *Guiding Families* will help you more generously live out the gospel of Jesus Christ.

Bill Henson
Founder and President
Lead Them Home

DEDICATIONS

To Jesus Christ for dying in my place;

To my parents for modeling unconditional love;

To my wife and children for being the joy of my life;

To our trustees for leading our ministry with excellence;

To Fr. Ray Pendleton for supporting and encouraging me during the toughest times;

To our tireless staff and volunteer editors for laboring long and hard;

To faithful friends for endorsing, reviewing, and contributing inspiring articles;

To each individual interviewed for opening the most vulnerable parts of your life to help others;

To Dr. Paul and Christie Borthwick for modeling a life-long commitment to mobilizing missionaries;

To 11-year-old bullycide victim Carl Joseph Walker-Hoover for awakening my heart to do something;

To Dr. Caitlin Ryan for graciously venturing across the belief gap to educate me on what to do;

To my home church, Grace Chapel, for offering personal care and practical support since my coming to Christ;

To pastors, ministry leaders, and administrators for trusting me to teach Posture Shift;

To countless LGBT+ young people and parents of LGBT+ loved ones for trusting me with your stories;

To our prayer partners, Guiding Families *readers, and donors for encouraging and supporting Lead Them Home.*

POSTURE SHIFT BOOKS

Guiding Families of LGBT+ Loved Ones: Second Edition

© 2006 – 2018 Lead Them Home. All Rights Reserved.

Second Edition, May 2018

Unless otherwise noted, Scripture quotations taken from the Amplified® Bible (AMPC), Copyright © 1954, 1958, 1962, 1964, 1965, 1987 by The Lockman Foundation. Used by permission. www.Lockman.org

Guiding Families of LGBT+ Loved Ones is an individual rights purchase. No distribution is permitted. No copying, scanning or posting online is permitted. Those using *Guiding Families* as a small group study must purchase a copy for each study participant.

100 Powdermill Road, Suite 325 | Acton, MA 01720

info@leadthemhome.org | (978) 212-9630

leadthemhome.org
postureshift.com

CONTENTS

PART 1
UNDERSTANDING LGBT+ LOVED ONES

PART 2
DEVELOPING A CARE PLAN

PART 3
FAQ, BELIEFS, & FAMILY MATTERS

PART 4
BEYOND LESBIAN & GAY

PART 5
PRAYING IN FAITH & TRUSTING GOD

PART 6
GUIDANCE FOR ALL WHO CARE

SPECIAL SECTIONS

PARENTS HELPING PARENTS

REAL LIFE PROFILES

GUEST ARTICLES

KEY TERMS

As we enter into *Guiding Families*, here is a list of key terms that may or may not be familiar to you. This is not an exhaustive list of all the terms we encounter in engaging LGBT+ people, but it will help us begin the conversation. You may be uncomfortable with or have concerns about some terms, and that is okay. As a missionary organization, we strive to use honoring language in extending Christ to LGBT+ people.

ACCEPTANCE

An honest and full acknowledgement of the reality of a situation; a love toward someone as they are, not as one would like them to be. Acceptance does not inherently mean approval of a situation or of other people's dealings with that situation. Acceptance also does not mean feeling good about a situation. It is a state in which each person (loved ones and self) can move forward owning their respective roles and responsibilities in a situation — no more, no less.

BAIT AND SWITCH

Occurs when intentions, beliefs, or attitudes are initially misrepresented and later found to be different than expected. An example would be expressing a love for LGBT+ people, only to later disclose a significant aspect of belief that was not clearly communicated earlier. A bait and switch can leave someone feeling hurt, betrayed, or lied to. While the purpose of a bait and switch tends to be avoiding difficult confrontation, it can ironically end up being more hurtful than an honest disclosure.

COMING OUT

When a person shares with other people their sexual orientation and/or gender identity, as well as the process that individual goes through to discover and understand their sexual orientation and/or gender identity. Originated from the phrase "coming out of the closet." Coming out does not necessarily mean "living it out" — a person may share about their experience without an intent to date the same gender or transition their gender. Conversely, a person may come out while they are already in a relationship or in the process of a gender transition. When someone's sexual/gender identity is announced by someone else without consent, it is called being **outed.**

HOMOPHOBIA/TRANSPHOBIA

A fear of LGBT+ people that triggers unthoughtful or even hateful ideas about their personhood, intentions, faith, conduct, and character. These attitudes often arise from not knowing LGBT+ people personally. They are typically based on inaccurate ideas leaning heavily on cultural stereotypes rather than on facts.

TRAUMA

A psychological shift resulting from a distressing event or series of events. Trauma may result from a one-time occurence, such as a death of a loved one. Trauma may also result from (often seemingly "smaller") distressing events occurring repeatedly over a long period of time, such as repeated physical or verbal harm at home or at school. The latter form is often called **complex trauma, developmental trauma, historic trauma, traumatic stress, toxic stress,** or **"little t" trauma.**[1]

LESBIAN

Adj./N.

(A woman who is) attracted exclusively or most significantly to other women.

"She is lesbian." "She is a lesbian woman."

GAY

Adj.

Attracted exclusively or most significantly to the same gender. Historically used only for males, but increasingly used also for females.

"He is gay." "He is a gay man."

BISEXUAL

Adj.

Attracted to more than one gender, but not necessarily at the same time, in the same way, or to the same degree.

"She is bisexual."

TRANSGENDER

Adj.

(Or **Trans**) Describes a person whose internal sense of gender identity does not correspond with their birth sex.[2]

"He is transgender."

[1]Paynter ML. (2017). *Exploring a School Culture and Climate Where Students Can Flourish: Using Focus Group Methodology to Capture Key Stakeholder Perceptions About School Culture and Climate in an Alternative Education High School.* San Jose State University, ProQuest Dissertations Publishing, 10635374.

[2]Yarhouse MA. (2015). *Understanding Gender Dyshporia: Navigating Transgender Issues in a Changing Culture.* InterVarsity Press.

QUEER/NONSTRAIGHT

Adj.

Umbrella term referring to individuals who are not **straight** (exclusively attracted to the opposite gender) and/or who experience a level of discomfort with their birth gender. Queer is a formerly derogatory term that has been presently reclaimed as an empowering identifier.

"He identifies as queer."

QUESTIONING

Adj.

Unsure of the exact nature of one's own gender identity and/or sexual identity, and thus unable to confidently identify by a particular sexuality/gender label in the present.

"She is questioning her sexuality."

INTERSEX

Adj.

Having been born with sex characteristics (ex: genitals, gonads, chromosomes, endocrinology) that do not correspond with the typical notions of male or female bodies.

"My child is intersex."

ASEXUAL

Adj.

Experiencing minimal to no sexual attraction to other individuals. Asexual people can experience a range of romantic inclination, from none (**aromantic**) to some (**gray-romantic**) to full (**romantic**).

"He is asexual, but not aromantic, so he still enjoys going on dates."

ALLY

N.

A person who is not LGBT+ but who affirms progressive LGBT+ social, political, and/or theological causes.

"His best friend is an LGBT+ ally."

PANSEXUAL

Adj.

Attraction to people not limited by the people's biological sex, gender, or identity. Whereas "bisexual" tends to denote two gender categories ("bi" = "two"), someone who is pansexual may not view gender as limited to two categories ("pan" = "all").

"She identifies as pansexual."

GENDERQUEER

Adj.

Not conforming to or identifying with typical notions of masculine or feminine appearance, roles, traits, or identity. Synonymous with **gender nonbinary, genderfluid, gender non-conforming, pangender, androgynous, or androgyne.**

"They are gender nonbinary, or 'NB' for short."

GENDER DYSPHORIA

N.

The experience of distress associated with the incongruence wherein one's psychological and emotional gender identity does not match one's biological sex.[2] A person with no or low gender dysphoria is said to have **gender coherence** or **gender congruence.**

"She experiences gender dysphoria."

TRANSITION

N./V.

A process of bringing one's gender presentation and/or sex characteristics into accord with one's internal sense of gender identity.

"My son has announced plans to transition."

HOMOSEXUAL

Adj./N.

A person who is attracted to the same sex/gender. Generally considered an outdated or offensive term to LGBT+ individuals.

SAME-SEX ATTRACTION (SSA)

N.

(Or **same-gender attraction**) This term is common for those who consider attractions toward the same gender to be a sin struggle, yet it is offensive to many LGBT+ people because it has "behavior" connotations and diminishes the "identity" aspects of sexual orientation. (Many LGBT+ people prefer the term **same-gender loving.**)

"He experiences same-gender attraction."

STRAIGHT/HETEROSEXUAL

Adj.

Attracted exclusively or most significantly to the opposite sex/gender.

"She is heterosexual."

CISGENDER

Adj.

(Or **Cis**, pronounced "/sis/") Describes a person whose internal sense of gender identity corresponds with their birth sex. (The prefix "trans" means "across" while the prefix "cis" means "on the same side of.")

"Being cisgender, I don't face the challenge of having to question my gender."

WELCOME
LGBT+ READERS

I WROTE *GUIDING FAMILIES* TO MAKE FAMILIES AND CHURCHES SAFER FOR LGBT+ PEOPLE. Whether you are a teen, a young single, a married couple, or in your retirement years, our ministry strongly believes that you deserve a loving family and a safe church home in which to worship God.

There is a risk that you may feel like *Guiding Families* is labeling you as a "them." To the contrary: you are "us" — our children, siblings, parents, grandparents, close relatives, friends, neighbors, and coworkers.

For decades, many (but not all) LGBT+ people have been treated as:

- an issue to ignore
- a problem to solve
- a threat to fight
- a danger to exclude
- a person to preach at
- an embarrassment to hide

- a schoolmate to bully
- an oddity to mock
- a son to shame
- a daughter to disown
- a brother to abandon
- a sister to reject

Treating LGBT+ people (or anyone else) in such denigrating ways neither honors one's humanity nor reflects God's love. In Galatians 5:22-23, the Apostle Paul powerfully writes:

> "But the fruit of the Spirit [the result of His presence within us] is love [unselfish concern for others], joy, [inner] peace, patience [not the ability to wait, but how we act while waiting], kindness, goodness, faithfulness, gentleness, self-control. Against such things there is no law."

You are a beloved child of God. You deserve a family that unconditionally loves you and welcomes you home (yes, with your partner). Love can and must transcend religious belief differences. True love is beautifully captured in 1 Corinthians 13:4-8,13. It reads:

> *"Love endures with patience and serenity, love is kind and thoughtful, and is not jealous or envious; love does not brag and is not proud or arrogant. It is not rude; it is not self-seeking, it is not provoked [nor overly sensitive and easily angered]; it does not take into account a wrong endured. It does not rejoice at injustice, but rejoices with the truth [when right and truth prevail]. Love bears all things [regardless of what comes], believes all things [looking for the best in each one], hopes all things [remaining steadfast during difficult times], endures all things [without weakening]. Love never fails [it never fades nor ends].*
>
> *And now there remain: faith [abiding trust in God and His promises], hope [confident expectation of eternal salvation], love [unselfish love for others growing out of God's love for me], these three [the choicest graces]; but the greatest of these is love."*

With no agenda — only as a matter of honest disclosure — our ministry holds to a traditional biblical belief regarding marriage and sexuality. However, *Guiding Families* does not shove theology at LGBT+ people. Its purpose is increasing family acceptance and enhancing church inclusion.

It is unlikely that your parents will change your beliefs. It is equally unlikely that you will change theirs. When parents (or their children) let differences divide, relationships are fractured. For this reason, your parents may need as much acceptance from you as you need from them. It is my prayer that *Guiding Families* will prevent fractured family relationships — and heal relational trust where it has been lost.

Love should never be defined by differences, but rather by every action, attitude, and word. In prayer and faith, I believe we can **eliminate family rejection** of LGBT+ loved ones **in this generation**. Amidst any differences in belief, let's work toward this goal together.

Finally, I do not presume to tell your story. I understand that not every LGBT+ person experiences bullying or family rejection. Many do, though, which is why our ministry focuses so intently on working with families and churches to prevent mistreatment of LGBT+ people.

I hope *Guiding Families* honors LGBT+ family and friends. I invite you to contact me if you have any concerns or helpful insights. Thank you for reading *Guiding Families.*

Bill Henson

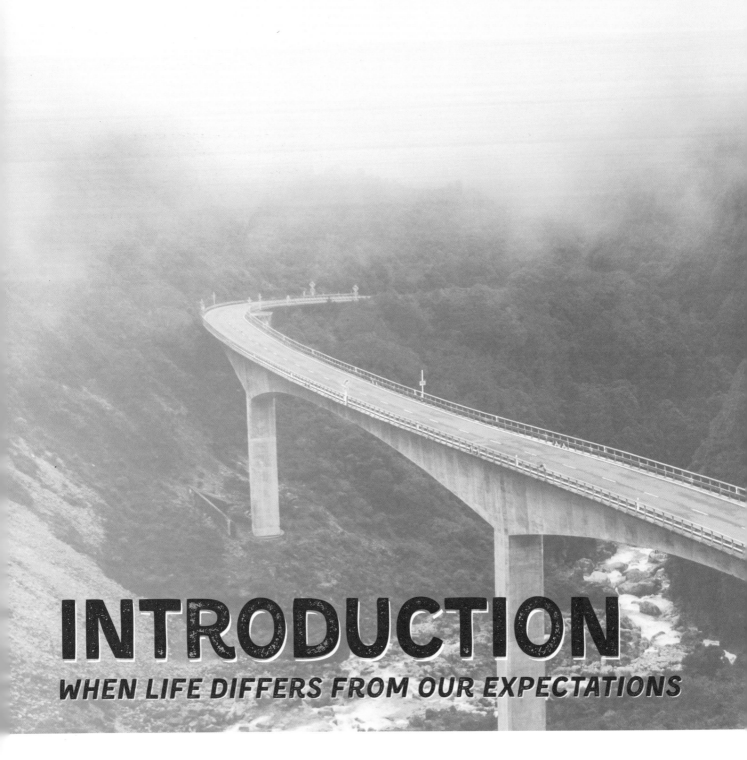

INTRODUCTION
WHEN LIFE DIFFERS FROM OUR EXPECTATIONS

WATCHING OUR CHILDREN GROW from babies into toddlers and from adolescents into young adults is one of the greatest privileges and miracles that a parent can experience in life. By the time our kids reach adulthood, they will have made us cry tears of joy and filled our lives with much laughter and love.

Finding out unexpected things about our children begins early on in parenthood. Some things that we discover involve their propensity to sin. We may be shocked to find out that our son lied to hide a bad test result. Or maybe he stole something from his friend or the neighbor. Possibly we overhear our daughter using language with her middle school friends that betrays the person we know her to be.

No doubt, our children are sinners. Just like us. They need God's grace. Just like us.

Other unexpected discoveries involve developmental gifts or vulnerabilities: We may discover that our daughter is particularly brilliant, artistic, or athletic. Or that our son struggles with learning. Maybe our child struggles to maintain attention. Or maybe they lack the initiative or drive it will take to succeed.

Some of our children's weaknesses are related to character flaws, but many of their failures and mistakes arise from vulnerabilities they face. More broadly, every child is growing up in this world for the first time and trying to figure out how life works.

These realities apply to every human being. As parents, these realities apply to all of our children.

When the unexpected discovery involves our child's sexual orientation and/or gender identity, we can suddenly feel very alone. Maybe shocked. Possibly fearful. For some, shameful. For many, big questions arise: *Why did this happen? How did this happen?* Lurking under these questions is often a deeper question that we may not want to face: *Did I cause this?*

Is this my fault?

As parents, this question can hit us hard. Our minds may be flooded with memories of our worst mistakes. Maybe I am a mother who became exhausted and neglected my child. Possibly I am a father who worked too many hours. We may remember yelling at or exasperating our children with overly high expectations. Our thoughts may go something like this:

Impatience. It's every parent's struggle, right? Oh, how many times I was impatient and demanding! Did my lack of gentleness cause my child to be gay? Did our divorce cause my daughter to be transgender?

While it is tempting to focus on causation, I want to resolve this question up front: **the origins of sexual orientation and gender identity are highly complex, multi-factorial, and likely rooted in both nature and nurture.** For any one person, it can be impossible to

know the exact cause. For this reason, I propose that we shift our focus from *causation* to *compassion*. Your LGBT+ loved one, regardless of their age, needs your faithful presence, understanding, and compassion in their life.

"I PROPOSE THAT WE SHIFT OUR FOCUS FROM CAUSATION TO COMPASSION."

You deserve the same compassion. In that spirit, *Guiding Families* is designed to help you increase understanding and build trustworthy relationships with LGBT+ loved ones. To accomplish this, we address common mistakes that many parents make. This is not about shaming or blaming you. It is our heartfelt intention to help you.

Our resource will not "fix" sexuality or gender identity, but it *will* equip you to lay down your life for your LGBT+ loved one.

As you move through our resource, you may discover ways that you've damaged relational trust with your loved one. Please remember: even loving parents make many mistakes. *Guiding Families* offers action steps you can take to begin the process of repairing trust and healing relational wounds.

I pray that you find this resource to be comforting. May God give you hope that He will bless your family.

"REMEMBER [FERVENTLY] THE WORD AND PROMISE TO YOUR SERVANT, IN WHICH YOU HAVE CAUSED ME TO HOPE. THIS IS MY COMFORT AND CONSOLATION IN MY AFFLICTION: THAT YOUR WORD HAS REVIVED ME AND GIVEN ME LIFE."

– PSALM 119:49-50

"AND JESUS WENT ABOUT ALL THE CITIES AND VILLAGES, TEACHING IN THEIR SYNAGOGUES AND PROCLAIMING THE GOOD NEWS (THE GOSPEL) OF THE KINGDOM AND CURING ALL KINDS OF DISEASE AND EVERY WEAKNESS AND INFIRMITY.

WHEN HE SAW THE THRONGS, HE WAS MOVED WITH PITY AND SYMPATHY FOR THEM, BECAUSE THEY WERE BEWILDERED (HARASSED AND DISTRESSED AND DEJECTED AND HELPLESS), LIKE SHEEP WITHOUT A SHEPHERD.

THEN HE SAID TO HIS DISCIPLES, 'THE HARVEST IS INDEED PLENTIFUL, BUT THE LABORERS ARE FEW.

'SO PRAY TO THE LORD OF THE HARVEST TO FORCE OUT AND THRUST LABORERS INTO HIS HARVEST.'"

– MATTHEW 9:35-38

PART 1:

UNDERSTANDING LGBT+ LOVED ONES

THE COURAGE IT TAKES
FOR A LOVED ONE TO COME OUT

THE DAY YOUR CHILD COMES OUT is one of the most critical days of their life. On the following pages, you will learn just how scary this moment can be for young people. Imagine knowing that your parents are loving yet worrying that one disclosure could mean that you are rejected — or even disowned.

As a parent, it might seem unthinkable that your beloved child could possibly fear you — or wrestle with anxious thoughts of being rejected.

Yet many *do* fear family rejection and disownment, which still occur today. Additionally, prior traumas (such as bullying) may be fueling some of your child's fears of being rejected.

For this reason, we must start with the premise that coming out may be the most risky and vulnerable moment of their life. What they are sharing with you often has been processing inside them for a long time, possibly for years. For them to share with you reflects deep courage, which can be described as "trusting in the midst of fear."

Your response is so critical. It will determine the difference between safety or fear, peace or anxiety, secure love or sense of rejection.

Similar to how young people can fear their parents' response, some parents fear, *What will happen when our pastors and others in our church find out?* Sadly, this fear can disable a parent's natural inclination to radically love and demonstrate acceptance.

We begin *Guiding Families* by addressing this fear. We train thousands of pastors across all geographical regions, from metro cities and college towns to rural communities. Every single pastor we have encountered shares the same love for your family that you have for your child.

In light of these things, we join your pastors in supporting you as you walk in love with your LGBT+ children. Your natural inclination to accept and love your child is God-given. At times, you might be tempted to withdraw in disappointment or grief, but it is a critical time to gently engage and assure your child of your love.

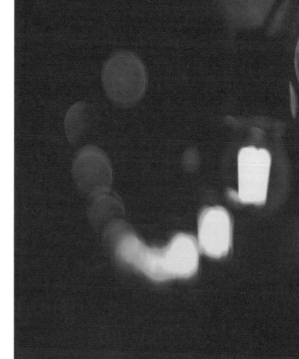

We asked pastors and church leaders what they would say to the parents of an LGBT+ child. Here is how they responded.

PASTORS ARE SHEPHERDS. We walk with people. We don't choose the path or destination; we simply are there for the journey. Yes, pastors preach, but pastoring is really about proximity. A good pastor's heart is to be near God's people to be dual advocates.

We pound heaven when one of our flock is distraught. We embrace the downtrodden and remind them, 'You are never alone.' In fact, our greatest fear is that anyone in our church would ever walk alone.

We aren't here to fix, criticize, or cast out. We are right here standing next to you to listen, understand, and contend for Heaven's grace.

It's a tragedy to attend a church and not be pastored. Please, please, please don't rob us of the privilege to walk beside you. It's why we're here.

— Roger Valci, Lead Pastor of Valley Christian Center (San Francisco Bay Area)

WHEN YOUR TEEN COMES OUT AS LGBTQ, the whole family goes through a vulnerable time. Your teen may exhibit a tremendous euphoria from finally deciding to speak up, yet the next day wrestle with feelings of depression and the fear of being rejected. Parents fear saying the wrong thing, judgment from others, and may sense a rush to abandon long-held beliefs. So you need to know that your pastors are here to listen, to pray with you, and to point you toward healthy responses. Today we need church leaders who are equipped to enter into the messy process of grace that triumphs over judgment.

We will stand with you and storm the heavens alongside you. And we will work to provide a safe place for your teen to belong and to experience the love of God in action.

— Paul Atwater, Senior Pastor of North River Community Church (Greater Boston)

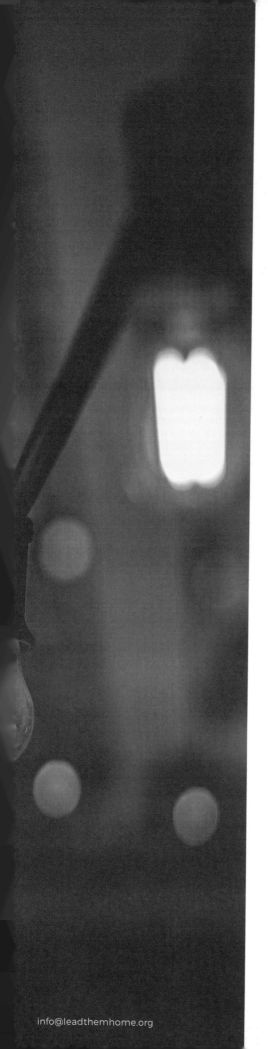

"

AS THE CHRISTIAN PARENT OF AN LGBT+ TEEN, you may feel a great deal of isolation, shame, and fear. Isolation may stem from real rejection from other Christians in whom you've confided. Shame may arise from questioning your own role in your child's gender identity or sexual identity. You may fear your own past actions, your present challenges, or your family's future. Despite a sense of isolation, you're not alone.

Discovering that your teen is LGBT+ can present itself as a daunting challenge. At the same time, before you is an enormous opportunity to minister the compassion of Christ.

Be assured that a posture of **unqualified love** toward your LGBT+ child is not only *compatible* with a traditional sexual ethic, but it is actually *required* by the gospel itself.

If, on this journey, you can trust God with your child even more deeply, He will show you how it is possible to effectively communicate **unconditional love** to your LGBT+ child without compromising your personal convictions about sexual morality.

— Dr. Nate Collins, Ph.D in New Testament at Southern Baptist Theological Seminary and author of *All But Invisible* (Louisville)

"

"

MANY PEOPLE PROBABLY THINK that if they have a solid, ortho-dox priest, he won't be compassionate enough to minister to a parishioner who is sexually atypical. And while every priest is dif-ferent, and some require more help than others, I think priests are much less naïve and much more loving on these issues than you might assume.

I am one of many priests who supports Church teaching and also realizes that people who are dealing with sexual or gender issues are precious and delicate people who deserve our utmost care.

I would like to humbly apologize on behalf of any of my brothers who may have treated you or a loved one in a way that falls short of Christ.

— Fr. Joseph Van House, Catholic Priest (Dallas)

"

GROWING UP LGBT+

THE WEIGHT TEENS CARRY

TEENS DO NOT DECIDE TO COME OUT ON A WHIM. They have likely been trying to sort out their identity for many years. They often experience isolation and depression as they seek answers with little social support.

It is critical to avoid stereotypes that misrepresent others' experiences and result in the patronizing of people. Put another way, it is disrespectful to presume that we know another person's story. Just because someone identifies at LGBT+ does not necessarily mean that they have been bullied or mistreated.

While stereotypes are dangerous, statistics do not lie. Victimization of LGBT+ young people occurs at a much higher rate than that of heterosexual peers. For this reason, it is critical that we understand what it can be like to grow up LGBT+.

LGBT+ young people routinely report feeling "different" at an early age. This internal difference may or may not be visible to their peers. If it is visible, peers may begin to exclude such a child. Even if it is not visible, LGBT+ youth feel discomfort inside and may withhold themselves from interacting with peers.

During elementary school years, this withdrawal can amplify perceptions of difference, leading to name-calling, overt attempts to exclude, and assigning labels to areas of differences. Sadly, this exclusion gets infused into the social lives of many LGBT+ young people. As middle school years approach, there is a greater risk of bullying.

When LGBT+ teens come out to themselves, they often wrestle not only with their past pain but also their future fears. They may fear their parents. They may fear their pastors. These fears can lead many young people to isolate, repress, and attempt to "pray the gay away."

The weight that many LGBT+ teens carry is too heavy. And we cannot lighten their burden if we are unaware of what they have been through. In a young life, feeling intrinsically different from peers over a long period of time can be a trauma. Being routinely *treated* differently — possibly even being repeatedly threatened or harmed — is an additional trauma.

Fearing parents' reaction to sexual or gender identity adds yet another layer of trauma. These past, present, and future traumas shape brain chemistry to continually anticipate condemnation, threat, or harm.

The cumulative impact of the above traumas can yield growing isolation, lower self-worth, and, for some, trouble in academic performance.

Understanding one's own sexual orientation or gender identity can be a confusing and frustrating process that takes time. **This is a very real experience: you cannot demand that these feelings go away — or deny the reality of what your child experiences.**

THE WEIGHT THAT MANY LGBT+ TEENS CARRY IS TOO HEAVY. WE CANNOT LIGHTEN THEIR BURDEN IF WE ARE UNAWARE OF WHAT THEY HAVE BEEN THROUGH.

4

10 COME OUT?

9 MAY HAVE ATTEMPTED OR CONSIDERED **SUICIDE**

8 TEND TO "REPRESS" TO A POINT OF **EXHAUSTION***

7 ANTICIPATE **JUDGMENT** AT CHURCH

6 HIGHER **ISOLATION**, DEPRESSION, AND POST-TRAUMA STRESS

5 WONDER IF GOD HAS **DISOWNED** THEM

4 FEAR FAMILY **REJECTION**

SELF-REALIZATION: "I AM GAY"

3 HIGHER **VICTIMIZATION** (BULLYING, TEASING)

2 DIFFICULT **PEER** INTEGRATION (ESPECIALLY SAME-GENDER)

1 FEEL "DIFFERENT" AT AN EARLY AGE

*Repression is the mental and emotional energy expended in an attempt to subdue or shut down unwanted feelings through self-effort. This process commonly leads to mental exhaustion, or even a psychological break-down. This can lower hope, increase feelings of self-contempt, and increase suicidality.

INITIAL REACTIONS

 EAD THEM HOME CONDUCTED ITS **Survey of Parent Engagement of LGBT+ Children (October 2017)** soliciting online survey responses from our email contact list. Over 110 parents across North America provided detailed anonymous insights into relational mistakes and successes they have experienced with their LGBT+ children. They further shared how relational damage was repaired and how God has been faithful to bless their families. Every "Parents Helping Parents" section features qualitative insights from this survey.

In this section, parents share about their initial reactions when their child came out.

WORDS TO DESCRIBE EMOTIONS

Love	In Disbelief	Relief
Disappointed	Shaken	Breathless
Grieved	Sad	Embarrassed
Fearful	Sorrowful	Frustrated
Loss of Dream	Calm	Brokenhearted
Shocked	Devastated	Heavy
Despairing	Stunned	In Denial
Hopeless	Shame	Loss
Depression	Not Surprised	Curious
Guilt	Bewildered	Compassion
Uncertain	Confused	Worry
Surprised	Distressed	Panic
Concerned	Hurt	Empathetic
Angry	Upset	Overwhelmed

I was shocked and disappointed. I felt that everything I had taught him and believed in was not real any longer. My world crumbled.

I was surprised that she would tell me over the phone. I was hurt she had told others before me.

It was hard to hear, I thought she was standing strong in her faith. She was going to college and was involved in a campus ministry. I started trying to reason it out and went over the past to figure out why she might be feeling this way.

Our son dated several girls through high school, and one he planned to marry after they graduated college. In his junior year of college, he broke up with her. Several months later, he called me on the telephone, and when I answered, he burst out (while crying): "I'm gay, Mom!" My answer to him was, "It's alright. I love you. That will never change." He was afraid to tell my husband, but I encouraged him to do just that. The next night, we had dinner together, and he told my husband. My husband told him he loved him as well. Behind closed doors, my husband and I didn't know how to fully handle all of this because of our Christian beliefs. But one thing we did know was that we loved our son and didn't want this to separate us.

My family, friends, church, and community turned their backs on me when I came out over 25 years ago. Five years ago, God softened my heart to the truth of the gospel, and I am now a new creature. Recently, loved ones have come out to my wife and me. We immediately assured them of our love. Privately, I struggle with knowing what my relationships should look like with these loved ones. I want to continue living Christ in front of them without pushing them out of our lives.

I was shocked and fearful. He wrote us a letter and wasn't home when we read it. I was worried he'd run away. We texted him, and he was at a friend's house and came home. That was the beginning of a journey to understand our son.

Internally, we felt shock and disbelief. Externally, we demonstrated acceptance and love.

THE DANGER OF
FAMILY ⟶ REJECTION

DIANE SHARES HOW GOD'S GRACE — AND A CHANGE OF HEART IN HER FAMILY — BROUGHT HER ACCEPTANCE AND RESTORATION IN CHRIST.

MY FIRST SAME-SEX RELATIONSHIP was with my best friend during my freshman year at a Christian college. When we were discovered, she was moved out of the dorm in the middle of the semester. We each were required to attend weekly counseling sessions with a psychology professor and the dean of students.

I felt humiliated. And when the semester ended, I went back home in shame. I don't know what ever happened to my friend.

For the next 30-plus years, I had tumultuous, short-lived relationships, mostly with women. Twice, I married men in an attempt to please my mother — and, of course, God.

> **TWICE, I MARRIED MEN IN AN ATTEMPT TO PLEASE MY MOTHER — AND, OF COURSE, GOD.**

During my second marriage, I was at my wit's end, full of anger, and seriously contemplating suicide. It was when I was in this dark, low place that I began to see God.

I had believed the lie that He had left me. But in truth, He was there the whole time, teaching me to lean on Him. Rather than shame me for being drawn to women, He quickly let me know that I was not condemned (Romans 8:1). I began to understand real grace and experience my relationship with God on an intimate level that I had never known before. No matter what I had done or would ever do, He loved and accepted me. When I felt alone, I knew I must go — no, run — to the throne of grace (Hebrews 4:16). He taught me about His unending love, mercy, and grace during all those years.

For a long time after my second marriage ended, there was an emptiness in my soul that I sought to fill with other female relationships. Eventually, I found a woman with whom I would spend many years of my life.

My parents' rule was that if I was in a gay relationship, I was never allowed to come home and be part of the family. This ultimate rejection only served to push me further into the gay community to try to find another place to belong.

Years went by, and my father passed away. My mother eventually became engaged to another man. Two years before their marriage, he told her, "You are missing out on your daughter's life. You need to accept this woman."

After 11 years of being with my partner — and out of contact with my mother — she decided to invite both of us to their wedding. When my mother met my partner for the first time, she hugged her.

When God led my mother to accept me unconditionally and embrace my partner as her own daughter, He completely restored our relationship. My spirit was restored in a way that I never thought it could be. God was so gracious to bring my mother and me back into relationship — with no pretense or strings attached. I knew without a doubt that she loved me completely and without condition.

> **GOD WAS SO GRACIOUS TO BRING MY MOTHER AND ME BACK INTO RELATIONSHIP — WITH NO PRETENSE OR STRINGS ATTACHED.**

After four years of restored relationship with my mother, my 17-year relationship with my partner ended. Given my deep relationship with Jesus, I could now accept how God wanted me to live my life. The God of miracles filled the emptiness of my heart once and for all. God has loved me unconditionally, and it is my strongest conviction that His kindness is what brought me to repentance (Romans 2:4).

Today, at 63 years of age, I am enjoying my life — me and Jesus. And my mother? Well, I love her with all my heart, and she is now my dearest friend.

SIX DEVELOPMENTAL STAGES
HOW TEENS COME OUT

REPRESS

Discovering same-gender attraction or gender dysphoria can be a shock to youth. For many, this reality may not match their family's biblical beliefs. They want to be a "good Christian" or meet parent expectations, so they try to deny their experience or "pray the gay away." If they have not experienced spiritual surrender, or if they are under high parent expectations, a young person may fall into repression using their own strength.

Youth do not always understand how critical adult support is. Some do, but they fear rejection or judgment. Many withdraw, isolate, and hide. Some want to hide physically for fear that people will guess that they are gay. Others hide emotionally so that their secret is not at risk.

HIDE

IDENTIFY

After some time of denial, repression, hiding, and attempts to "pray the gay away," many teens reach a place of accepting their attractions or internal sense of gender. They begin to internally think in terms of *identity* rather than *inclination*. This internal identification can occur while a young person is still repressed and isolated. It should not be a shock that teens consider sexuality and gender to be core elements of personal identity. *Everyone* tends to experience "whom I love" and "who I am" as core elements of our human identity.

Even teens who identify as LGBT+ may not be outwardly "open" about their sexuality or gender expression. It is common for teens to say to themselves, "I know that I am gay" yet carry on in isolation, repression, and fear. Any teen who lets all of this stress build up for too long without adult support runs the risk of escalating depression and suicidal ideation. Mental, emotional, and spiritual exhaustion can overtake a teenager when anxiety and distress from past pain and future fears accumulate for too long.

SHUT DOWN

COME OUT

It is critical for teens to be able to share without fear. Some who cannot imagine a path forward attempt to avoid anyone ever knowing by *checking out* (trying to take their life). Others who believe that their life is precious take a risk in sharing their sexuality or gender identity with another person by *coming out*. (Remember: just because a loved one "comes out" does not necessarily mean that they are currently "living it out" or even that they intend to "live it out.")

When teens come out, it is an opportunity to seek recovery from isolation, bullying, or self-hatred. Hurt can turn into anger if people around them do not accept their identity. It is very important for parents and pastors to offer unconditional love and acceptance during this time.

FIGHT

SAVE A LIFE! BE A SAFE PERSON WHEN A TEEN COMES OUT.

8

WILL (24) — REPRESS

"I was so afraid of disappointing my parents. I also feared my friends finding out. I was never bullied; I was just a guy who loved to play basketball. And while I always felt different from other guys, I had a strong father who was present in my life. I grew up fully engaged in a guys' world, loving adventure and sports. Yet I still felt so isolated because that 'one small thing' that no one could ever know about me kept weighing me down. **I repressed for 12 years. It nearly killed me.**"

HIDE — JESSICA (14)

"I haven't shared with my parents because I'm worried that they won't believe me, respect me, or accept me. **My parents are loving and safe, but it will cause me great anxiety if they find out.** They keep saying that being gay is something that people can change. This worries me because I'm not sure if they'll be kind and accepting or have an opposite response of doubt and anger."

CRYSTAL (22) — IDENTIFY

"When I was 12 years old, I remember telling my adoptive mother that I was born in the wrong body. **Even though I was born a boy, I knew in my mind that I was a girl.** It was at this point that she became even meaner to me. She would hit me, bend my thumb backwards, and yell at me for painting my nails or dressing as a girl."

SHUT DOWN — RILEY (25)

"I was 22 and still hadn't told my parents. I could no longer control my emotions. It was a very isolated, lonely place. It was so bad that I actually wrote a suicidal letter. In the letter, I said I love my parents and told them I experience same-gender attraction. I had also just found out my brother and sister-in-law were going to have a kid, so I wrote my brother to have him tell my future nephew or niece that I love them. After 10 years of repression, isolation had destroyed all my hope. **Having that secret all by yourself can be a very exhausting thing. You can only stuff your feelings down for so long.**"

JOHN (16) — COME OUT

"My parents don't know. **I don't want to hide my life, and I don't want to feel like I'm lying or living a double life.** I don't know how much longer it will be before I tell them. A part of me feels like it could happen within the next year. Another part of me feels like I'll never find the right time, like the years will just keep passing by. Another part of me wants to believe that they *never* need to know — but I know deep down that they do."

FIGHT — RACHEL (26)

"I am tired of constantly living on Mount Everest. You know what that's like? You die if you stop moving, it's impossible to go backwards, and you may die even if you *do* keep going — but it's your only chance. I'm tired of judgment and self-hatred. I am not going back into a horrible closet. **This is who I am. I deserve what every human longs for: to give love to and receive love from a life partner.**"

IN OVER MY HEAD

AMIDST EXPECTATIONS TO BECOME THE MAN EVERYONE ELSE WANTED HIM TO BE, LIAM (20) SHARES HOW GOD LED HIM TOWARD ACCEPTANCE AND HOLINESS AS THE UNIQUE MAN OF GOD THAT HE IS.

GROWING UP, I WAS THE HOMESCHOOL NERD WHO hung out with my sisters' friends. At times, I tried to socialize with boys, but once they discovered what I was like (can't throw a ball — and don't want to), they stopped inviting me to join them. I grew isolated and remember thinking, *Why do I have to do what they like? Why can't they do what I like for once?*

In middle school, I went on my first retreat, which was also the first time I heard the word "gay." When I got home, I asked my parents about it. Their response: "We don't talk about that."

Unsatisfied with their answer, my middle school curiosity drove me to Google. Its answers were, well, far more descriptive. And in this way, my young mind was inundated with gay pornography.

The physical closeness I saw didn't scare me away, but I remained confused about why the boys called me "gay" with such a disgusted tone. I knew then that I was undoubtedly attracted to guys and guys alone.

This reality clearly went against my Christian faith and family. From the way they talked about it, I concluded that the church hated people like me. This scared me, so I hid. I became isolated and depressed, and I spent many years trying to "pray the gay away."

Meanwhile, my youth pastor taught that gay people had chosen an evil lifestyle. He said that they could become heterosexual if they were willing. He added that if they had not yet "changed," they were not repentant enough. Despite my youth pastor's subtle prods of "If you ever have any struggles, just talk to me," there was absolutely no way anyone would hear from my own lips that I was gay, lest I be rebuked and "straightened out" before the entire church.

I eventually got involved with a military auxiliary with the dream of being stationed in West Point, NY. This finally gave me a means to relate to other guys, and I thought it would be my perfect cover-up. No one would ever have to know.

Having my first crush at 17, though, didn't help matters. I didn't tell him — or anyone. By this time, I was 5 years into repression, isolation, depression, and suicidal ideation. My friend's father read into my situation and began spreading rumors about my "sexual dirtiness," going as far as telling my parents directly, "Get your son under control."

The rumor took off like wildfire through my homeschool cooperative, youth group, and military auxiliary. All of my friends, including my crush, eventually just cut me out of their lives due to pressure from their parents. My parents eventually came to me about what was happening, inquiring the seemingly innocent, "Is … any of this true?"

In terror, I refused to offer the truth. My parents wanted to comfort, protect, and encourage me through whatever was going on — but I was sure all of that would drastically change if they knew the truth. So instead, I offered myself an out.

I queued up a mental checklist: a bridge, a patch of trees, a rainy night, an "accidental" skidding off the road. It was the perfect cover. I was suicidal and had a plan.

One night, it was raining, and with the key in the ignition, I knew it would be my checklist rainstorm.

I was done with this life and this impossibly overwhelming struggle. Yet, driving down that rainy road, I thought of my little sister — my closest friend. If I took my life, I would not be there to encourage and support her. The more that thoughts of my family flooded in, the more my hands became locked in position. No life would be taken that night.

During that drive home, I turned on some music, and the voice of Jenn Johnson filled the depressed interior of that car. Suddenly, I was "In Over My Head" as the love and presence of God crashed over me.[1]

*Johnson, J. (2015). In Over My Head (Crash Over Me) [Recorded by Bethel Music and Jenn Johnson]. On *We Will Not Be Shaken* [Digital]. Shasta Lake, CA: Bethel Music. (2014).

At this point of complete hopelessness, I experienced God's saving presence. To this day, whenever life gets tough, I return to that song.

My last effort at hiding was dating a beautiful girl. Over our 2 years together, my attempts to "fake it until you make it" were coming undone. Our talk of engagement and marriage fell apart as she slowly found that her dream "manly man" was not someone I could just become. I could never love her in the way she desired, so I broke everything off as gently as possible.

Just a few months later, in the summer of my 19th year, I came out to my parents in the form of a lengthy letter. I shared my orientation, but I was also clear of my commitment to a path of celibacy.

Over a week went by after I mailed it off. No response. Then, the moment came, their reply letter was in my hand, and in just a few of their opening words, 7 years of fear melted away:

"Liam, we are *not* ashamed of you. We love you so much."

CELIBATE AT AGE 20

Today, Liam is 20 years old. In his pursuit of God, he has taken a vow of singleness and celibacy. "This life, though filled with plenty of blessings and freedoms," he says, "is not always easy."

Here are a few challenges Liam faces within Christian community even as he seeks to surrender his sexuality to God.

RESILIENCE

I cannot stop people from seeing me in denigrating ways that discount, deconstruct or doubt who I am in Christ. Throughout my life, as I have faced a number of threatening medical issues, I learned by faith that the devil has power, but no authority. I can find joy, peace, rest, and victory — even in injustice.

There is a time for being sad, but I have found that the intensity of suffering will pass; God does not enjoy seeing me suffer; rather, He desires to see me have life abundantly (John 10:10).

I cannot live under the stress of others' expectations. I choose to live each day in Christ, surrendered to His love and presence. I take this journey seriously, and I even wrote my own celibacy vow to help me focus my intentions.

FAMILY

While my parents love me, I sense pressure from them to consider marriage to a woman. I understand their good intentions, but the reality of my orientation means it is not healthy for me to live in the shadow of this expectation.

SCHOOL

Even in my Christian college, I have sat through classes where the professor taught how the LGBT+ community is the reason for the downfall of society, that people like me corrupt and destroy family, media, culture, and politics.

VOLUNTEERING

My passion for children's ministry is met with great opposition. One mother said to me, *"Liam, a fag* has no place in children's ministry."* I've been given many scolding looks as they shield their children from me like I have some fatal disease.

WORK

Working for a Christian non-profit, I was recently notified, "We cannot disclose a reason, but we will not be welcoming you back to your role next year." While I cannot be certain, circumstances during my tenure led me to believe that they saw me as a risk.

*This is an extremely offensive, derogatory term.

info@leadthemhome.org

SIX ACCEPTANCE STAGES
HOW PARENTS OFTEN REACT

*NO LGBT+ CHILD IS **A GRIEF**, YET PARENTS (AND OTHER FAMILY MEMBERS) OFTEN EXPERIENCE DEGREES OF **GRIEVING** WHEN A CHILD COMES OUT. SOME EXPERIENCE ALL STAGES. OTHERS EXPERIENCE ONLY CERTAIN STAGES. SOME CYCLE THROUGH THE STAGES MANY TIMES, OFTEN NONLINEARLY, BEFORE REACHING ACCEPTANCE. FOR OTHER PARENTS, ACCEPTANCE COMES IMMEDIATELY.*

THERE IS NO ONE RIGHT WAY TO GRIEVE.

Even parents who already suspect that their child is LGBT+ can experience shock. Others who had no idea may experience little to no shock. No one can predict how a parent will respond. One unsuspecting mother said, "While I had no idea, it is just one more thing we know about him. I am so thankful he told us." Others feel their world has been turned upside down — like their understanding of life, family, and faith is collapsing.

Initial shock may draw parents into a self-protect mode. Similar to the fight-or-flight switch designed to protect us, a panic can cause parents to deny the reality before them. It is similar to what a child experiences during the **Hide** stage. If not careful, parents will minimize or discredit their child's disclosure. One mother said: "You are not lesbian. You have dated boys." One father said: "We don't have homosexuals in our family."

When denial fails, parents may try to force their preferred reality. When this fails, frustration can spill over into anger. Underneath that anger is their own hurt, but expressions of anger will hurt their child. Anger can cause a teen to fight to *validate* their identity just as parents fight to *deny* it. Parents and LGBT+ youth often experience identical emotions. The difference is timing: an LGBT+ child is at the finish line when parents are not even wanting to be at the starting gate (see Navigating Relational Gaps on page 42). Parents and children need one another during this time; patience, listening, and respect are critical to preserving relational connection and trust.

Many LGBT+ youth think or are led to think they can "pray the gay away." Thinking it might work, they conclude that there is no reason to tell anyone. Sadly, this leads LGBT+ youth to languish in isolation. Coming out, then, is not just a declaration of identity; it is also an exit from isolation. Parents in the **Bargaining** stage may try to negotiate their child into silence. One father told his son: "This is not you. Don't tell anyone." Lost in translation is the reality that most LGBT+ teens have already been waiting a long time. Attempts to bargain an LGBT+ child into continued isolation is often internalized as parent rejection.

Parents (or other family members) who deny reality, express anger, and propose impossible demands usually damage relational trust. Acceptance begins when parents realize that they cannot change their child's sexuality or gender identity. This recognition can fuel a new cycle of grief. Giving up control of hopes and dreams for our children leads to sadness — and for some, serious depression.

There are quick-and-easy or long-and-difficult paths toward acceptance. While there is no one right way to grieve, it is critical for parents to handle any grief within a loving posture. No parent can just turn off their hurt or disappointment. But we must bring grief to Christ and our support system, rather than pouring it onto our children. Otherwise, our grief will likely layer additional trauma (family rejection) upon our child's heart. It is important to remember that acceptance of your child does not mean you are approving of gay relationships.

WE SHOULD AIM TO GRIEVE WELL.

www.leadthemhome.org

PAT & KATHY

SHOCK

"Internally, our personal reaction was one of deep grief and being stunned, feeling like we had failed as parents. We were so afraid. It was shocking. We never expected this to happen to someone in our family. We felt that surely it must be a choice. Externally, our response was to convey our love for our son no matter what — and to tell him that he is a valuable member of our family. We acknowledged that many things were changing but that our love for him would never change."

DENIAL

JERRY & TRACY

"Our reaction was pure disbelief and denial. Our son was always shy, and we felt like he must be experiencing confusion. We just could not let go of the belief that this would pass. We just kept thinking, 'Surely it's just a phase.'"

THERESA

ANGER

"I felt a little bit of anger. I was fearful for my daughter and what a gay life would mean for her. I was disappointed in myself that I must have done something wrong to cause her to feel this way."

BARGAINING

JEFF

"I regret telling my daughter things like 'Why won't you just give change a try?' and 'How can you know unless you give dating a guy a chance?' Ultimately, I was trying to negotiate her out of her orientation. I wanted to be able to say something or make some suggestion that she would just get all excited about — or at least agree to. This approach was only delaying our daughter being able to experience our acceptance of her as a person. Looking back, it was not a wise move."

WAYNE

DEPRESSION

"I feared for my son's physical and emotional health. I worried he might walk away from Christ. And I felt extreme sadness and grief that I didn't know sooner. Though there were subtle clues that he was struggling with his sexuality, I missed them and wasn't there for him. His life would now be fraught with complications, disappointment, and heartache, which overwhelmed me. It was frustrating trying to seek support from my family, church, and the Christian community at large. How was I supposed to lovingly engage him in conversation and provide support while still being faithful to God? I worried that any wrong response might push him over the edge to self-harm — or that he might walk away from our family. The fear, grief, frustration, and deep sadness were overwhelming."

ACCEPTANCE

DANICA

"As my son came out, my mind raced back to all the thoughtless and insensitive remarks I had spoken about gay people. Suddenly, I felt a deep need to show my son how sorry I am for my words and to tell him how much I love him."

A CLOSET OF OUR OWN

DAVID AND TINA SHARE INSIGHTS FROM THEIR JOURNEY THROUGH GRIEF AFTER THEIR DAUGHTER, AMANDA, CAME OUT.

SHOCK

My husband David and I found out via social media. We were in shock. Everything in our world changed that day — everything except God. While David had noticed curious clues during our daughter Amanda's college days, he had quickly dismissed them. Now, they were proving true.

We could barely focus since being stunned by the news. David and I had difficulty functioning at work and at home. We couldn't eat or sleep. I spent many days in my bathrobe the whole day. We isolated ourselves in fear of how our church community would respond. **As our daughter was coming out of the closet, we were experiencing what it was like to go in.**

LGBT+ teens can be fearful of people finding out about their sexuality. We've now felt those same fears. Amanda had put her faith in Christ when she was 10. Will church people say she must not really be a Christian? Will friends stop calling and drop away? Will they misunderstand aspects of our journey and mischaracterize what we believe?

Our minds raced to find answers and solutions to lessen our pain and make us feel like we had some control over our circumstances.

DENIAL

The first remedy we tried was to simply deny reality. Maybe we could convince ourselves that this was just a phase. It didn't work. We also tried distorted logic: **maybe if we caused this, we can fix it, too.** We searched for ways to help "change" Amanda — because it seemed hopeless otherwise. But staying in denial would not fix our hopelessness and growing anger.

ANGER

We understood how difficult it might have been for Amanda to tell us about her sexuality, given our deep church involvement. But did she have to use social media to express her romantic feelings toward her partner — even posting photos — all while giving her parents no heads-up? We didn't stumble upon those postings until months after they began dating. We didn't know who knew by then, but we figured many of her followers were dear Christian friends and family members.

We were livid — not that she didn't tell us, but that she didn't tell us before going public. We had no privacy to process our sorrow and get our hearts wrapped around this shocking revelation.

Amanda's posts revealed a person overjoyed and in love. But we were far from a place of joy.

Thankfully, God got ahold of our hearts before we told Amanda how we felt. He pulled us close to Himself. **We heard our God of love and mercy telling us He wanted to teach us a better way, a way that can only be walked out in His power.** So in the midst of our darkest days, our precious Lord started a new thing within our hearts.

Rather than expecting Amanda to have empathy for *us*, we began feeling empathy for *her* — and for all LGBT+ people. We began to feel angry on their behalf for having been stigmatized as the "worst of sinners" by many who say they follow Christ. We now have eyes to see the hypocrisy that can exist. We are sorrowful over our own hypocrisy and silence as these attitudes and behaviors have been deeply ingrained into much of our Christian culture for far too long. We want to capture a more Christlike love for Amanda, her partner, and the wider LGBT+ community.

Our more subtle attempts to escape our new reality would surface at unexpected times. We prayed for God to use these circumstances to change us. Though sincere in that prayer, **we admit that we may still (at times) secretly hope that our cooperation with God in changing our hearts would move His Hand in changing our Amanda's heart, too.** But as our relationship with Christ grows closer, it becomes harder to play those bargaining games.

For the first year and a half, it felt like we were stuck in a deep, dark pit of depression. It ebbed and flowed, but was an ever-present part of our experience. I had many appointments with our Christian counselor who has provided much grace and wisdom for the journey. We also got a significant amount of relief simply as time passed.

But the depression can still hit in unexpected waves. It has now been 3 ½ years since we started down this road. **Recently, Amanda and her partner Dana became engaged. David and I sank into depression once again.** It started to subside as we spent more time with God and supportive friends. God has put people in our lives who are there for us when the going gets tough. Their prayers and love make a world of difference in the quality of our lives on this journey.

What breaks our hearts the most is that Amanda seems to want nothing to do with Jesus. Thinking about that reality can depress me. Another trigger involves my longing for closeness with her. Sometimes she holds me at bay — or even attacks me for no reason. It hurts when that occurs.

Much has changed in our hearts in the last several years. **As we learn to place our full dependence upon God, this experience becomes less about Amanda and more about our journey with Christ.** I can honestly say that most of our days are filled with gratitude and contentment in Him. We are learning to love our precious daughter from hearts that are being re-shaped to look like His. We believe Amanda is experiencing our love in a fresh (yet still imperfect) way. We pray that it is beginning to feel more like Christ's radical love.

David and I are committed to journeying through life together with Amanda and Dana. Dana is a wonderful young woman. We love her dearly as family. We have fun visiting them out of state and hosting them in our home. We enjoy making cherished memories together, leaning on God as He unfolds His purposes.

Without this journey, we might have continued to live with a blind spot that minimizes LGBT+ people. We share their hunger for love, acceptance, and belonging. David teaches high school, and his classroom has become a safe spot for LGBT+ youth to hang out. He wants them to know that they have a place where they are loved and wanted.

We thank God for the privilege of walking alongside other parents in any stage of this journey. **Know that your family is not alone.** There are others who will stand with you and declare that all our children are made in the image of God. Each is incredibly valuable and deserves our deepest love.

This is my prayer: *Lord, help us not miss out on what we have today because we miss what we thought would have been a better path. We trust the uniquely perfect path You have already prepared for us, and we trust Your promise to be with us every step of the way. We release our desire to know what is yet to come, and we trust Your abundant grace to be ready to meet every future need. Keep us in Your peace as we seek to know and to walk in Your will each day. In Jesus' name, amen.*

RISKS LGBT+

THE 2 LEADING RISK FACTORS

1 BULLYING

RELATIVE TO THEIR HETEROSEXUAL PEERS,

LGBT+ YOUTH ARE...[1,2]

2-4X more likely to attempt suicide (in accepting families)

4-8X more likely to attempt suicide (in rejecting/disconnected families)

91% more likely to be bullied

46% more likely to be victimized

3X more likely to miss school (out of fear)

2X more likely to skip college

[1]Schuster MA, Bogart LM, Klein DJ, et al. A longitudinal study of bullying of sexual-minority youth. *N Engl J Med* (2015); 372:1872-1874.

[2]Ryan C, Russell ST, Huebner D, Diaz R, & Sanchez J. Family Acceptance Project™. Family rejection as a predictor of negative health outcomes in white and Latino lesbian, gay, an bisexual young adults. *Pediatrics* (2009), 123 (1) 346-352.

[3]Durso LE & Gates GJ (2012). Serving our youth: Findings from a national survey of service providers working with lesbian, gay, bisexual, and transgender youth who are homeless or at risk of becoming homeless. Los Angeles: The Williams Institute with True Colors Fund and The Palette Fund.

[4]Kosciw JG, Greytak EA, Giga NM, Villenas C. & Danischewski DJ. (2016). The 2015 National School Climate Survey: The experiences of lesbian, gay, bisexual, transgender, and queer youth in our nation's schools. New York: GLSEN.

LGBT+ YOUTH HOMELESSNESS[3]

20-40% of homeless youth identify as LGBT+

62% have attempted suicide

59% have been sexually victimized

Many are forced to trade "services" (such as survival sex) for food and housing

94% of youth homeless shelters report serving LGBT+ youth in the last year

75% report working with transgender youth in the last year

68% of homeless LGBT+ youth report serious family rejection

Percentages of LGBT+ teens who have already experienced bullying and victimization:[4]

85% VERBAL HARASSMENT

49% ELECTRONIC HARASSMENT

27% PHYSICAL HARASSMENT

13% PHYSICAL ASSAULT

58% DID NOT REPORT (OUT OF FEAR)

62% REPORTING TO SOMEONE DID NOT STOP HARM

INCREASED VICTIMIZATION =

Lower GPA
Increased depression
Increased self-harm
Increased suicide attempts[1]

Bullying for all students declines as age increases, but it **remains higher at every grade level** for LGBT+ students relative to heterosexual peers.[1]

TEENS FACE

FOR LGBT+ TEEN SUICIDE:

2 FAMILY REJECTION

FAMILY REJECTION

FAMILY DISCONNECTION

LGBT+ YOUTH IN EVANGELICAL FAMILIES[5]

85% felt uncomfortable coming out to parents

81% feared being viewed as disgusting by family

57% feared being disowned by parents

42% forbidden to share with others

9% literally kicked out of their home

[5]VanderWaal, C.J., Sedlacek, D. & Lane, L. (2017). The Impact of Family Acceptance or Rejection among LGBT+ Millenials in the Seventh-day Adventist Church. *Journal of Social Work and Christianity*, 44(1-2), 72-95.

A teen comes out. Her parents hug her. They cry. They say, "We love you no matter what." **Afterward, the topic is never raised again** because her parents are uncomfortable with homosexuality. This silence leaves a young person **isolated, carrying internal stress** out of her own strength. Holding this stress in, rather than verbalizing it in safe conversation, **raises the risk of suicidal ideation.** We can say that "family disconnection" — even in a loving home — operates similarly to active forms of rejection. **Although family disconnection is not intended to reject, it can produce dangerous risks for young people.**

IS THIS AN EMERGENCY?

Many people who are suicidal are not *imminently* suicidal. Here are 4 factors indicating that help is *urgently* needed:

1. SUICIDAL THOUGHTS
2. SPECIFIC PLAN
3. STATED INTENTION
4. ACCESS TO MEANS

NATIONAL SUICIDE PREVENTION LIFELINE:

(800) 273-8255

Bullying and family rejection are the leading risk factors for LGBT+ teen suicide.

Contact a licensed counselor if your loved one is suicidal. **If they are imminently suicidal, call 911 or take them to the hospital immediately.** If uncertain, call the National Suicide Prevention Lifeline for further evaluation.

Remain calmly alert about these risks. Stay present in your loved one's daily life.

info@leadthemhome.org

HOMELESS & TRANSGENDER

CRYSTAL IS 22 YEARS OLD, TRANSGENDER, AND CURRENTLY EXPERIENCING HOMELESSNESS. SHE SHARED WITH US ABOUT HER LIFE AND HER FUTURE HOPES TO RECAPTURE A SENSE OF FAMILY.

I WAS BORN WITH THE NAME "CRAIG" to my biological parents. They had my little brother and sister soon after they had me. Because of alcoholism and neglect, we were removed from our home. My siblings were both placed in one foster home together, but I was placed separately in another foster home.

Over time, my biological parents regained custody of my siblings. But they never pursued getting me.

At age 4, I was adopted by a single woman named Maggie. At first, she was nice, but only for a short period of time. The abuse started well before I knew anything about gender identity.

All my life, I always wanted to spend time with my biological brother and sister. Sadly, not only did my biological parents not want me back home, but they also actively prevented me from finding my brother and sister. I never stop thinking about them. I miss them dearly.

When I was 14 years old, I remember telling my adoptive mother that I was in the wrong body. Even though I was born a boy, I knew in my mind that I was a girl. I began identifying as Crystal. It was at this point that she became even meaner to me. She would hit me, bend my thumb backwards and yell at me for painting my nails or dressing as a girl.

I was kicked out of my home by my adoptive mother at age 21. She disowned me, but it was also necessary for me to get out of that home and escape the abuse I had endured for years. I am now 22 years old and homeless.

Maggie was really no mother to me at all. I shared that she's my adoptive mother so that you can learn about my story, but I don't consider her to be any kind of mother. In the past year since being disowned, Maggie has not reached out even once to help me. She has never apologized for hitting me, hurting me, or kicking me out.

In fact, I recently needed foot surgery, and Maggie purposely withheld medical insurance benefits. I've only ever known her as someone trying to control me, deny my experience, reject me, and disown me. I don't remember any kind of love or care in that home.

Life on the streets is really difficult. I sleep at a city-run mission, but it's not the safest place for someone like me. Just outside the mission, there is drug use and prostitution. Many people come into the city to sexually take advantage of homeless people.

I may be homeless, but I work hard, and I want to be happy and healthy. I'm a responsible person, and I'm even the boss of the cleaning crews at the mission.

LIFE ON THE STREETS IS DIFFICULT..... JUST OUTSIDE THE MISSION, THERE IS DRUG USE AND PROSTITUTION. MANY PEOPLE COME INTO THE CITY TO SEXUALLY TAKE ADVANTAGE OF HOMELESS PEOPLE.

"If you are leaving home because you can't stand 'the rules,' understand that the street has its own rules and will be very dangerous. Your family's rules are most likely much safer. Friends, relatives, a shelter, child protective services or foster home will all be much safer alternatives than the streets."

– Hatch Youth, a program of the Montrose Center[1]

1 The Montrose Center. "No Home?" Hatch Youth, 26 Sept. 2008, http://hatchyouth.org/index.php?option=com_content&view=article&id=37&Itemid=59

I enjoy getting coffee, playing soccer, hanging out with friends, and playing games. Part of doing what makes me happy is changing my gender to match who I am on the inside.

Many residents smoke synthetic marijuana outside the mission. As for me, I don't use any kind of drugs or alcohol. Alcohol is what cost me my biological family to begin with. I don't want to ever destroy my life with alcohol and drugs. Smoking will make your lungs black and ruin your mind. I've seen the impact of alcohol and drugs on many other people's lives.

I like to stay positive. I have many gifts, I work hard, I am trustworthy, and I believe in doing the right thing. I care about my family, even though I haven't been able to find my brother and sister since we were separated when I was little. I think about them a lot.

Music is one of my talents and something I really enjoy. I like listening to music, but I also plan to make music one day. I like putting together musical beats with my mouth and showing my music skills online through videos. It helps me cope with the pain of my life. It's probably one of the biggest things that gives me purpose and helps me to avoid using drugs.

Life on the streets can place young people at risk to many dangers. One is survival sex, which is where young people feel they have no other option but to trade their bodies for sex to obtain food, money, or a place to stay. There are a lot of people out there who know you have no choice but to give them what they want sexually, because you're hungry or cold on the streets.

I shared that I don't use alcohol or drugs. Well, I also want to tell you that I refuse to get involved in survival sex. I just won't do it. What men don't realize is that I was born with a male body, and also that I earned a black belt in Karate growing up. If anyone tries to do anything to me, they'll be in for a surprise. I don't want to hurt anyone, but I know how to defend myself and my friends if necessary.

I feel homeless, but I do have a home at the mission. That said, I don't want to be there for too long because it's so messy, and it's also not the most secure place.

I'm currently working hard to get a better paying job. I plan to save up money and get an apartment. I'd like to have roommates and share a home together. We could take care of the house together and help with the expenses.

I'd like to buy a big house one day so I can live with a bunch of friends. We'd be together like a big family. We'd cook together and take care of the house together. I'd adopt children and give them the love they need. I want to help vulnerable children know that they are truly loved. That is my dream.

I also hope to have a store one day. I enjoy cutting glass and making earrings out of metal. I could work with my friends, and we'd make items and sell them. We'd take care of the store together and help each other.

The biggest impact of homelessness is that I lost my relationship with Maggie. She was not nice to me at all, but she is the only person I've ever known as a mother. I'm sad that she blamed me for my gender instead of helping me. I forgive her, but you should never disown your child.

I can't look back because I'm now grown up. I have to find hope in the future — not the past.

I WANT TO HELP VULNERABLE CHILDREN KNOW THAT THEY ARE TRULY LOVED. THAT IS MY DREAM.

Outreach Indiana is a drop-in shelter for homeless youth (ages 14-24). They provide a safe place for youth to enjoy a hot meal, launder clothing, take a shower, search for jobs online, and access a host of services designed to protect and rebuild young lives. Ryan, a staff member at Outreach Indiana, shared with us his thoughts on Crystal and her personal growth.

RYAN, STAFF MEMBER AT OUTREACH INDIANA

"Crystal has been an inspiration in her strength of adapting to the challenges homelessness brings, as well as overcoming being kicked out of her family's home and separated from her siblings. I've been honored to walk with Crystal in overcoming barriers to better employment while modeling a healthy, caring friendship.

I am incredibly impressed with Crystal's resilience in overcoming emotional, relational, and financial obstacles. She has leaned on her faith in God despite coming from a broken family that struggled to embody Christ's love and even caused Crystal physical harm. She writes poetry and songs and is often the one who tries to help others solve their concerns.

Crystal needs continued encouragement from other peers and friends. This helps motivate her forward in her career path. I and other staff at Outreach have spoken the truth of God's love over her. But it has been a challenge for her to find peers who can positively encourage her. Crystal has a strong internal constitution: she has the will to follow the shelter's rules and is a very compassionate person.

Sadly, there are individuals who attempt to take advantage of her by pressing against her boundaries into sexual situations and generally preying upon her. We do everything possible to be a place of refuge where she can be safe and invest in her future."

LGBT+ TEEN

WHO KNOWS THAT YOU'RE LGBT+?

JESSICA (14): Only a handful of friends know. One from my church, one from school, and a few others who are not associated with a church. No adults are aware of my story.

YOUR PARENTS DON'T KNOW YET. WHAT IS THE REASON YOU HAVEN'T SHARED WITH THEM ALREADY?

JESSICA: I haven't shared with my parents about my sexual orientation because I'm worried that they won't believe me, respect me, or accept me. I don't want them to think any differently of me after I tell them, but I'm worried that they will. I'm afraid my parents will not fully understand that this is something I can't control. My parents often say that being LGBT+ is something that can be changed.

WHAT IS THE MOST INSENSITIVE THING YOU'VE HEARD SAID ABOUT LGBT+ PEOPLE?

JOHN (16): It hurts when I hear Christians say that homosexual attraction is a choice — as if I purposely chose these feelings. It minimizes my struggle and makes me feel isolated, misunderstood, and judged. My brother has made gay jokes that really hurt me, but I didn't say anything because I don't want him to know about my struggle.

WHAT IS THE IMPACT OF FAMILY REJECTION AND JUDGMENT IN THE HEARTS OF LGBT+ YOUNG PEOPLE?

JOHN: I think rejection and judgment make it easy for LGBT+ people to ignore Scripture. How can anyone accept a "biblical truth" that rejects, judges, and mistreats people who are hurting? It also makes it impossible for LGBT+ people to trust their own families, much less their churches. No wonder so many LGBT+ young people find support in the LGBT+ community! Rejection leads people to get support outside their faith community. I'm personally blessed not to have been bullied or rejected, so I can more easily trust God's good plans for my life — even though it will be challenging.

RATE YOUR FEAR ABOUT SHARING WITH YOUR PARENTS FROM 1 (NONE) TO 100 (HUGE).

JESSICA: I would rate sharing with my parents at about 60. One of my parents has a gay brother whom they both treat with respect, acceptance, and support in his marriage. That makes me want to think they would be kind and accepting of me, too. But I still don't know how they would react. Sometimes they say that being LGBT+ is a choice, and I am worried they won't understand that it wasn't a choice for me. I'm not sure if they'll be kind and accepting or if they'll have an opposite response of doubt and anger.

HOW BIG OF A RELIEF WILL IT BE FOR YOUR PARENTS TO LEARN ABOUT YOUR SEXUAL ORIENTATION?

JESSICA: It definitely would be a huge relief if I could come out to my parents. With most every problem I experience, my mom is my biggest supporter — except for my sexuality since I have never talked to her about it. If she knew about my sexual orientation and reacted positively, then she could help me with relationships or questions I may have.

HOW HAVE PEOPLE IN YOUR SUPPORT NETWORK MOST HELPED YOU?

CRYSTAL (22): The people at Outreach Indiana are really good people who have given me a safe place to talk about my life. They care about me. They have also helped me get a social security card. Now I can look for a better job.

HOW DOES GOD COMFORT OR ENCOURAGE YOU?

CRYSTAL: God comforts me by helping me forgive people. I believe God wants me to help people believe in Him. I do that by helping them when they're hurting.

WHAT DO YOU MOST NEED TO HELP YOU FACE YOUR FUTURE WITH HOPE?

CRYSTAL: I want to get a good job. That will make a big difference in my life. Now that I have my new social security card, I have a better opportunity to get a good job. I want to learn to cook so I can take care of myself. I also want more friends and to take care of kids in tough situations.

JOHN: I can't make it by myself or in my own strength. Doing it alone over a long time is isolating and exhausting. It doesn't work. The only way I'll make it is with God's presence and my family's support. I need people to see me without a label, no different than before. I'm just a human with problems, but I also have gifts and talents that have been given to me by God. That's how I hope people will see me. I also need friends and family who understand that I have a difficult struggle. I can't make it if those closest to me minimize my struggle, ignore it, or play like it doesn't exist.

WHAT WOULD YOU SAY TO PARENTS WHO HAVE JUST FOUND OUT THEY HAVE AN LGBT+ CHILD?

CRYSTAL: I would tell parents to love their child no matter what. Your child may be male-to-female or female-to-male, but they need your love no matter what. Be kind to your child. Don't make fun of them. Don't insult them. Help them! To love someone is to help them.

JOHN: Be loving, supporting, and encouraging. Don't place impossible demands and expectations upon them. Think about what your child has possibly been through (depression, fear, mistreatment). Show understanding and be patient. Ask them questions that allow them to safely talk about their thoughts and feelings. You cannot do all this if you are not present, so be present. Be a safe and accepting family that will walk with your child.

(SEE CRYSTAL'S STORY ON PAGE 18, JESSICA'S STORY ON PAGE 32, AND JOHN'S STORY ON PAGE 33.)

info@leadthemhome.org

REFLECTION QUESTIONS

1. Were any **Key Terms** unfamiliar to you? If so, which one(s)?

2. What are some of the burdens a young person might carry **Growing Up LGBT+**?

3. Did you resonate with any parent survey responses from **Initial Reactions**?

4. Compare and contrast the **Six Developmental Stages** for teens with the **Six Acceptance Stages** for parents. Which stage(s) do you most relate to? Please discuss.

5. Which statistic on **Risks LGBT+ Teens Face** impacted you most? As pastors and parents, what should be our response to LGBT+ youth? What will it take to reduce the burdens they carry?

6. Which **Real Life Profile** impacted you the most? Identify common themes flowing through the stories of Diane, Liam, David and Tina, and Crystal. Please discuss.

7. At just 20 years old, in wholehearted commitment to honoring God, Liam is pursuing lifelong celibacy. Even in sacrificial obedience to biblical morality, he *still* encounters mistreatment in the church. What does it say when a church rejects fully repentant people?

8. *Guiding Families* states that "acceptance does not equal approval." Is this claim possible? If so, how is it possible? Identify the threshold where acceptance becomes approval.

9. As a pastor, do you face any personal barriers in demonstrating acceptance of LGBT+ youth? As a parent, do you face any barriers in offering acceptance to your LGBT+ child?

10. Identify the stated concerns of young people in the **LGBT+ Teen Q&A**. Which of their statements most caught your attention? What do young people in their shoes need from us?

"IF, HOWEVER, YOU ARE [REALLY] FULFILLING THE ROYAL LAW ACCORDING TO THE SCRIPTURE, 'YOU SHALL LOVE YOUR NEIGHBOR AS YOURSELF [THAT IS, IF YOU HAVE AN UNSELFISH CONCERN FOR OTHERS AND DO THINGS FOR THEIR BENEFIT]' YOU ARE DOING WELL."

– JAMES 2:8

Churches are seeking practical, loving, biblically sound guidance on LGBT+ inclusion and relational care.

Is your church ready?

POSTURE SHIFT

POSTURE SHIFT TRAINING SEMINAR

Posture Shift is a private, at-your-site leadership training seminar designed to equip your team for effective LGBT+ outreach and care. This missiological teaching educates your team on **historical victimization of LGBT+ people, vulnerabilities of LGBT+ youth, and key language mistakes that damage trust.** Walk away with a **10-step best practice care plan** that includes coverage of complex matters such as church inclusion. Join tens of thousands of Evangelical leaders across North and South America. Equip your team today!

REQUEST A PROPOSAL AT
POSTURESHIFT.COM

LEAD THEM HOME

"BEAR (ENDURE, CARRY) ONE ANOTHER'S BURDENS AND TROUBLESOME MORAL FAULTS, AND IN THIS WAY FULFILL AND OBSERVE PERFECTLY THE LAW OF CHRIST (THE MESSIAH) AND COMPLETE WHAT IS LACKING [IN YOUR OBEDIENCE TO IT]."

– GALATIANS 6:2

PART 2:

DEVELOPING A CARE PLAN

RESPONDING WELL WHEN LOVED ONES COME OUT

T CAN TAKE TREMENDOUS COURAGE for LGBT+ loved ones to come out. For teenagers, it can be a frightening prospect.

Lead Them Home cares for LGBT+ teens and young adults who are on the verge of coming out to their parents. Some are frozen in fear. Others cannot ever imagine getting the words out.

Listen to 19-year-old Eric:

I realized I was attracted to guys at 13 years old. I feared what this would mean for my relationship with God. I feared my parents finding out. I prayed, but the gay did not go away.

I so wanted to tell my parents. I wanted them to comfort me and make it go away. I wanted to be a kid again so I wouldn't have to grow up. At times, I just wanted to die. After all, I didn't ask to be gay.

Every time I felt emotionally close to my parents, I came so close to telling them. Conversations on long drives. Dinners with my dad on father-son nights. Bedtime talks with my mom. But every time, I backed away as though from a cliff's edge.

The longer I wait, the harder it gets. Sometimes, I wish I would die in an accident so they never have to know. I can't have peace without them knowing. But I can't have peace with them knowing, either.

They love me. I just don't want to disappoint them.

At our Posture Shift seminars, we ask church leaders to pay close attention when LGBT+ teens come out. **You never know what history lies behind a young person's disclosure.**

What if, when Eric comes out, he is suicidal? What if he has been bullied? What if isolation has worn him out emotionally? What if depression has left him hopeless?

Eric's isolation did finally wear him down. He reached a point of hopelessness. One night, he seriously considered taking his life. But he had an unexpected thought:

> *As my last hope, I'll tell my pastor. If that doesn't go well, then I'll have my answer: I'll take my life.*

Importantly, Eric is an emotionally secure young man. He is successful in academics and sports. He has many friends. He was never bullied. Eric worships God and loves to serve on mission trips. He works part-time to help pay his living expenses at college. His parents' marriage is healthy. Eric lives out the gospel. He knows that God has a purpose for his life.

TEENS CAN BE VULNERABLE JUST AS PARENTS FACE A STEEP LEARNING CURVE.

Eric is a *best-case scenario,* yet even he has felt suicidal.

Recall the "Growing Up LGBT+" profile (page 4). What if we add social exclusion to Eric's life experience? Name-calling, teasing, and bullying? Judgment? Denigration? Isolation?

Add these factors to Eric's story, and suicidality skyrockets.

Now, let's bring parents into this situation. Parents can be caught off guard by what their child is sharing. As we learned in "Six Acceptance Stages" (page 12), parents can be instantly launched into the early stages of grief that include shock, denial, or anger.

IN THIS SECTION, OUR BEST PRACTICE CARE PLAN INCLUDES:

- Response script for the moment LGBT+ loved ones come out.
- Follow-up questions that demonstrate compassion and awareness of vulnerability.
- Parent survey responses detailing common mistakes parents make.
- Language inventory detailing words and phrases that can damage relational trust.
- Vision plan for preventing and reducing lateral wounds that can impede spiritual growth.
- Navigational tool to educate parents on relational gaps that can trigger mistakes.
- Reset plan for seeking forgiveness and restoring trust with LGBT+ loved ones.

Because of the steep learning curve they face, parents can unknowingly inflict their own grief upon their child. This issue results from a time gap: while LGBT+ young people often have been acclimating to their sexual orientation or gender identity for months or years, parents are dealing with brand new information.

While youth are crossing the finish line of a coming out journey, their parents do not even want to be at the starting gate of having an LGBT+ child. Many parents experience unexpected grief at the very moment when their LGBT+ children are embracing identity, joy, and possibly the pursuit of romantic love. Adult children may come out *and* share news of a partner all in one disclosure.

This scenario is a perfect storm for relational mistakes. Parents and teens alike are bound to say words or express emotions that are hurtful or disappointing. Mutual patience, understanding, and forgiveness will be necessary.

In Part 2, we will attempt to prevent parents from making unintended relational mistakes or to quickly recover from any initial missteps. We offer a best practice care plan that parents, church leaders, and all who care can follow when LGBT+ loved ones come out.

Along the way, you may discover mistakes you have already made. Remember: you are not alone. Many parents have gone before you. We include many of their self-reported miscues to educate parents who are earlier on in this journey.

Even loving parents can make some very regrettable mistakes. Sadly, the church's historical failure to thoughtfully engage LGBT+ people fuels many of these relational mistakes. As Christians, we have often spoken of nonstraight people as though they are an issue. We need to fix this.

As renowned author Dr. Preston Sprinkle says in the title of his book, your LGBT+ loved ones are not an issue. They are part of us. They are *People To Be Loved.*

NO ONE HAS TO GIVE YOU PERMISSION

TO LOVE YOUR LGBT+ CHILD.

LGBT+ loved ones need your presence. No one has to give you permission to love your LGBT+ child, yet many parents report feeling criticized as fellow Christians question their efforts to demonstrate unconditional love and acceptance.

Whether you are a parent, grandparent, relative, friend, pastor, teacher, or counselor, young people need a thoughtful response from us when they come out. We must offer vulnerable young people acceptance, listening, understanding, and affection. **Your comforting, listening presence is so important.**

For the most part, Christians have no prior history of relating well to LGBT+ people. We speak; they run. It turns out that no matter how sincerely we want to love, our words often hurt and propel gay and transgender people away from the church — and sometimes away from their family.

Words matter. We will look at words, phrases and clichés that can damage relational trust with LGBT+ loved ones. Do not dismiss or underestimate the impact of language. At Lead Them Home, we operate carefully with language. One of our core values is that every word counts.

Every word has the power to build trust or destroy trust; nourish faith or chop at the roots of faith; construct personal worth or tear it down; draw people toward Jesus or propel them away from Him.

As parents, family members, and church leaders, we must do everything possible to avoid offensive words. Language mistakes can damage the efforts you are making to build and maintain a close relationship with LGBT+ loved ones. Be sure to pay careful attention to "Words Matter" (page 38).

Since relational mistakes are so common, we will close Part 2 by detailing how to repair past relational mistakes and how to reset the relationship with your LGBT+ loved one.

AS WE PROCEED, IT IS IMPORTANT TO REMEMBER SEVERAL THINGS:

- Identifying mistakes is not a search for the cause of your child's sexuality/gender.

- Preventing mistakes can reduce vulnerability to isolation, depression, and suicidality.

- Parent mistakes are from actual self-reports from our 2017 parent survey responses.

- Parents participated in the survey to help other parents not repeat their mistakes.

- No parents are being shamed or blamed for mistakes they have made.

- *Every* parent of *every* child (gay, straight, or trans) makes many mistakes raising children.

- It is never too late to take inventory of mistakes and apologize to LGBT+ children.

DUE TO HIGHER TRAUMA FACTORS DETAILED IN PART 1, LGBT+ YOUTH ARE SUSCEPTIBLE TO INTERNALIZING AN EXPECTATION THAT THEY WILL BE MISTREATED. MANY LOSE HOPE, AND SOME GIVE UP ON LIFE.

HOW TO EXPRESS
ACCEPTANCE
WHILE HOLDING
TO YOUR BELIEFS

"
Mom and Dad love you.
We will always love you.

We are so thankful you told us.
You are very courageous.

We are going to walk with you
no matter what.

This is your home — always!
We are your family — always!

We really want to hear your
whole story.
"

LGBT+ YOUTH ARE **2-4X MORE VULNERABLE TO SUICIDE** THAN THEIR HETEROSEXUAL PEERS. THEY ARE **8X MORE VULNERABLE** IF **FAMILY REJECTION** OCCURS.

28

FOLLOW-UP CONVERSATION
ENSURING YOUR TEEN'S SAFETY

1. YOU HAVE LIVED SEVERAL YEARS WITHOUT MOM AND DAD'S SUPPORT.

2. WE'RE SO SORRY WE DIDN'T KNOW — AND WEREN'T THERE FOR YOU.

3. WE'D LIKE TO HEAR MORE ABOUT WHAT THAT WAS LIKE FOR YOU.

4. ARE YOU FEELING OR HAVE YOU EVER FELT SUICIDAL?

5. ARE YOU BEING OR HAVE YOU EVER BEEN TEASED OR BULLIED?

6. HOW HAVE YOUR FRIENDS RESPONDED TO YOU?

7. HOW HAVE PEOPLE AT CHURCH RESPONDED TO YOU?

8. IS THERE ANYTHING ELSE YOU WOULD LIKE US TO KNOW RIGHT NOW?

9. DO YOU PREFER WE SHARE WITH OTHERS OR MAINTAIN YOUR PRIVACY?

AVOID 2 EXTREMES:

ALLOWING SILENCE TO CUT OFF ANY DIALOGUE

CONSTANTLY TALKING ABOUT YOUR CHILD'S GENDER/SEXUALITY

Even parents who respond in a loving manner are often grieving. **Shock, sadness, or discomfort** can result in a **growing silence** that lowers family connection. This silence can convey to your child that you are not happy with them. **Healthy conversation that values our children is essential for a strong parent-child connection.**

info@leadthemhome.org

29

SUSTAINABLE SU

Given what we learned in Part 1 about risks that LGBT+ teens face, it is critical to stress the importance of helping LGBT+ youth and young adults build effective support.

*Many LGBT+ young people lack adequate **adult** support. **Quickly correcting relational mistakes** will make space for you to play a critical role in a young person's development.*

PARENTS: *If your child has been judged, he or she may have lost hope or given up on faith (or the church).* ***You must help them build a support system.***

MINISTRY LEADERS: *You may be the very first person to whom a teen comes out. Make yourself known as a safe person and **help students access other safe adult support.***

Whether your loved one is lesbian, gay, bisexual, transgender, questioning, queer, intersex, asexual, pansexual, genderqueer, or any other identity or inclination involving sexuality or gender, the process of self-discovery and the risk factors many youth face are similar. For this reason, our guidance on how parents should respond remains the same.

**AVOID 2 BIG ERRORS:
ASKING YOUR CHILD
TO HIDE THEIR
SEXUALITY/GENDER &
"OUTING" YOUR CHILD
WITHOUT PERMISSION.**

**YOU MAY BE ONE OF ONLY

A FEW PEOPLE WHO KNOW.

YOU MUST SERVE AS PART OF

THEIR SUPPORT SYSTEM.**

PPORT SYSTEM

JESUS

PARENTS	OTHER FAMILY MEMBERS	PASTORS (1-3)
COUNSELORS (1-2)	MENTORS (3-5)	PEERS (SEE BELOW)

KEY INSIGHTS ON A HEALTHY SUPPORT SYSTEM

PARENTS can ask helpful questions that allow you to determine how well your child internalizes God's love and their family's acceptance. Such questions could include:

"In your spiritual identity, is God for you or against you?"

"Do you feel like Mom and Dad truly love and accept you?"

"What additional support do you think you most need?"

PASTORS can ask a young person which pastoral staff they'd feel safe sharing with in order to expand support.

COUNSELORS are needed not because a child is LGBT+, but because they are a critical help for *any* person who might be experiencing anxiety, fear, hurt, or trauma.

OTHER FAMILY MEMBERS can play a critical role adding to parent support (or offering acceptance) for young people whose parents are grieving, angry, rejecting, or not yet *in the know*.

ADULT MENTORS are men and women from 3 to 30 years older than your child. Never underestimate a young person's need for both father (or older brother) and mother (or older sister) figures speaking value into their lives. Mentors are critical for every human being.

IF YOUR CHILD IS UNDER 21: Allow, but do not encourage, additional peer support. Immature peers sometimes gossip, tease, or reject. This can potentially raise the risk of suicidal ideation. Do not block healthy friendships, but be aware of this risk.

NEVER DISCLOSE A YOUNG PERSON'S SEXUAL ORIENTATION OR GENDER IDENTITY WITHOUT THEIR PERMISSION. EVEN IF

MANDATED REPORTING IS NECESSARY DUE TO A THREAT OF SELF-HARM OR HARM COMMITTED AGAINST A MINOR, SUCH

REPORTING CAN BE PERFORMED WITHOUT DISCLOSING SEXUAL ORIENTATION OR GENDER IDENTITY.

info@leadthemhome.org

HOW SUPPORT UNFOLDS

14-YEAR-OLD JESSICA REACHED OUT TO US VIA EMAIL. WE DISCOVERED THAT ONLY ONE PERSON (A PEER) KNEW ABOUT HER SEXUALITY AND THAT SHE WAS DEPRESSED AND SUICIDAL. HERE'S HOW WE HELPED HER EXPAND HER SUPPORT NETWORK.

JESSICA: Hi, my name is Jessica, and I have bisexual attractions. I attend Gateway Church. I am afraid to tell my parents. I feel unable to change my attractions. I worry that my parents won't believe me or respect me. Any advice?

JESSICA: Thank you for the quick response! I'm 14. I prefer email since I'm a bit uncomfortable.

I've never told anyone at Gateway, except my friend Joseph from small group. He actually encouraged me to email you, and I'm really glad he did!

I hope to come out to Pastor Todd. I know he is loving. I just haven't found the courage.

BILL: Hi Jessica, I'm so thankful that you reached out. I want to ask if it's possible for us to have a phone call or if you need to limit our conversation to email.

Also, do Pastor Todd or any of the parent leaders know about your sexuality? Pastor Todd is super loving. I will never "out" you to anyone. I am just thankful that you attend such a loving church. I want to ensure that you are connected with local support (if possible).

Oh, also please let me know your age. That's so important. I am here for you and look forward to hearing from you.

JESSICA: Emailing Pastor Todd would be great! That would help me get more comfortable.

Unfortunately, I am suicidal. I just started counseling. My therapist is a Christian. She knows about my depression. I'm planning on coming out to her next week since I know I can trust her.

BILL: Jessica, it is an honor. Jesus loves you so much. Your friend Joseph is very wise. Hey, here is an idea. Without mentioning your name (or gender), and with your permission, I can email Pastor Todd and ask him to share how he would respond if an LGBT+ teen came out to him. Would that be helpful? I know that he will let me share his response with you. I will remain here for you. I just want you to have even more safe support.

JESSICA: Thank you so much. You truly have blessed my day with your words, speaking with me, and helping me find ways to come out to my pastor and family. This encouragement will bless me for the rest of my life. Please let me know when Pastor Todd replies.

BILL: Oh Jessica, you are so special. God has a plan for your life, and it's a plan you don't want to miss. I think sharing with your counselor is a great next step! Please let me know how that conversation goes. Now that I have your permission, I will contact Pastor Todd. Just think: in a matter of days, Joseph's encouragement for you to talk to an adult is leading to multiple safe people to help you. I am here for you. Your counselor is here for you. Joseph is a great friend. And I bet Pastor Todd's email reply will prove to be another safe source of support. Soon, your support will be wrapped around you, and that might open the door for you to share with your parents. No pressure. I am just saying that support is great news!

BILL: Hi Jessica, here is Pastor Todd's reply. Jessica, I just want to say that I am very proud of your courage. I hope Pastor Todd's words demonstrate the safety with which you will be embraced. Let me know if you need anything — I am here whenever needed.

TODD: Dear Bill, below is a note you can pass along to the student:

First and foremost, I'm so incredibly happy you had the courage to come speak with me today. I want you to know that I will always love you and that love is completely unconditional. We want every student at Gateway to be loved, cared for, and encouraged to share about the good things and the tough things going on in their lives. Not only do we want to hear what you're dealing with, but we also want to come alongside you and support you however we can. I really want our youth group to be a safe, welcoming, and warm environment for every student — LGBT+ or straight. I'm more than willing to support you in any way you might need. Know that we have great resources to help you and your family when you feel comfortable and ready to share what's on your heart. I'm here for you, I love you, and I'm always ready to listen!

JESSICA: Hi Bill, I thought Pastor Todd's response was really good! I feel more confident that he'll accept me. I'm planning to come out to him after small group next week. Also, thank you so much for your help. I feel like I can come out now without having to worry so much. If it wasn't for your help, I'd probably still be sitting here wondering through these worries alone. I know that God loves me no matter what :)

www.leadthemhome.org

JOHN IS A 16-YEAR-OLD WITH EXCLUSIVE ATTRACTION TO OTHER GUYS. WE MET HIM AT A BOSTON-AREA CHURCH. AS JOHN IS JUST BEGINNING TO BUILD HIS SUPPORT NETWORK, HE SHARED WITH US ABOUT THE FEW PEOPLE WHO DO KNOW ABOUT HIS SEXUALITY, THE BARRIERS HE FACES TO TELLING OTHERS, AND WHAT ADDITIONAL SUPPORT WOULD MEAN TO HIM.

JESUS: When I first discovered that Scripture doesn't support gay relationships, I worried about being lonely the rest of my life. It's a scary thought. Today, I'm comforted that God has provided guidance for my life as a follower of Christ. My plan for the future is to live in obedience to God in singleness and celibacy.

PARENTS

OTHER FAMILY MEMBERS

PASTOR: My youth pastor Bryan encourages me in my Christian faith and "gets" the reality of my struggle. We talk about Scripture, but he mostly asks how I'm doing. He's a good listener.

COUNSELORS

MENTOR: I met Bill just recently. He listened to my story, offered to be a part of my support network, and has even offered to help me expand my support.

PEERS: My friend Conner is available to just listen and encourage me. With my friend Ian, I feel like I have to watch what I talk about. He keeps pressuring me to date a girl.

Bill is concerned about the fact that my family doesn't know yet. I want them to know, too, but the prospect of telling my parents bothers me. **Even though *I know that I know* my mom and dad are super loving parents, I still live in fear of being . . .**

BURDENSOME: I don't live in fear of being rejected or disowned by my parents, but I do fear stressing my family out — and being stressed out myself by their response. I fear how long it might take them to get over any shock they feel when I come out. I just can't carry the weight of their anxiety. I don't want to burden them with my struggle. My sexuality is already enough of a burden!

MISUNDERSTOOD: I worry that if I open up, they'll figure I'm "deciding" or "choosing" to live a "gay lifestyle." I don't want them to slap a label on my sexuality or start seeing me differently. I don't have a label, but if I had to pick one, it would be "awkward."

OVERSIMPLIFIED: I've made my decision to follow Christ, but even with that commitment, the road ahead will be challenging. Just like any aspect of following Jesus, it's not as simple as flipping a switch. How am I, at age 16, supposed to imagine living the rest of my life without experiencing a date or falling in love? With God's help, I can make it, but I need support from my family, too.

MINIMIZED: I fear being minimized. I fear they'll minimize the challenge I face by saying things like, "You're young! You may just find a young woman you like one day." In reality, they can't know that, and neither can I. These expectations about my future — or about what it means to be a good Christian — only add to the burden.

BAD AT TIMING: I do want to share with them about my sexuality, but it's hard for me to know when the time is right. I'm kind of waiting to see what happens. It'll eventually come out. It has to — for their sake and mine. Right? I don't want to hide my life. I don't want to feel like I'm lying. I don't want to feel like I'm leading a double life. I don't know how much longer… a part of me feels it could happen within the next year. Another part feels like I'll never find the right time, and the years will just keep passing by. Another part wants to think they never need to know, but I know deep down that they do.

COMMON MISTAKES
EVEN LOVING PARENTS MAKE

HAVE YOU ALREADY MADE MISTAKES?

Even loving parents, in a time of shock or grief, can respond in hurtful ways. Sometimes, parents are even connected with "support" that encourages mistakes that will lead to a toxic relationship. We share these common mistakes to help other parents prevent mistakes — or identify past mistakes — that can hinder a close relationship with their child.

REJECTING

Yelling at, scolding or mocking. ● Threatening to reject or disown. ● Saying things like, "You are not the person I thought you were." ● Refusing contact or excluding from family activities. ● **ASKING YOUR CHILD TO LEAVE YOUR HOME.** ● Refusing to meet or welcome your child's partner. ● Refusing to call your child's partner by their preferred title (ex: husband, spouse, son-in-law). ● Homophobic or transphobic comments or actions.

NEGLECTING

BEING UNAWARE OF HOW YOUR CHILD IS BEING TREATED BY PEERS, RELATIVES, AND OTHER ADULTS. ● Contributing to family gossip. ● Quoting Scripture when a child is suicidal. ● Not standing up to bullies on your child's behalf. ● Communicating more about doctrine than expressing love for your child. ● Exhibiting favoritism toward your other child(ren).

FALSELY ASSURING

Suggesting that your child just needs a positive opposite-sex sexual experience. ● **TELLING YOUR CHILD THEY CAN CHANGE OR "PRAY AWAY THE GAY."** ● Telling your child that God will make them straight. ● Getting overly excited about your child's attempt at a heterosexual relationship (especially when it's unhealthy or harmful).

ACCUSING

Accusing your child of "choosing the gay lifestyle." ● Blaming your child for failing to share their sexuality/gender identity sooner. ● Saying, "Being gay/transgender is a mental illness." ● Accusing your child of faking self-harm to get attention. ● Blaming or threatening to divorce your spouse. ● **TELLING YOUR CHILD THEY ARE NOT A CHRISTIAN – OR A BAD CHRISTIAN.** ● Saying, "Thinking you are a (fe)male is delusional." ● Trying to get your child to explain why (s)he is gay. ● Saying, "It's like our child is dead." ● Telling your child things like, "This will kill your grandmother." ● Telling your child, "You broke my heart." ● Blaming your transgender child for being a homosexual (confusing gender identity with sexual orientation). ● Saying, "It's simple: genitals determine gender!"

DENYING

Saying, "You just need to get over this." ● Telling your child that they are really heterosexual — or that they better be. ● **TRYING TO EXPLAIN AWAY YOUR CHILD'S SEXUALITY FOR THEM.** ● Failing to recognize past gay jokes or judgmental statements. ● Questioning your child's recollection of painful memories. ● Doubting gender dysphoria as a real experience. ● Blaming your child's gender dysphoria on culture or the "gay agenda."

www.leadthemhome.org

CONTROLLING

Forcing your child to see a counselor with the intent of "fixing" them. ● **WITHHOLDING COLLEGE FUNDING, INHERITANCE, OR FINANCIAL SUPPORT.** ● Limiting attendance at family gatherings. ● Attempting to limit what ideas or worldviews your adult child is exposed to. ● Constantly telling your child you are praying about their gender/sexuality. ● Reassuring your child with unbiblical promises (ex: "temptations will be healed"). ● Seeing your child's wedding as your loss of control over their life. ● Saying, "I am going to hire a prostitute to teach him about sex with women." ● Assigning causation to nurture-related wounds or declaring the reason why your child is gay or transgender. ● Expecting your child to experience orientation change by discussing and processing nurture-related wounds. ● Using "tough love" to attempt to force healing. ● Demanding that your child come back to Jesus.

PERSONALIZING

Seeing your LGBT+ child as a threat to your career or integrity. ● Fixating on who to blame ("Who caused this?"). ● Leaning on your child to support you in your grief. ● **THREATENING TO COMMIT SUICIDE.** ● Making your child's sexuality or gender all about you (your grief, guilt, or reputation). ● Asking where you went wrong as a parent. ● Focusing on your pain and disregarding your child's pain. ● Telling others, "It would have been easier had my child not been born."

"UNDERSTAND [THIS], MY BELOVED BRETHREN. LET EVERY MAN BE QUICK TO HEAR [A READY LISTENER], SLOW TO SPEAK, SLOW TO TAKE OFFENSE AND TO GET ANGRY. FOR MAN'S ANGER DOES NOT PROMOTE THE RIGHTEOUSNESS GOD [WISHES AND REQUIRES]."

– JAMES 1:19-20

MISCOMMUNICATING

Using unhelpful clichés like, "Love the sinner, hate the sin." ● Asking, "How could you do this to us?" ● Asking leading or loaded questions rather than open-ended questions. ● Failing to make time and create emotionally safe space for your child to talk about sexuality or gender. ● **NOT FOSTERING RESPECTFUL COMMUNICATION.** ● Wrestling through your own theology in front of your child (sending mixed messages). ● Not talking with your spouse after your child comes out (within a reasonable time frame). ● Making assumptions before seeking understanding. ● Assuming that what you intended to say is what was actually heard.

DOUBTING

Refusing to recognize Christ's presence in your child's life. ● Not leading your child spiritually by modeling a dependence on God's promises.

IT IS NEVER TOO LATE TO APOLOGIZE – EVEN FOR REALLY BIG MISTAKES!

*Some teens or young adults are so hurt and angry that they cannot quickly forgive you. **Others will immediately open their heart and be deeply touched** as they realize that you understand how your response hurt them.*

35

(See page 93 for how an LGBT+ adult child responded with grace.)

OVERCOMING RELATIONAL MISTAKES

PARENTS TOLD US ABOUT THEIR BIGGEST RELATIONAL MISTAKES, HOW MISTAKES IMPACTED RELATIONAL TRUST WITH THEIR CHILD, AND HOW LONG IT TOOK TO RECOVER FROM MISTAKES.*

	MISTAKE	IMPACT	DURATION
KAY	When our son came out, our biggest mistake was not asking more questions to try to understand where he was coming from first before making any judgements or assumptions.	Knowing he was secure in our love — and later having our extended family share their love and acceptance of him — lifted a huge weight off of him. We realized that first and foremost, our child needed to feel love and acceptance from us.	We started realizing the pain and torture he had been experiencing inside after a few discussions. Since then, we've tried to keep open discussion, acknowledging hurts and struggles instead of trying to "fix" them, and encourage him in his faith.
DENNIS	Our mistake was feeling like we could "fix" our son. We offered to find a counselor, and even to pay for counseling. We'd mention churches we thought would fold him in and help. We thought if we could just get him to a good Christian counselor that we could shorten this journey. As parents, we're geared to help our children out of their messes, and this instinct kicked in strongly when he came out to us.	These tactics to "help" just put up walls between us. Now, we pray a lot and let God do this work in him and we practice love and kindness — as *that* is what God says leads toward repentance. This has opened up communication between us, and now, we can get to deeper issues more often.	Our son *does* need our support and our love, but we had to realize that God is his Savior — not us. Our realizing this mistake came slowly over the first 2 years. We find the common ground and enjoy spending time with him, and often, his partner. The more interest we show in his life, his accomplishments, and his partner, the more he opens up to us.
KIRK	Our biggest mistake was harboring the thought that "one good woman" might change him. As I started listening to and learning from my son, I realized that my desire for his life was for my own benefit, not for his.	My son did not feel like he could come to me to talk about ongoing insecurities he has had from his years of being in the closet.	Realizing my own mistake took months to accept. Now, we focus on loving him as our son and taking pride in his many achievements. He is more willing to talk to me about his own desires and relationships.
NORA	Our mistakes included rejecting our daughter, arguing Scripture, believing that she could choose to change, and believing that she was doing this to purposely hurt us.	We have learned a lot from our daughter and have a close and accepting relationship with her and her partner. I would say the healing is in being teachable. I still sink into guilt at times, so I am working on boundaries.	I've confessed my mothering mistakes in her childhood, but not those related to coming out. It took us 10 years to recognize those mistakes. Now, I have the privilege of doing "Grammie daycare" for my daughter's children.

*Lead Them Home Survey of Parent Engagement of LGBT+ Children (October 2017)   www.leadthemhome.org

MISTAKE	IMPACT	DURATION	
My biggest mistake was not asking more open-ended questions to draw out his story and thoughts. I lacked knowledge of LGBT+ culture and history, so I had to learn as I was dealing with the revelation. What I learned fueled my fear for my child. I was too emotional in front of him at times, too pushy with doctrine at times, too self-revealing as I explored my own values and beliefs on same-sex relationships.	My child is now married to his partner, working, and earning a living. But I know that he still carries unspoken hurts about his journey — and I'm at a loss how to help him. Distance, his desire to move on, and my overbearing history with him makes healing a challenge. I really desire relational reconciliation, but I'm not sure he feels the need for it. I've apologized for some of my mistakes and tried to re-engage him in conversation — with limited success.	It took a few years to be able to look back and evaluate my response. Even now, after 5 years, there is still so much more that needs to be discussed and shared. My best success has been working at staying connected to him during the very difficult first few years. I made an effort to get to know his partner and educate myself about LGBT+ culture and history. I attended his wedding and provide support in areas where I feel like I can.	**SONYA**
I didn't realize how vulnerable she was and wasn't as careful about voicing my concern. She took my concern as disapproval. She believed we thought she was going to hell. We have since made efforts to show and tell her of our unconditional love.	We didn't know the impact because she withdrew from us and did not share her feelings and fears. We didn't realize how much of this was a result of our own relational mistakes.	It took us several months to realize our mistakes. Her counselor gave us the heads-up, and we immediately began a campaign to show her that we love her and that nothing about this struggle will stop us from continuing to love her.	**ROY**
By God's grace, we listened to his story, asked a lot of questions, and asked him to be patient with us as we worked together in navigating this new territory. We assured him of our unconditional love and our respect for the courage it took to share his news with us. At the same time, we initially had the mindset that his being gay was a choice, and we told him so.	Fortunately, we have maintained a very open and loving relationship with our son. He has been understanding and forgiving, all while desiring that we respect him as an individual. We found out that our son had spent 10 years pleading with God to "take the gay away and make him normal" — to no avail. He even tried dating a couple of girls hoping this would spark a reverse interest.	After much prayer, conversation, and reading books on the subject, it took almost 2 years before we were willing to accept the fact that our son's same-gender attraction was not a choice. We have also realized that this is not about us! This is *his* life and the story that God has allowed. After many years, we have come to trust that God has a purpose beyond our expectations.	**ROSETTA**

"WORDS MATTER"

LEAD THEM HOME'S POSTURE SHIFT SEMINAR for church leaders is built upon the historically established best practice that missionaries must understand a people's history, culture and **language** in order to effectively share the gospel.

This is especially true when missionaries attempt to share Jesus with people who have been ostracized, condemned, or denigrated by Christians. Every Posture Shift Seminar addresses the reality that a so-called gospel of exclusion or condemnation has no power to reach already-banished persons. They have already heard too many hurtful **words and clichés** that have propelled them out of the church.

Family Care, our seminar for parents and families of LGBT+ loved ones, teaches that love is never limited by differences. Love can endure belief gaps in all human relationships, but only if love is proven by our every action, attitude, and **word**. In families, **words** have the power to build trust or destroy it.

Our support sessions give us the privilege of directly reaching LGBT+ people and their families across the globe. Earlier in our work, even as a ministry specializing in LGBT+ care, **our words** were the source of deep hurt for several LGBT+ young people. More than a decade of experience has sensitized our staff to the importance of favoring a listener-learner posture over a teacher-teller posture. **Too much speaking** can lead to the unintentional spilling of hurtful words.

In totality, thousands of encounters with LGBT+ people have built into Lead Them Home a core value that **every word counts.** Our staff, volunteers, and interns routinely hear this reminder as we seek to maintain a consistent, thoughtful core ethic that **language matters.**

"DO NOT LET ANY UNWHOLESOME TALK COME OUT OF YOUR MOUTHS, BUT ONLY WHAT IS HELPFUL FOR BUILDING OTHERS UP ACCORDING TO THEIR NEEDS, THAT IT MAY BENEFIT THOSE WHO LISTEN."
– EPHESIANS 4:29

"A TRANSGENDER"
"A TRANS"
"TRANSGENDERISM"
"TRANSGENDERED"
"TRANSGENDERING"
"TRANNY"
"I REFUSE TO USE THOSE PRONOUNS"

"THE GAYS"
"SEXUALLY BROKEN"
"HOMOSEXUAL STRUGGLER"

Sometimes, Christians use language to talk about LGBT+ people that LGBT+ people do not even use themselves. When we do this, it gives off the impression that **we are not listening to them – and do not care what they have to say.** Resolve not to speak a "foreign language." If in doubt, ask what terms, names, or pronouns someone prefers.

Note: Many people use homosexuality and transgender interchangably, but sexual orientation and gender identity are two distinct matters.

"GRACIOUS WORDS ARE A HONEYCOMB, SWEET TO THE SOUL AND HEALING TO THE BONES."
– PROVERBS 16:24

"A GENTLE ANSWER TURNS AWAY WRATH, BUT A HARSH WORD STIRS UP ANGER."
– PROVERBS 15:1

"[T]HE TONGUE IS A SMALL PART OF THE BODY, BUT IT MAKES GREAT BOASTS. CONSIDER THAT A GREAT FOREST IS SET ON FIRE BY A SMALL SPARK."
– JAMES 3:5

"THE WORDS OF THE RECKLESS PIERCE LIKE SWORDS, BUT THE TONGUE OF THE WISE BRINGS HEALING."
– PROVERBS 12:18

"SET A GUARD OVER MY MOUTH, LORD; KEEP WATCH OVER THE DOOR OF MY LIPS."
– PSALM 141:3

"HOMOSEXUAL"

If your loved one identifies as gay, and you insist on referring to them as a "homosexual," they will interpret your use of this word as **religious judgment.**

What you may refer to as "the sin" is what many LGBT+ loved ones call "my identity." They will hear, **"God loves me, He hates me."** Choose authentic conversation over catchy clichés.

"LOVE THE SINNER, HATE THE SIN"

"MY DEAR BROTHERS AND SISTERS, TAKE NOTE OF THIS: EVERYONE SHOULD BE QUICK TO LISTEN, SLOW TO SPEAK AND SLOW TO BECOME ANGRY...."
– JAMES 1:19-20

"THOSE WHO CONSIDER THEMSELVES RELIGIOUS AND YET DO NOT KEEP A TIGHT REIN ON THEIR TONGUES DECEIVE THEMSELVES, AND THEIR RELIGION IS WORTHLESS."
– JAMES 1:26

"THE WORDS OF A WISE MAN'S MOUTH ARE GRACIOUS AND WIN HIM FAVOR, BUT THE LIPS OF A FOOL CONSUME HIM.... THE FOOL MULTIPLIES WORDS."
– ECCLESIASTES 10:12-14

"REMIND THE PEOPLE TO ... SLANDER NO ONE, TO BE PEACEABLE AND CONSIDERATE, AND ALWAYS TO BE GENTLE TOWARD EVERYONE."
– TITUS 3:1-2

"GAY LIFESTYLE"
"LIFESTYLE CHOICE"

"SEXUAL PREFERENCE"

Your loved one will feel blamed for choosing same-gender attractions. **Many teens are blamed** for living a "gay lifestyle" when they are **not even dating anyone.**

Gay married couples will **assume you think they are promiscuous** if you refer to their relationship as a "lifestyle."

These phrases are demeaning, **convey judgment,** and demonstrate a lack of understanding.

"PRACTICING HOMOSEXUAL"

"ALTERNATIVE LIFESTYLE"

"ADAM & EVE, NOT ADAM & STEVE"

Your LGBT+ loved ones will sense that they are being **ridiculed for being so stupid.** This kind of statement screams, "Don't you get it?!"

If sinners can't be Christian, we're all in big trouble. We may not place a "prefix" in front of our own Christian identity *with our language.* But we add the prefix "sin" *with our actions* every time we choose other identities and inclinations over God. While it is true that every person is accountable to God for their life, **it is counterproductive to deny the authenticity of our loved ones' spiritual identity.** (Note: Many who identify as a gay Christian maintain a traditional biblical belief and do not act on same-gender sexual desires.)

"THERE IS NO SUCH THING

AS A GAY CHRISTIAN"

info@leadthemhome.org

REDUCING LATERAL DISTRACTIONS

The Apostle Paul teaches that a spiritual journey that culminates in repentance requires the seeds of "patience, tolerance, and kindness" (Romans 2:1-4). But how can teens and young adults begin this journey toward God — and hear His voice — when the path is heavily blocked by injustice, mistreatment, and fear?

Clearing roadblocks and healing wounds gives spiritual identity a chance to grow.

GOD

VERTICAL WHISPERS

SPIRITUAL IDENTITY FORMATION

EXPERIENCING GOD'S WORD

UNCONDITIONAL LOVE

DISCERNING GOD'S STILL, SMALL VOICE

BELONGING & INCLUSION

RECOGNITION OF GOD-GIVEN TALENTS

FAMILY ACCEPTANCE

PROTECTION FROM HARM

FELLOWSHIP & SUPPORT SYSTEM

LATERAL DISTRACTIONS

THE FLESH

DEPRESSION & SUICIDALITY

FAMILY REJECTION

SOCIAL EXCLUSION

ISOLATION & LONELINESS

BULLYING & VICTIMIZATION

MORALIZING & MINIMIZING

PERSONAL PAIN

HURTFUL WORDS

JUDGMENT & CONDEMNATION

THE ENEMY OF OUR SOUL

THE WORLD

LGBT+ PERSON

"THE FARTHER I RUN AWAY FROM THE PLACE WHERE GOD DWELLS, THE LESS I AM ABLE TO HEAR THE VOICE THAT CALLS ME THE BELOVED, AND THE LESS I HEAR THAT VOICE, THE MORE ENTANGLED I BECOME IN THE MANIPULATIONS AND POWER GAMES OF THE WORLD."

– HENRI J.M. NOUWEN, THE RETURN OF THE PRODIGAL SON

www.leadthemhome.org

REMOVING ROCKS THAT BLOCK GROWTH

When the Pharisees brought to Jesus the woman caught in the act of adultery (Jn. 7:53-8:11), they were confident in their resolve that she be stoned to death. Jesus, on the other hand, bent down, and began to draw in the sand. One by one, the Pharisees dropped their rocks and walked away. By identifying their sins, Jesus disabled the power of "rocks" intended to reject, condemn, and literally kill.

Jesus protected a sinful (and vulnerable) person. Against a long history of men simultaneously using and condemning this woman, **Jesus transcended these "power games" to bring God's presence to her wounds. In doing so, she immediately felt safe and valued enough to tell the truth about her life to Jesus.**

When someone has a traumatic history involving bullying, exclusion, family rejection, or religious condemnation, there is no space for them to recognize and reveal the truth of their life. All their energy is distracted by the "clanging cymbals" of this world. They are so beaten down that most of their energy is focused on self-protection from real and perceived threats.

My 13-year-old son was talking about feeling ridiculed for his beliefs at school. He made a very simple but powerful statement: "Dad, **when people attack me, it just makes me want to prove them wrong.** But you know what, Dad? That feeling of wanting to prove them wrong — it's just human nature."

Every wound in a person's life can become a "lateral distraction" that prevents the ability to hear the whispers of God in their life. These "rocks" have tremendous power to block someone from vertical spiritual growth. Further, it causes them to hunker down into a defensive posture, needing to prove

PEOPLE CAN GROW IN FAITH IDENTITY WHEN THEY ARE GIVEN SPACE TO OWN THEIR STORY BEFORE GOD.

they are right or worthy or talented. **The trouble with "lateral distractions" is that they can actually cloud a person's ability to see their life as it is.** How can I tell the truth of my life if I cannot see it?

What Jesus did for the woman caught in adultery was an act of justice. In our world today, many Evangelicals see all the focus on "justice" as an affront to biblical truth. Yet what Jesus did was sheer justice. His act to protect her was equally an act of spiritual warfare.

EVERY WOUND IN A PERSON'S LIFE CAN BECOME A "LATERAL DISTRACTION" THAT PREVENTS VERTICAL SPIRITUAL GROWTH.

When we protect, care for, serve, comfort, invite, and encourage LGBT+ people, we are in essence taking a justice action step, entering into the spiritual warfare of blocking "religious rocks" that have repeatedly been used to judge and exclude them.

When we abide in Christ, bathe our efforts in prayer, and posture ourselves to learn from, listen to, and love LGBT+ people, God can anoint our efforts to produce something spiritual — something that "love the sinner, hate the sin" has no power to ever accomplish. God can use us to work against "power games" and "clanging cymbals" and "trigger clichés" that shut people down. When this happens, don't be surprised if people start revealing the truth of their lives.

In one support session, a young gay man unexpectedly confessed his uncer-

tainty about his sexuality. For months, he insisted — in front of his parents — that gay relationships are absolutely okay with God.

In the power of *safe space*, provided to him week after week for many months, he unintentionally whispered: "Just because I say it's okay doesn't mean it's okay with God — and it doesn't mean I always feel like it's okay. Sometimes, I worry if I am living in sin."

Instead of jumping all over him with "you finally get it," my response was confessional in nature:

"Trust me, I know that feeling! It is not comfortable. Given how much I know you love your boyfriend, what is it like for you when you feel this uncertainty or fear?"

When we disarm condemnation, it creates space for people to tell the truth of their story because they no longer have to hide to self-protect. When you commit to creating safe space for honest conversation, don't be surprised if God shows up.

"IF I SPEAK IN THE TONGUES OF MEN OR OF ANGELS, BUT DO NOT HAVE LOVE, I AM ONLY A RESOUNDING GONG OR A CLANGING CYMBAL."
– 1 COR. 13:1

info@leadthemhome.org

NAVIGATING RELATIONAL G A P S

THE OBJECTIVE FOR PARENTS (and other family members) is to **grieve well** and **avoid inflicting shock, denial, anger, bargaining, or depression** upon LGBT+ loved ones. That said, no parent is perfect. As we've said, even loving parents will make mistakes on this journey. Every parent of every child makes many mistakes.

We never want to minimize the pain or mistreatment that LGBT+ young people may have experienced, and we certainly must be committed to doing everything possible to prevent mistreatment within homes, schools, neighborhoods, and churches. Without lessening this focus, let us for a moment consider all the gaps that parents are processing in the hours, days, weeks, months, and years after their child comes out.

TIME GAP #1: MATURITY GAP

Whether a teen is gay, straight, or transgender, all teens desire to exercise autonomy in decision making. The Maturity Gap captures the age distance between an **LGBT+ loved one's desire to exercise autonomy** in decision making versus a **parent's sense of responsibility to oversee such decisions**. As detailed below, authority must be incrementally released as loved ones age — but capturing the right balance can generate tension for all involved. Further, while some requests that LGBT+ youth make of their parents are very similar to other teens' requests (like permission to date), others are quite unique (like asking to take hormone blockers). Do you hold the line? Maybe, but if so, for how long?

There is a season to say "no" and a season to let our adult children make their own decisions before God. Parents who exercise an absolute "no" eventually send their young adult children into the world with no parental guidance in making personal decisions. Progressively permitting your teen to make more of their own decisions is necessary for their emotional, mental, and spiritual maturity.

MOVING FROM AUTHORITY TO INFLUENCE

MOST EFFECTIVE STYLE

AUTHORITY

INFLUENCE

13-15
YEARS OLD

16-18
YEARS OLD

19-21
YEARS OLD

RETAIN AUTHORITY	RELAX AUTHORITY	RELEASE AUTHORITY
FIRM BOUNDARIES	FLEXIBLE BOUNDARIES	FREE BOUNDARIES
PROTECTOR	ADVISOR	INFLUENCER
MORAL TEACHER	SHEPHERD GUIDE	TRUSTED FRIEND

EVERY PARENT OF EVERY CHILD, GAY OR STRAIGHT, MUST EVENTUALLY LET GO AND TRUST GOD.

PARENTAL POWER MUST TRANSFORM INTO TRUSTED INFLUENCE AS TEENS GROW INTO ADULTS.

TIME GAP #2: DISCLOSURE GAP

The Disclosure Gap represents the time distance between **when a teen realizes their LGBT+ experience** and **when they come out to their parents.** Often times, this gap can be 2 to 8 years wide. For some, it can be 10 or more years wide. Loved ones have been self-discovering and working toward self-acceptance for years. For many parents, though, it's like an instant, unexpected breaking news headline.

GAP #3: EXPECTATION GAP

The Expectation Gap expresses the emotional distance between **the relief (or even celebration) that LGBT+ loved ones experience** and **the shock (or grief) that their parents often experience.** LGBT+ loved ones are shedding what may be a years-long repression in order to joyfully embrace self-acceptance and potentially pursue a romantic interest. Some parents, at this same point in time, could feel very angry. Other parents, even while intending to demonstrate love and acceptance, may inwardly be feeling extreme loss, sadness, and shock.

GAP #4: BELIEF GAP

The Belief Gap describes the difference between **an LGBT+ loved one's religious beliefs about marriage and sexuality** and **their parents' beliefs.** Christian parents may have just heard their child express a biblical belief related to sexuality only weeks ago, but suddenly those beliefs are wobbly or entirely abandoned. This can add frustration to the relational mix for both LGBT+ loved ones and their families.

GAP #5: LANGUAGE GAP

The Language Gap constitutes the relational distance between an LGBT+ loved one's and their parents' **understanding of, and vocabulary related to, sexual and gender identity.** Parents may question whether sexuality and gender are even legitimate aspects of identity, while their children are operating in a world that is rapidly expanding both the categories and spectrums for sexual and gender identity. As indicated in Words Matter (page 38), language mistakes can severely damage relational trust. *Every word counts.*

IMAGINE ALL 5 OF THESE GAPS CRASHING INTO A PARENT-CHILD RELATIONSHIP IN A SINGLE POINT IN TIME! PARENTS *AND* TEENS ARE BOUND TO MAKE MISTAKES. MUTUAL FORGIVENESS IS A NECESSITY.

PARENTS LOVING WELL

DESPITE PAST MISTAKES, MANY PARENTS ARE MOVING FORWARD AND TAKING THE NEXT POSITIVE STEP IN LOVING THEIR LGBT+ CHILDREN.*

We have started praying about everything: our interactions, our words, and for the grace of Christ Jesus to pour out of us in genuine love for our daughter. We have started seeing all aspects of her as a person, not getting stuck on this one issue. **We make it a point to delight in her, make memories with her, and accept her where she is, trusting that God is at work in her life.** Also, we have surrendered our own hearts and wills to God for His transformation of *us*, depending on and seeking to know Him more intimately day by day.

When we met her partner, we hugged her and treated her like a friend of the family. **Our daughter was in an LGBT+ volleyball league, and we went to watch her play in the finals.** I'm sad to say we were the only spectators in a room where six different games were going on at the same time. We whooped and shouted, learned her teammates' names, and tried to encourage them on the court, just like we did in her younger years. Her teammates came up to us afterward and thanked us for being there.

I always keep the door open, loving freely and telling him frequently that I love him. **I have stopped fearing that he will misinterpret my love as a change in belief.** I have also learned to appreciate and enjoy his partner and friends instead of being afraid.

I accept him as he is and tell him how much I love him. We make sure he's included in all family discussions and activities. When he finally told us he was gay, **I made it a point to fly out to see him and tell him he is always welcome at our home.**

We have realized that we need to look at both our child and their partner as beloved creations of God, creations with whom He desperately wants a relationship.** That is at the core of my posture. This realization did not happen overnight, and I'm still not completely there. But sin affects every human being on the planet. No one is exempt. That truth has helped me to find common ground. If the love and grace of God that I have experienced is received by either or both of them, it is 100% worth it!

Our greatest successes: **We have allowed space for the Holy Spirit to work and speak to our daughter.** We have loved her partner and received her without judgment. Praying with confident belief in God's love and faithfulness toward our daughter, we have begun to let the Lord do His cleansing, healing work in our own hearts.

I continue to love them and frequently let them know how precious they are to me. **I hug them often and demonstrate loving physical affection.** I get to know their friends.

I've never let the door of our communication close. Regardless of circumstances, I've held that as a top priority since my children were little.

I have come to accept my role as her father. I am not the one for her to share all her sexual struggles with. She has other people in her life to trust with this information. This helped me accept my role. I must respect her and trust her to make her own decisions. My role is to help her know that she is loved no matter what.

We all met as a family when he came out a year ago. **We led our family to agree to love him unconditionally.** Then we met as a family with Lead Them Home to ask questions and get help in keeping our son close. Our son lives hundreds of miles away, so he wasn't there, but he knew about both family meetings. Since then, his boyfriend has spent a weekend with us.

*Lead Them Home Survey of Parent Engagement of LGBT+ Children (October 2017)

I have changed for the better through committing this struggle to God and surrendering my son to His loving care. **I have started praying that my son first and foremost would know and understand the love Jesus has for him.**

Our greatest successes have been open communication and unconditional love. I started to see and express to my son that this was *his* journey and that he needed to seek out God's guidance in his life for himself. We didn't shove our theology down his throat. **He knew what we believed about homosexuality. Even so, we encouraged him to find out the answers for himself and to own his faith.** We told him that no matter where his journey took him, we love him and want a close relationship with him.

What pleases me the most is how our relationship with our daughter's partner has developed over the years. Initially, she was a difficult person to get to know — very closed to us emotionally. She came from a dysfunctional family background, and you could tell that she had been hurt in many ways. Over the years, though, she has come to trust and care for us. We love her very much.

Our success came when we started approaching him with humility, and without mentioning our prayer life to him, we sought the Lord for healing in our relationship.

My best success is that my child still loves coming home and being with us. I know that he loves to spend time with all of us.

Our success was communicating our unconditional love right away. We have continued to follow that up with ongoing tenderness and care for her. At the same time, **I think talking about this topic — as an important one, but not the only topic to discuss in life — has been healthy.**

About 2 years after she came out, we started reading many books and resources. **We learned about the high rate of suicide for gay teens whose families reject them. That was a wake-up call.** After that, we resolved to just love and support her. We confessed how truly sorry we are for all the hurtful things we said. Now, we just shower her with love. We invite open conversation — even about her partner. She was so tired of hiding.

I freely and lovingly share about Jesus. He grew up in a Christian home, so he "knows" the gospel message, but I think he received a legalistic version and felt that he couldn't be a follower of Christ and be attracted to men. **This journey has opened up new dialogue and has allowed us to present the true gospel: that salvation is open to all and that the Holy Spirit will sanctify us throughout our lives.**

I express to him often about how deep my love is for him. **I have learned to listen without reacting or pushing for information.** I no longer "preach at" him or pressure him to go back to church.

Our success was helping our child feel like we were "on their side" enough that we could take steps together slowly and not rush into big, life-changing, irreversible decisions.

We maintain contact and relationship with him through all the drama. We offer unconditional love. **He was once suicidal and is now doing much better, even though there is still much healing needed.**

Even though he lives in another state, **he told us that wherever his dad and I are — that is his home.** Needless to say, we got teary-eyed.

HOW TO RESET THE RELATIONSHIP

Specifically confess every mistake you know you have made.

Ask your child if they have been hurt in ways you don't recognize.

Apologize and seek forgiveness for any way you've hurt your child.

Ask to start again — and reset your attitude, tone, and language.

Invite dialogue without letting differences take over every conversation.

Declare that you accept your child and dearly love them.

Admit that this is all new, but you are willing to listen and learn.

Immediately take any "threats" off the table.

Pay back any financial penalties or withholding of college tuition.

Tell your child how valuable they are to you.

If your adult child has a partner, invite them both to dinner.

Win your adult child's trust by loving their partner generously.

Invite your adult child (and partner) home for the holidays.

Resetting a fractured relationship is more likely to occur with thoughtful language. Before proceeding, review "Words Matter" (Page 38) carefully.

SAMPLE "RESET" LETTER

Dear Matthew,

We want to apologize for things that we have said to you since you came out 3 years ago. You are our precious son, and we are so proud of you. You are not a grief to us. Yet in our grieving, we have said hurtful words. I am sure there are things we said unconsciously or even words we cannot recall, but we do remember the following.

- We yelled at you for being gay instead of comforting you.
- We blamed you for being gay rather than listening to you.
- We accused you of choosing to be gay when we needed to learn more.
- We told you to "change" as if you had some power that you refused to use.
- We labeled your personhood a "gay lifestyle" and an "alternative lifestyle."

There is so much more. I am sure you recall things that we cannot. We invite you to share anything with us that was, or remains, hurtful to you. The one thing we feel most sad about is that we never even asked what it was like for you to live the entirety of your teenage years without Mom and Dad knowing about your sexuality. It has haunted us that you feared we would reject you since age 12 or so. Then, when you finally had the courage to share with us, we nearly did exactly that. It grieves us.

When you started dating Jack, we refused to meet him. We want to say that we actually enjoy Jack. He is so thoughtful and kind. We see his compassion for others. We also see the way he has honored us even as we did not welcome him so warmly. We want to apologize to you both as a couple for our disrespect. We also want to invite the two of you home this weekend to join us for dinner.

Finally, we made threats when we felt very out of control. We denied your Christian faith. We told you that you cannot come home as long as you are living a life of abomination. We demanded that you not tell your brothers and other family members. We treated you as if you were a danger to your nephews. We even withheld monetary gifts from you that we gave to your brothers at Christmas.

Son, enclosed is a check equal to the gifts that we withheld from you. We will never again ask you to hide your story, and we will not avoid sharing our life with you. We are not ashamed of you. You are our precious son — and we are ready to receive Jack into our family as a son. You both are always welcome home.

We see Jesus in you. We applaud your Christian faith, and we encourage you to keep diving deep into Christ and the Bible. Except this time, we just encourage you to cultivate your personal relationship with God. Keep on making Him your Savior and Lord. We will no longer judge you. We ask you to seek God with your whole heart, soul, strength, and mind — but we no longer have an agenda. Just seek God with all you've got.

We let our hurts and fears become a hammer over your head. We did not realize it at the time, but it is very clear to us today. We sinned against you.

Son, we want to express our sincere apology. You are so precious to us. We never want to lose you. We long for a restored relationship and ask for the opportunity to earn trust with you and Jack.

We are asking for your forgiveness. We would love to treat you and Jack to a nice dinner this weekend. We invite you both to stay over with us if your schedule is free.

Please forgive us. Know how much we love you. In the midst of any differences that remain, we will make it together because there will no longer be an "us versus them" attitude in our family. There is only us: you and Jack are part of us. Come home. A long hug, warm welcome, delicious meal, and much love await you both.

Thank you for being such a wonderful son. Since the day you were born, we have been amazed by our Matthew. You have always been and will always be our precious son. We hope to see you guys this weekend.

We love you,
Mom and Dad

FOR HELP STARTING YOUR RESET LETTER, VISIT LEADTHEMHOME.ORG/RESET.

REFLECTION QUESTIONS

1. In **Responding Well When Loved Ones Come Out,** 19-year-old Eric is on the precipice of coming out to his parents. He does not feel sufficiently safe to do so. Discuss what Eric is facing. He is described as a "best-case scenario." Discuss why. What does this imply for other LGBT+ teens?

2. In **How To Express Acceptance**, identify important messages for pastors and parents to convey to LGBT+ loved ones. From **Follow-Up Conversation**, develop a few of your own questions that can generate safe dialogue with LGBT+ young people. Please discuss.

3. As you review **Sustainable Support System**, what role can you play as a pastor or parent? What is the one rule you should never break in attempting to expand someone's support system?

4. *Guiding Families* suggests that *even loving parents* (and *loving pastors*) will make mistakes in relating to LGBT+ loved ones. Which of the **Common Mistakes** can you most relate to? What underlying factors play a role in yielding relational mistakes?

5. The parent survey responses in **Overcoming Relational Mistakes** offer compelling data on the impact of relational mistakes. Take note of the *impact* and *duration* of some mistakes. Which survey response most impacted you? Please discuss.

6. **Words Matter** describes words and phrases that we, as Christians, frequently use when engaging LGBT+ people. Why is language so important in relating to LGBT+ loved ones? Are there any adjustments you need to make in your language usage? Why or why not?

7. How would you define a **Lateral Distraction**? How do lateral distractions affect a person's ability to receive spiritual nourishment? In **Removing Rocks That Block Growth**, what does Jesus do for the woman? How can you follow Jesus in protecting LGBT+ loved ones?

8. In **Navigating Relational Gaps**, *Guiding Families* describes five gaps between parents and LGBT+ teens. Importantly, these gaps can exist between LGBT+ young people and pastors as well. What happens when all five gaps collide in a parent-child relationship? As pastors and parents, how do we build *influence* in the lives of LGBT+ young people?

9. Parents don't just make mistakes! In **Parents Loving Well**, we learn of the many positive steps parents are taking to care for and generously love LGBT+ children. In what ways are you, as a pastor or parent, already caring well for LGBT+ loved ones? Please discuss.

10. **How To Reset The Relationship** offers a pathway to making amends for any past mistakes. What are key points you would include in writing a **Reset Letter**? Pastors, would you ever consider writing a Reset Letter to an LGBT+ person you have cared for?

"SEARCH ME [THOROUGHLY], O GOD, AND KNOW MY HEART; TEST ME AND KNOW MY ANXIOUS THOUGHTS;

AND SEE IF THERE IS ANY WICKED OR HURTFUL WAY IN ME, AND LEAD ME IN THE EVERLASTING WAY."

– PSALM 139:23-24

INDIVIDUAL AND FAMILY support

> " In 2010, I faced some of the most confusing and painful years of my life. I was 19 and had been struggling with my sexuality since I was 13. I was out on my own for the first time at college, and my relationship with my family was gone because I had come out as lesbian.
>
> The depression I had been battling for years came down upon me even harder as I felt everything I had known was being ripped out from under me. Stability was far from me, and I kept pushing God away because I was tired of rejection. I couldn't imagine Him offering me any kind of acceptance.
>
> That year, I exchanged multiple personal emails with Lead Them Home. The ministry's support calls gave me a shred of stability and pointed me back to the Cross. Founder Bill Henson truly cared for me and understood how I was suffering. Even still, I still had a long road toward a close relationship with Jesus.
>
> After many years of back-and-forth wrestling with God's will for my life, I finally completely surrendered my life to Jesus, falling wholly dependent on His grace to rebuild my life and faith identity. God has blessed me in ways I can't describe. He continues to build me a life I could never have imagined before. "
>
> – Noelle

IF YOU OR YOUR FAMILY NEED ADDITIONAL SUPPORT, WE INVITE YOU TO CONTACT US AT INFO@LEADTHEMHOME.ORG.*

IN PERSON SKYPE PHONE EMAIL

*If your situation is an emergency, please dial 911.

"I WARN AND COUNSEL THE ELDERS AMONG YOU (THE PASTORS AND SPIRITUAL GUIDES OF THE CHURCH) AS A FELLOW ELDER AND AS AN EYEWITNESS [CALLED TO TESTIFY] OF THE SUFFERINGS OF CHRIST, AS WELL AS A SHARER IN THE GLORY (THE HONOR AND SPLENDOR) THAT IS TO BE REVEALED (DISCLOSED, UNFOLDED):

TEND (NURTURE, GUARD, GUIDE, AND FOLD) THE FLOCK OF GOD THAT IS [YOUR RESPONSIBILITY], NOT BY COERCION OR CONSTRAINT, BUT WILLINGLY; NOT DISHONORABLY MOTIVATED BY THE ADVANTAGES AND PROFITS [BELONGING TO THE OFFICE], BUT EAGERLY AND CHEERFULLY;

NOT DOMINEERING [AS ARROGANT, DICTATORIAL, AND OVERBEARING PERSONS] OVER THOSE IN YOUR CHARGE, BUT BEING EXAMPLES (PATTERNS AND MODELS OF CHRISTIAN LIVING) TO THE FLOCK (THE CONGREGATION). AND [THEN] WHEN THE CHIEF SHEPHERD IS REVEALED, YOU WILL WIN THE CONQUEROR'S CROWN OF GLORY."

– 1 PETER 5:1-4

PART 3:
FAQ, BELIEFS, & FAMILY MATTERS

ADDRESSING THE HARDEST QUESTIONS

WE WILL NOW ADDRESS A NUMBER of delicate matters. We start by offering answers to some of the most common questions parents and pastors face when LGBT+ young people come out. Many Christians have *strong* but *uninformed* views on the toughest questions. It can lead to unfruitful arguments and unnecessary fractures in relationships.

For example, **Christians (of all stripes) often think *any* inborn cause of same-gender attraction or gender identity necessarily suggests that God "makes" people gay or transgender.** This is a false presumption. Being born a certain way does not necessarily imply God's intention. Is it God who "makes" babies born with painful, debilitating, or fatal conditions?

As another example, **Christians (of all stripes) routinely think that a conversation about biblical beliefs only honors God's character if "I" win the debate.** This sets up a dividing wall and fuels a combative or condemning spirit.

It is not actually so easy to change another person's deeply held beliefs. Reducing the gospel to "convincing others to agree with me" is unhealthy. We are not called to "win" a debate; we are called to love and honor God and to love and serve one another.

We have no power to convince others to change their views. It works both ways: our beliefs are deeply held. No one can simply flip a switch to change our beliefs.

We have no power to control people, and we have no interest in judging people. Rather, we strive to follow Jesus in laying down our lives to care for vulnerable people. God has the power through his Holy Word and Spirit to convict our hearts if he wants us to change what we believe. This can happen instantly or over many years!

Along the way, we have found that answering distant, complex, and controversial questions with accessible, simple, and accurate answers is a bridge to building trust across differences.

Relationships built upon respectful dialogue, unconditional acceptance, and secure love will allow a parent and teen (or a pastor and student) to transcend differences of belief without destroying relational trust.

After gaining better answers to common questions, we will then learn how to discuss biblical truth. We want to cultivate a healthy belief that goes beyond mere *right beliefs*. The Pharisees had all the right beliefs, but all the wrong ways of engaging people. Jesus spent lots of time confronting legalism because it tends to dehumanize people. Finally, we will look at several unique family situations that require specific guidance.

DID MY PARENTING CAUSE MY CHILD'S HOMOSEXUALITY?

We encourage families to focus on relationship rather than causation. Scientists believe the causes of same-gender attraction and gender dysphoria entail complex nature and nurture inputs. If you know that you have sinned in parenting your child, then — unrelated to sexuality — confess, apologize, and improve how you love your child.

WHY DO PEOPLE SAY THEY WERE BORN GAY?

Some people likely are born gay. Many more are likely born with a predisposition toward same-gender love and attraction that builds into their sexuality as they develop. If you knew you never made a "choice" to be gay, and if you knew that you simply always felt these feelings, wouldn't you also conclude you were born gay? This does not minimize the many nurture-related inputs that can play a role in the formation of sexuality.

DOES GOD MAKE PEOPLE GAY?

Does the condition in which any of us are born imply God's intent? With sensitivity to differently-abled children, does God intend for a child to be born with little brain development or missing limbs? Or chemical imbalance? Or anxiety? Or Zika virus? God certainly set in motion the capacity for human reproduction, but sin and suffering result in every person being born with human brokenness. How we are born does not necessarily imply God's intent.

ISN'T ACCEPTANCE REALLY A FORM OF APPROVAL?

Acceptance means that God loves us even when we fall short of His glory. It means that we, as parents, love our children no matter what. It means our children always have a family and a home. Acceptance becomes approval if my beliefs and actions depart from God's Word. I can fully honor God in my beliefs and actions — and simultaneously love my children even when they depart from God's Word.

CAN GAY PEOPLE CHANGE?

Most people, gay or straight, do not experience a material change in their orientation over their lifetime. When change is reported, it primarily involves three common scenarios: (1) a young person growing through a questioning stage of development; (2) a woman finding security being in an intimate relationship with another woman for a time; and (3) a man or woman recovering from molestation or sexual experimentation.

COMMON QUESTIONS

DOES REPARATIVE THERAPY WORK?

Lead Them Home has never engaged in reparative therapy (RT). Adults making an informed and voluntary decision to pursue RT should not be ridiculed. Parents, however, should never force a minor or young adult into such treatment. In many states, RT is illegal. Adults report varying levels of success. Some have reported that it worked for a while, but that "change" was unsustainable over time. To claim that a treatment effectively works, (a) it should be helpful across a wide range of individuals and (b) healing should be sustainable over the long-term (permanent). In truth, a number of former proponents who once claimed "healing" (orientation change) are today living in a same-gender relationship. While we do not criticize or want to limit the rights of adults who voluntarily find value in it, we do not recommend reparative therapy. Lead Them Home has direct reports of RT severely damaging the emotional and mental health of both teenagers and adults, as well as their family members. For every person, regardless of sexual orientation or gender identity, the biblical objective is holiness rather than the elimination of temptation.

ARE YOU CONCERNED ABOUT QUEER IDEOLOGY IMPACTING CHILDREN?

Many damaging forces impact our children daily: issues like divorce, substance abuse, and pornography. While a new generation holds that gender and sexuality are fluid across a lifetime, research demonstrates that 99.4% of adults are binary male or female[1] and roughly 95% are heterosexual.[2] This generation's cause is about correcting mistreatment of marginalized people. Queer ideology is unlikely to move hard science. Why fight a battle that likely will self-correct for most people? We should instead lay our lives down for this emerging generation in the name of Christ.

[1] Flores AR, Herman JL, Gates GJ, & Brown TNT (2016). How Many Adults Identify as Transgender in the United States? Los Angeles, CA: The Williams Institute.
[2] Gates GJ (2016) In U.S. More Adults Identifying as LGBT [Data set]. Gallup U.S. Inc.

IS IT A SIN TO EXPERIENCE SAME-GENDER ATTRACTION?

Jesus was "tempted in every way" (Hebrews 4:15). We know that He never sinned, and thus we can conclude that temptation is *not* a sin. One Christian college student was told by another student: "Unless your same-sex attraction entirely goes away, you cannot go to Heaven." Thoughtless statements like this are untrue and can have tragic consequences. It is an indisputable fact that to experience temptation is to be human. As a caution, though, every human knows there is a thin line between feeling temptation and falling into sin (see James 1:15).

WHY DO LGBT+ PEOPLE IDENTIFY BY THEIR SEXUALITY OR GENDER?

While being in Christ should be our primary identification, many other roles in life, such as being a parent, spouse, grandparent, or sibling, play core roles in the formation of our personal identity ("who I am"). While we may have biblical beliefs that forbid same-gender romantic or sexual relationships (including gay marriage), the ultimate desire LGBT+ people have for love or a life partner is a core human longing. For this reason, they will experience "who I love" as a vital element of personal identity — as deeply as any heterosexual person would. Acknowledging that this experience is just as true for LGBT+ people does not unwind or threaten our theological convictions.

SHOULD MY 15-YEAR-OLD LESBIAN DAUGHTER BE INCLUDED IN YOUTH GROUP?

Absolutely! How tragic it would be if we excluded any youth when we should be nourishing their faith identity. All people — gay, straight, or transgender — need salvation through Christ. As Paul indicates in Romans 2:1-4, the path toward salvation includes five ingredients. The first three are explicitly stated: *patience, tolerance*, and *kindness*. The other two are implied by the word "toward" — *space to belong* and *time to grow*. Acts of exclusion squash spiritual growth. We should include LGBT+ youth, reduce their vulnerability to bullying, call out their gifts, foster God's purposes for their life, and encourage their families toward acceptance.

PEOPLE SAY "DON'T JUDGE," BUT I DISOBEY GOD IF I IGNORE THE BIBLE'S INSTRUCTION TO JUDGE SIN.

"Believers, do not speak against or slander one another. He who speaks [self-righteously] against a brother or judges his brother [hypocritically], speaks against the Law and judges the Law. If you judge the Law, you are not a doer of the Law but a judge of it. There is only one Lawgiver and Judge, the One who is able to save and to destroy [the one God who has the absolute power of life and death]; but who are you to [hypocritically or self-righteously] pass judgment on your neighbor?" (James 4:11-12, AMP).

I WOULD NEVER HAVE MY CHILD BRING THEIR ALCOHOLISM OR A DRUG DEALER INTO MY HOME. WHY THEIR SEXUALITY OR PARTNER?

Alcohol and drugs are addictive, mind-altering substances that can kill. When loved ones attempt to manipulate family for money to abuse substances, parents might limit home visits. The basis for such a boundary is to guard against manipulation or threat of physical harm. Who in anyone's family is not struggling with sin? Building relationship, establishing better communication, and nourishing our children's faith identity all outweigh any reason to reject our children.

AM I SUPPOSED TO JUST LET MY CHILD LIVE IN SIN?

On page 42, we discuss how parents must transition from authority to influence as our children become adults. The biblical goal is not for parents to dictate how their adult children live their lives — the ultimate objective is for every one of us to understand that we will be held accountable to God for how we live our lives. To accept this is not a biblical compromise. Rather, it is a spiritual reality that we, as parents, cannot control our adult children. There is a point at which we are no longer responsible for the decisions they make.

"DO NOT JUDGE AND CRITICIZE AND CONDEMN [OTHERS UNFAIRLY WITH AN ATTITUDE OF SELF-RIGHTEOUS SUPERIORITY AS THOUGH ASSUMING THE OFFICE OF A JUDGE], SO THAT YOU WILL NOT BE JUDGED [UNFAIRLY]. FOR JUST AS YOU [HYPOCRITICALLY] JUDGE OTHERS [WHEN YOU ARE SINFUL AND UNREPENTANT], SO WILL YOU BE JUDGED; AND IN ACCORDANCE WITH YOUR STANDARD OF MEASURE [USED TO PASS OUT JUDGMENT], JUDGMENT WILL BE MEASURED TO YOU." – MATTHEW 7:1-2, AMP (JESUS)

HOW DO I DISCUSS
BIBLICAL BELIEFS
ABOUT SEXUALITY & GENDER IDENTITY?

LEAD THEM HOME HIGHLY DISCOURAGES *FOCUSING ON THEOLOGY* WHEN TEENS ARE HURTING. *SAFETY AND FAMILY CONNECTION* MUST BE THE TOP PRIORITIES.

Your child is not a sinner because of their sexual orientation or gender identity, but for the same reason we are **ALL** sinners: *we all sin!*

Unintentionally, many Christians have so judged LGBT+ young people that it has actually *deconstructed their faith identity.*

Avoid positioning God *against* your child's identity. Remember that many continually anticipate condemnation due to **trauma.**

Take your child to Psalm 23 or Psalm 91 or Psalm 103 or a parable of Jesus. **Nourish a holistic faith identity** to build trust in God.

You can *humbly* ask your child thoughtful questions (see next page).

Regardless of their responses, prove that *dialogue* can be safe. Do not shame them if they no longer share your belief.

SIX GUIDING PRINCIPLES FOR A HEALTHY CONVERSATION ON FAITH, SEXUALITY, AND GENDER

1 Attest to your child's Christian identity.

2 Suggest dialogue, but do not force it.

3 Ask thoughtful questions and listen well.

4 Avoid hurtful labels or accusations.

5 Respond to belief differences with respect.

6 Foster a holistic conversation about faith.

For additional help, please contact Lead Them Home.

"LIVE IN HARMONY WITH ONE ANOTHER.... NEVER OVERESTIMATE YOURSELF OR BE WISE IN YOUR OWN CONCEITS.... IF POSSIBLE, AS FAR AS IT DEPENDS ON YOU, LIVE AT PEACE WITH EVERYONE." – ROMANS 12:16,18

www.leadthemhome.org

HONORING QUESTIONS

YOU CAN ASK ABOUT BELIEFS

Lead Them Home must stress that the following discussion questions are exclusively intended for emotionally and mentally healthy persons. **If your loved one has a recent history of victimization, suicidality, or emotional distress, you should place on hold any questions about biblical beliefs.** The safety of loved ones is a top priority.

What does your **sexual or gender identity** mean to you?

How do you describe your **faith identity?** What does your faith mean to you?

How does your sexual or gender identity **intersect** with your faith identity?

Have you ever experienced **conflict** between your sexual or gender identity and your biblical beliefs?

Do any spiritual conflicts about your sexual or gender identity still bother you?

If so, how does God help you, and **who offers you support?** You can count me (us) as part of your support network if you ever need to talk when things are tough.

If not, how did you find **peace?** How did God guide you to **accept** your sexual or gender identity? **Who helped you develop your beliefs?**

Are you planning to stay connected at **church?**

Are you open to talking with a pastor about **what you believe?**

Are you open to Mom and Dad sharing with you **what we believe?**

IF YOU ARE WORKING THROUGH YOUR OWN THEOLOGY, WE RECOMMEND READING *PEOPLE TO BE LOVED* BY PRESTON SPRINKLE.

Christians tend to take on responsibility for others' lives, leading us to fall into the trap of considering it our urgent duty to confront or hold accountable those who *fall short of God's glory.*

The problem is that we apply our urgency quite selectively. It does not appear that Christians are super urgent about dealing with the widespread pornography pandemic, for example. Jesus warned the Pharisees and teachers of the law that they had **blind spots.** He angered them by even referring to them as **blind guides.** They could so easily see others' sins, but they barely even noticed their own sins.

We are no different today. As **"majority sinners,"** we seem to be automatic recipients of "Amazing Grace." Yet we can often exclude **"minority sinners"** from grace altogether. Or more commonly, the "grace" that we *say in words* often is short of any *real care* for people.

As an example, surely it is not *every* Evangelical's responsibility to tell LGBT+ people that God "loves the sinner but hates the sin." Yet ask many LGBT+ folks what they hear from Christians! They report that this cliché is nearly all that conservative Christians ever say to them.

It seems like many Christians carry an unhealthy fear that we are *condoning and enabling* gay sex if we fail in our *duty before God* to let LGBT+ folks know that they are living in a *sinful lifestyle.*

As noted in the Preface in "A Message For LGBT+ People," it is not our agenda to discuss theology in *Guiding Families.* Yet parents, pastors, and teens discuss sex and the Bible all the time. For this reason, it is worth clearly defining a healthy view of *biblical truth* (or orthodoxy).

> "THIS IS MY COMMANDMENT: THAT YOU LOVE ONE ANOTHER [JUST] AS I HAVE LOVED YOU. NO ONE HAS GREATER LOVE [NO ONE HAS SHOWN STRONGER AFFECTION] THAN TO LAY DOWN (GIVE UP) HIS OWN LIFE FOR HIS FRIENDS. YOU ARE MY FRIENDS IF YOU KEEP ON DOING THE THINGS WHICH I COMMAND YOU TO DO." – JOHN 15:12-14

7 CRITICAL ELEMENTS OF BIBLICAL TRUTH

*Jesus constantly confronts our tendency to have a **religious** "blind spot" — which we can define as critical elements of biblical truth that we are missing. **What am I missing?***

1. BELIEFS THAT HONOR GOD

2. BEHAVIORS IN OBEDIENCE TO GOD'S WORD

3. CHRISTLIKE TREATMENT OF OTHERS (WHETHER THEY ARE CHRISTIAN OR NOT)

4. COMPASSIONATE CONCERN FOR HURTING, VULNERABLE, OR MARGINALIZED PEOPLE

5. JOYFUL, WILLING, AND COMMITTED HEART TO LAY DOWN MY LIFE FOR OTHERS

6. HOLISTIC (NOT TARGETED) USE OF SCRIPTURE TO PLANT GOD'S WORD IN HUMAN HEARTS

7. ACTIVE PRAYER LIFE, EXPRESSED IN FAITH, BELIEVING IN GOD'S PROMISES FOR MY FAMILY

VIEW OF BIBLICAL TRUTH

To biblically honor God, we can never solely rely upon what we believe (see James 2:17). **Many Christians have *right beliefs* even as our own *wrong behaviors* materially betray those beliefs**. Others of us have *right beliefs*, and we're even striving for *right behaviors* — but we don't always *treat others* so well.

We can't achieve "biblical truth" only by knowing why others need to repent. We can't achieve it by believing in a Genesis version of marriage while privately using pornography. We can't achieve it by personal holiness if judgment easily bleeds out of our hearts toward others. We can't honor God with all the truth in the world *if the ground remains uneven at the foot of the cross*.

Honoring God is more than telling others that they are living in sin. We must ultimately do something about our own sins while treating others generously. If you want to do something about sin in our world, there is no greater power than for "majority sinners" to actually repent of our sins. Then, at least, we will offer a path for "minority sinners" to follow.

One last point: **By cultivating a healthy view of biblical truth, we necessarily infuse "patience, tolerance, and kindness" into our witness of Jesus Christ.** We become better missionaries. We become better pastoral caregivers. We become better preachers in the pulpit. We become better parents, better family members, and better friends to LGBT+ people.

Suddenly, living out the gospel is about much more than convincing someone that they are living in sin. **Healthy biblical truth means we seriously consider what is necessary to nourish faith identity in others.**

Nourishing faith identity in others starts by bringing Jesus in us to people where they are, as they are. We learn their story. We build relational trust. We serve and care for their needs. We protect them against any vulnerability to being wounded or condemned. Along the way, we can share Scriptures that meet them where they are in the needs, struggles, and joys they experience.

This isn't the end of our witness of biblical truth. But it's what is necessary to establish a holistic, fruitful foundation for gospel witness — a witness that humbly honors God and demonstrates the radical love of Jesus.

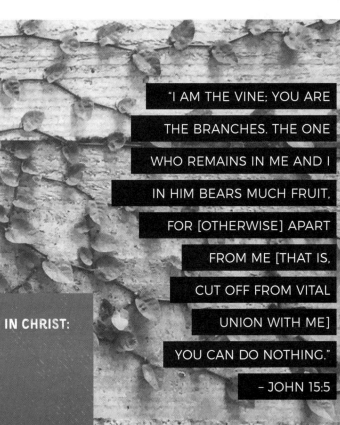

"I AM THE VINE; YOU ARE THE BRANCHES. THE ONE WHO REMAINS IN ME AND I IN HIM BEARS MUCH FRUIT, FOR [OTHERWISE] APART FROM ME [THAT IS, CUT OFF FROM VITAL UNION WITH ME] YOU CAN DO NOTHING."

– JOHN 15:5

HEALTHY ORTHODOXY IS NOTHING LESS THAN ABIDING IN CHRIST:

MY POSITION

+ MY PERSONAL PRACTICES

+ MY TREATMENT OF OTHERS

+ MY BRINGING CHRIST'S PRESENCE TO PEOPLE

info@leadthemhome.org

AN INTERVIEW WITH DR. PRESTON SPRINKLE AND DR. BRANSON PARLER

WE INTERVIEWED DR. PRESTON SPRINKLE AND DR. BRANSON PARLER TO ASK THEIR BIBLICAL GUIDANCE ON

CHALLENGING QUESTIONS OFTEN FACED BY PARENTS OF LGBT+ CHILDREN.

YOU BOTH HOLD TO A TRADITIONAL OR ORTHODOX BELIEF. THAT'S *WHAT* YOU BELIEVE. BUT PRACTICALLY SPEAKING, *HOW* DO YOU LIVE OUT WHAT YOU BELIEVE AROUND LGBT+ PEOPLE?

DR. SPRINKLE: I want to first be sensitive about history. While I do not believe that the traditional position itself causes harm to anyone, it is undeniable that legalistic Christians have mistreated or failed to care for LGBT+ people. No wonder our world sees traditional belief as the source of harm.

Next, we need a healthy view of marriage. **We should celebrate and honor God's design for marriage, but we cannot idolize it.** Straight and cisgender people are not superior to gay and transgender people. Married people are not superior to single people. Singleness and marriage are both wonderful — but each has its trials. Single people are not incomplete, and marriage will not complete us.

Finally, we must protect and defend LGBT+ people from harm. Mistreating gay and transgender people is not a Christian value — it dishonors God!

DR. PARLER: At the heart of the gospel, we find the amazing love and grace of Jesus who desires to reach even a sinner like me. Being a Christian is not about behavior modification; it's about heart transformation. So I want to live in a way that communicates to my friends (LGBT+ and straight) that we're all radically dependent on the grace of God — both to forgive us for our sins and to empower us to new life in the Spirit.

To emphasize Preston's last point, **I best honor God by treating people the way Jesus treats us.** We are defined first and foremost by the fact that God created and loves us.

MANY LGBT+ PEOPLE ARE FRUSTRATED (EVEN HURT) WHEN CHRISTIAN PARENTS HOLD TO A TRADITIONAL BELIEF. SOME SAY THEY CANNOT BE TRULY LOVED UNTIL THEIR PARENTS ADOPT AN AFFIRMING BELIEF. PARENTS CAN BE CONFLICTED BETWEEN HONORING GOD AND LOVING THEIR CHILDREN. HOW WOULD YOU GUIDE PARENTS?

DR. PARLER: You don't have to choose between honoring God and loving your children! I grew up in a legalistic church background, so I was in college before it really hit me that God loved me totally and unconditionally, based on nothing I did, but completely on what Jesus did for me.

Once we realize that Jesus' love is rooted in his grace, not our action, loving others becomes less of a mystery. Jesus didn't wait till we got our act together to show us love: "While we were sinners, Christ died for us" (Romans 5:8).

If Jesus would die for us while we were rebels, spitting in his face, what is he calling you to do for your child? Nothing could be more God-honoring than proving that love never gives up — and never walks away.

DR. SPRINKLE: With a God-honoring love, you can truly love your kids even as you hold to a traditional belief. That said, you may have to avoid overly stressing your beliefs in order to demonstrate your unswerving love for your LGBT+ child.

When LGBT+ people insist that the traditional belief is unloving, it is probably because many people who hold to that belief have harmed them. We cannot downplay the harm that has been done. It is not a flippant accusation — their frustration is based on well-documented mistreatment of LGBT+ people.

All that said, abandoning your biblical beliefs is not the answer. Scripture instructs us to love the Lord with all our heart, soul, strength, and mind — and like unto it, to love our neighbor as ourselves. You do not have to ditch your theology to love your children, but as Branson suggested, you must prove your love by being present in your child's life!

"YOU DO NOT HAVE TO DITCH YOUR THEOLOGY TO LOVE YOUR CHILDREN, BUT YOU MUST PROVE YOUR LOVE BY BEING PRESENT IN YOUR CHILD'S LIFE." – PRESTON SPRINKLE

MOST LGBT+ TEENS GROWING UP IN CHRISTIAN FAMILIES KNOW THEIR PARENTS' BIBLICAL BELIEFS ABOUT MARRIAGE AND SEXUALITY. MANY PARENTS WORRY, THOUGH, THAT THEIR CHILD MIGHT NOT BE AWARE OF WHAT THEY BELIEVE. HOW IMPORTANT IS IT FOR PARENTS TO TALK WITH LGBT+ CHILDREN ABOUT THEIR BIBLICAL BELIEFS?

DR. SPRINKLE: I agree that most LGBT+ kids do know what their parents believe. Assuming this is true, I would take pressure off parents: you do not have to keep reminding your child of your beliefs over and over again. What you need to emphasize so much more is how much you love your child.

At the same time, I don't want to take off the table a family studying Scripture or downplay the power of God's Word. But remember: this must be set within the context a loving relationship. If your child does not know they are loved, no Bible study will be effective.

Studying Scripture doesn't mean you target sexuality or gender identity. **Make sure Bible study, prayer, and family time are about all of God's Word — and how your child's day went!**

DR. PARLER: I can't believe I'm saying this (I'm a theology professor, after all), but it's less important than you might think. **Good theology plus bad timing is bad theology.** Your goal should not be to speak "timeless truths" but timely words of wisdom that will bring strength, healing, and life.

Be patient. Your child needs true biblical comfort that comes from resting in Jesus. It's his grace that will lead us, not more lectures or moralizing over what we should or should not do.

Now, as opportunities arise to talk naturally through various biblical teachings, I agree with Preston: I'm all for diving in. **But you have to trust that it's not on you and your words to control your child's life.** You have to trust God's Word to work with power over time.

SOME PARENTS GET FRUSTRATED WHEN BIBLICAL CONVERSATIONS FAIL TO CHANGE THEIR CHILD'S BELIEFS. THEY WORRY THEY DID IT WRONG OR DIDN'T MAKE IT CLEAR ENOUGH. HOW CAN PARENTS ADDRESS THIS ANXIETY?

DR. PARLER: Don't be anxious about anything, but in prayer, lay your heart and your requests before God. I think about Augustine, the greatest theologian in the history of Christianity, who lived most of his teens and twenties in an ungodly way that grieved his mother, a faithful Christian. When he reflects on her witness in his life, the main thing that stands out was her constant prayer for him. **Keep praying for your child.** As you pray, though, God will work in your heart, too!

DR. SPRINKLE: We cannot force our beliefs upon others — and beliefs are rarely cultivated simply because they were clearly articulated. Faith is not like a math problem in which brief instruction can help us immediately know the right answer. **Belief comes from within, and it is God who enables us to embrace his truth over time.**

More than just talking about biblical truth, we have to model it! You can share what the Bible teaches, but we must also embody the truthful grace of Jesus Christ in an unconditional way toward our kids. Kindness is truth. Love is truth. Grace is truth.

Even then, we cannot simply cause our children to believe it. Please do not feel guilty if your beliefs did not take root in your child's heart. God is not done yet! And that gets to Branson's point: never stop praying.

WHAT IS A PARENT'S RESPONSIBILITY BEFORE GOD? HOW CAN THEY HANDLE CONCERNS OVER WHETHER THEY HAVE DONE ENOUGH TO IMPACT THEIR CHILD'S LIFE AND BELIEFS?

DR. SPRINKLE: Our responsibility as parents is to be faithful to God. When we mess up (as all parents do), we must ask forgiveness and trust that God can overcome our mistakes and inadequacies. There are amazing parents whose children are not following the Lord. You are not alone.

Like you, as a father, I often wonder if there is anything I can do to ensure that my children will be faithful to Jesus. Our responsibility is to be godly parents, but our children will believe because God opens their hearts to believe. God is the one who brings our children to himself!

We can be a wonderful catalyst, but ultimately it is God's work to open their hearts to believe and follow him. The best thing we can do is surrender our own lives to God. **It is better to be an authentic witness than attempt to control our children's beliefs.**

DR. PARLER: As parents in a culture of control, as Preston indicated, we need to let go. We're constantly bombarded with the lie that our kids are plastic to be shaped and molded into a form of our engineering. That's false!

Your child is a person, an image-bearer of God who is both free and responsible for their life before God. As parents, our call is to be a faithful presence in our child's life.

We cannot manipulate or force them down the path we think they should go, even if it's the right one! We must remember that fear is from the enemy, and that the perfect love of Jesus casts out fear.

At the end of the day, we must rest in the sovereignty of God and trust that he can work out something even better than what we could ever hope or imagine.

WHAT ARE SOME SCRIPTURAL EXAMPLES THAT CAN HELP PARENTS AVOID LETTING ANXIETY OR FEAR DOMINATE AND DAMAGE THEIR RELATIONSHIP WITH LGBT+ CHILDREN?

DR. PARLER: I think of 2 Timothy 1:7: "We have not been given a spirit of fear, but of power and of love and of a sound mind." You might feel helpless to impact your child's life, but recognize that those natural feelings *must submit* to the Spirit and power of Jesus. God has not abandoned you. He is with you in a special way, I believe, as you walk a path you might not have expected to walk. He *will* give you the power to go on. He can give you love, rather than fear, as your main motive.

I also think of Joseph, Daniel, Paul, and ultimately Jesus. God takes people whose stories seem ruined and writes such amazing endings! Now I want to be careful here — God never promises to make your LGBT+ child conform to what you might want them to be. But you can trust that he's doing something even better: conforming them to the image of Jesus.

We really have to trust that God is able to work and write a story far better, even if far different, than we can. The story's not done. Trust the Master Writer.

Another is Philippians 1:6: "He who began a good work in you is faithful to complete it." **Most of our anxiety and fear around our kids has a theological root — we don't really trust that God is fully good.** We must ask ourselves whether we believe God is still good and whether Jesus is still on the throne. I cannot be the savior of my child, but I can witness to the One who loved them so much he gave his life for them.

Is that a good God? Absolutely! As I focus on his goodness, I begin to trust, to leave my anxiety and fear at his feet, knowing that he never stops working on my behalf — and on my child's behalf.

DR. SPRINKLE: Remember the father in the parable of the lost son. He allows free will to run its course. He lets his son make destructive decisions. This father knows he cannot control his son, but he also knows that with God, the story is not over. It was beyond difficult, but he cast all his hope upon God.

Always extend grace, kindness, and unconditional commitment to your children. **Whether they are home with God or far away, they must know that their parents love them no matter what.**

In Matthew 6:34, Jesus reminds us to not be anxious about tomorrow, for today has enough troubles. Our job — for today — is to be faithful to God as best we can, receive forgiveness when we mess up, and let God's sovereign and loving will run its course.

Parents have an opportunity to extend undeserved grace, love, compassion, and understanding for their child. Find delight in your LGBT+ child! This will not fix them, but it can help build and maintain a strong relationship. You can better witness the love and truth of Christ where there is trust between you and your child.

MANY PARENTS HAVE ASKED A QUESTION SIMILAR TO THIS: "OUR ADULT GAY SON HOLDS TO HIS CHRISTIAN FAITH. HE TRUSTS JESUS AS HIS SAVIOR. IF ANYONE LIVES OUT GODLY COMPASSION, IT IS OUR SON. BUT HE HAS A PARTNER. IF HE DIES, WILL HE GO TO HELL?

DR. SPRINKLE: Every Christian parent asks this question when their children are not walking with the Lord — or living within biblical Christianity. One of my life verses when it comes to difficult questions is Genesis 18:25 — "Will not the judge of all the earth do what is right?"

This is a rhetorical question: the answer is a resounding yes! God is good. **He is perfectly just and loving. He will always do what is right.** So, my trust must be in the character of God!

When considering our children's eternity, we should never place our trust in their goodness — nor should we lose hope because of their sinfulness! Further, **we should not place our trust in what we *think* the answer may be.**

Our trust must be in the goodness of God. People go to hell for rejecting Jesus. Only God knows who is rejecting Him. As parents, we join you in prayer — for all of our children — that they will choose Christ and surrender their lives to Him.

DR. PARLER: As Preston indicated, when the Bible talks about why people go to hell, it's because they refuse to believe in Jesus. No one is condemned to hell because of one specific sin or action. **If our salvation is not rooted in what we do, but in what Jesus does for us, then we cannot lose our salvation because of something we do.** That wasn't the basis of our salvation in the first place.

Christians are called to walk by and manifest the fruit of the Spirit in their life, but there are times when all of us are out of step with God's will for our lives. You cannot identify who's going to hell by looking at any one sin — gossip, murder, pride, bitterness, sexual immorality.

I always come back to Jesus' approach. He draws people to himself with compassion, mercy, and grace. This doesn't excuse or ignore sin, but it recognizes that the way to guide someone toward God's best for their life is through grace, kindness, and compassion.

WHETHER THEY ARE HOME WITH GOD OR FAR AWAY, THEY MUST KNOW THAT THEIR PARENTS LOVE THEM NO MATTER WHAT.

— PRESTON SPRINKLE

DOES THE BIBLE FORBID PARENTS FROM ALLOWING AN LGBT+ LOVED ONE TO COME HOME WITH THEIR PARTNER? PARENTS OF ANY TEEN, GAY OR STRAIGHT, MIGHT HAVE DATING RESTRICTIONS, BUT WHAT ABOUT AN ADULT CHILD AND THEIR MARRIED PARTNER?

DR. PARLER: When Bible passages speak about disconnecting a relationship with someone who is living in unrepentant sin (as in 1 Cor. 5), the goal is to help that person understand that what they are doing is out of step with the path of discipleship.

If we're talking about adult children raised in a Christian home where biblical sexual ethics have been communicated, then they are likely hyper-aware that what they're doing doesn't fit with their parents' views. In 2 Cor. 2:7-8, Paul cautions the church to avoid actions that will overwhelm someone with sorrow to the point that Satan gets a stronghold in their life. So **while there is a place for tough love, ostracizing a child further by refusing to engage with their partner misses the real point of Scripture.**

Furthermore, we must recall that Jesus scandalized the good religious folks of his day by his willingness to eat with the so-called sinners and outsiders. He understood that what people needed most was to encounter the deep wellspring of hospitality and embrace offered by his Father. What better example of parental generosity is there?

DR. SPRINKLE: There are few instructions in the Bible about specific parenting situations. Raise your children in the Lord. Don't exasperate them. Be godly parents. Love your children. Teach them God's Word. Parents should have the freedom to follow their conscience and the counsel of others.

I don't think you are sacrificing your convictions or approving of their relationship just because you love and welcome your child's partner. If you fail to love your child's partner, it likely will damage trust with your child.

When the Bible says to love your neighbor as yourself, it is not limited to certain neighbors or only those who are following God. In the parable of the Good Samaritan, we know nothing about the morality of the man who was beaten up. The Good Samaritan did not interrogate the guy! As long as you are not violating Scripture, you should work really hard to build a strong relationship with your LGBT+ child — and that requires loving their partner.

As Branson suggested, parental generosity and hospitality are critical. **There is no spiritual power in the act of excluding people.** By welcoming your child's partner into your home and treating them as a member of the family, God can anoint that kind of hospitality!

LGBT+ YOUNG PEOPLE CAN BE UNDERSTANDABLY FRUSTRATED WHEN THEIR PARENTS DO NOT EMBRACE AN AFFIRMING BELIEF. A CLOSE PARENT-CHILD BOND IS CRITICAL FOR ALL OF US. HOW WOULD YOU ADVISE LGBT+ CHILDREN TO RELATE TO THEIR PARENTS?

DR. SPRINKLE: As much as you want your parents to respect and understand you, extend this same courtesy to them. Your parents' beliefs are not intended to hurt you — they likely believe what they believe to love and honor God. **Would you really want them to abandon their beliefs if doing so, to them, would dishonor God?**

What your parents believe about marriage is held across the global church — as well as human civilizations across all of history and all major religions. They don't have an isolated belief.

In recommending that you respect your parents, this does not mean you must endure abuse. If that is happening, I am so sorry! Abuse is not a biblical expression of God's truth — or his love!

DR. PARLER: I agree with Preston: be patient and offer grace to your parents. Although you might be frustrated by their beliefs, realize that your relationship is rooted in much more than having the same beliefs.

It might seem strange, but you may have to lead your parents in that way. The parent-child relationship is complicated. I love my parents like you love yours, but I totally disagree with some of their views. **I've had to learn that love goes beyond simply agreeing with my parents!** Our relationship is far from perfect, but we're working at it. I encourage you to do the same.

WHEN A THEOLOGY QUESTION IS NOT A

"What do you believe the Bible teaches about same-gender relationships?"

How many times have LGBT+ people opened with this question? If you're a pastor, you've heard it. If you're in youth ministry, you've heard it. If you're involved in nearly any kind of full-time ministry work, you've likely heard it. If you're a parent, you've *definitely* heard it.

You're not alone. In our work at Lead Them Home, we've heard this question, too — countless times.

There are two mistakes to avoid. And take notice: trying to avoid one mistake can easily steer you right into the other. It can be quite challenging to navigate between messing up.

1. BAIT & SWITCH

We don't ever want to set up a bait and switch. This involves creating a generous welcome, coming across as supportive of gay marriage, and drawing someone into relationship, only to later share with them that we hold to a traditional belief. This is almost never done intentionally, but LGBT+ individuals may understandably interpret the circumstances as staged.

2. LEADING WITH THEOLOGY

We don't ever want to lead with theological talk. This entails a quick disclosure of theological beliefs soon after getting to know someone. The underlying motivations that lead Christians to fall into this error are multi-faceted. Let's look at several:

FEARS THAT DRIVE US TO LEAD WITH THEOLOGY

FEAR OF DISOBEYING GOD	Many of us fear that we **might be dishonoring God by not disclosing our beliefs.** This fear flows more from our personal hangups than from any biblical command. If this disclosure were a command, then we would have a duty to confront neighbors, coworkers, friends, and family about a lot of sin! We actually don't often take this approach, but we routinely do with LGBT+ people.
FEAR OF CONDONING OR ENABLING	For some evangelicals, we carry this fear that we **might be approving, condoning, or enabling gay marriage unless we tell LGBT+ people our beliefs.** The truth is that we aren't that powerful. Gay couples do not date, fall in love, or marry because of us. We must let go of this unhealthy fear.
FEAR OF BAIT AND SWITCH	Increasingly, many of us fear establishing a strong relationship with LGBT+ people and then **watching that trust come undone when they later learn about our beliefs.** In other words, we make this error in an attempt to avoid a bait and switch — and out of sincere love for LGBT+ people.

Disclaimer: it is impossible to avoid mistakes in human relationships. The harder we tiptoe trying to *avoid* mistakes, the more likely we'll *fall into* making mistakes. It is important to remember that Scripture offers us guidance: "Above all things have intense and unfailing love for one another, for love covers a multitude of sins [forgives and disregards the offenses of others]" (1 Pt. 4:8).

In this verse, love's covering goes both ways. We're called to forgive and disregard the ways others have offended us. Yet there is a promise embedded in this verse: if we genuinely love, honor, and think about the needs of other people, it is more likely that they will see our heart and be willing to forgive the ways we might unintentionally offend them.

At Lead Them Home, we have made four commitments in a sincere attempt to love LGBT+ people:

1. **We will not initiate, manipulate, or otherwise coerce** a conversation about theological beliefs.

2. We will not enter into a theological conversation without **first establishing a friendship.**

3. **Any theological conversation must be mutual.** We are committed to honoring LGBT+ people by asking about their stories and listening well when they share their beliefs.

4. **We will not play games** by refusing to answer a theological question …

… as long as the question is really a theological question!

Many times, it turns out, an on-the-spot theological question is not the real question on the heart and mind of an LGBT+ questioner. It may be, but often, it is not. Listen to the following telephone conversation unfold:

CALLER: Hi, my name is Brian. I am a college student. I was referred to your ministry. I wanted to ask about Lead Them Home's beliefs on homosexuality.

LEAD THEM HOME: Hi Brian, it's an honor to meet you. I am happy to answer your question. First, I'm curious — what's on your mind in asking about our beliefs?

BRIAN: Oh, so I joined a church on my college campus. The chaplain learned that I was gay. He told me that I needed to call Lead Them Home to talk about my beliefs.

LEAD THEM HOME: Oh, I see. So do you really want to talk theology?

BRIAN: It's not at the top of my list. But that's what the chaplain said I need to do.

LEAD THEM HOME: I am glad you let me know. I would love to hear more about you. If it's helpful for me to clarify our ministry's beliefs, I am happy to do that, too. But it would be an honor just to learn more about you.

BRIAN: Oh, thanks. My story is typical. I realized I was gay when I was 12. When my parents found out, I was 15. They told me I need to marry a girl. They pay for tuition at this Christian college as long as I talk with the chaplain. So, I do it because I need to graduate and find a job to provide for myself.

How tragic if we miss the real scenario playing out beneath the questions others ask. In over a decade of missionary work sharing Christ's love with LGBT+ people, here are just a few reasons why LGBT+ people approach us (and likely why they approach you!) when asking about theology:

"My parents sent me to ask you."

"My pastor recommended that I talk with you."

"I just thought you required us to talk about theology."

"I have to prove to my parents that I'm trying to be straight."

"I just wanted to find out if this would be a safe place for me."

UNDER THE SURFACE OF
THEOLOGICAL QUESTIONS
MAY BE HEARTBREAKING
MATTERS OF JUDGMENT,
CONDEMNATION, MISTREATMENT,
AND CONDITIONAL LOVE.

In hastily answering a question about theology, we may miss the opportunity to comfort and care for people who are being judged or mistreated. We need to surrender urgency and build *pause* into our response. Ask questions to find out what's behind their initial question.

If the interest really is theology, then invite your loved one or friend to share their beliefs. Discuss any differences with respect. You don't have to go into the guts of biblical interpretation. You can simply say, "I hold to a traditional belief. I don't intend to judge anyone. I believe what I believe to honor God based on how I understand the Bible. I understand why you believe what you believe, and I respect you."

But remember: don't lead with a theological answer, because not every theological question is *actually* a theological question.

info@leadthemhome.org

MY ADULT CHILD'S PARTNER

IF YOUR LGBT+ LOVED ONE HAS A PARTNER, GOD HAS GIVEN YOU THE PRIVILEGE OF SHARING THE GOSPEL WITH YET ANOTHER PERSON!

*If you attempt to **segregate** your child's partner from your family, you will **damage trust** with your own child.*

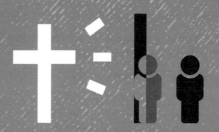

*If you **honor** your child's partner and **generously welcome** them into your family, then you have an opportunity to **gain relational trust** with your child — and their partner.*

HOLIDAYS: Invite your child and their partner home for all family holiday gatherings.

SLEEPING ARRANGEMENTS: Ensure that whatever your policy, it is applied evenly for all loved ones. If you require married couples in your family to sleep in the same bedroom, then gay married couples should be welcomed into your home similarly.

EVERYDAY LIFE: Invite your child and their partner to dinner and accept invitations they may extend to you.

FAMILY PORTRAITS: Gay or straight, few families include a dating partner in formal family portraits. Once a couple is married, however, it is appropriate to include every family member in formal portraits.

66

WEDDINGS

CHRISTIANS SOMETIMES FEAR condoning or enabling gay marriages. Gay couples marry because they are in love. We do not cause marriage — and **we cannot stop gay couples from marrying.**

While you cannot biblically *officiate* a same-gender wedding ceremony, you can **attend.** You can also **pray** at a wedding if asked to do so.

If you decide against attending your loved one's wedding, no one should judge your sincere effort to honor God. Yet you must **count the cost.** This decision not to attend the most special day of your loved one's life **can (and often does) yield deep and lasting relational damage.**

Being "right" for one day can damage the opportunity to be a witness for thousands of days into the future. Think long-term. Think into the next generation. **How can you best establish trust so that you have connection with future grandchildren?** Acts of rejection today may so damage trust that you are not permitted to have any meaningful relationship with your grandchildren.

Lead Them Home encourages you to attend your loved one's wedding. We are aiming for **long-term relational trust where a witness of Christ can be lived out and shared over many years.**

Every situation is unique. We are contacted by parents, siblings, and a wide range of relatives of LGBT+ loved ones who are marrying their partner. In some cases, not attending the wedding is possible without damaging the relationship. In other cases, failing to attend can entirely end even a close family relationship. We cannot address every scenario here in this guide.

For additional guidance, please contact us.

WELL-INTENDED ADVICE CAN HAVE SERIOUS LONG-TERM CONSEQUENCES:

Audrey, a grandmother from Oregon, was encouraged by Evangelicals to not attend her son's wedding to his partner 10 years ago. Tragically, her son has never trusted her to be part of his family's life. She has grandchildren that she has never been given the privilege to meet. She is deeply grieved. Today, those same believers attend their own loved ones' gay marriage ceremonies, have never apologized to Audrey, and have failed to grasp the consequence of their guidance to her.

AN EVANGELICAL PASTOR'S PRAYER AT HIS SON'S WEDDING

*"Lord, **we gather** today in our deep love for David and Caleb. **We welcome** Caleb and his family into our family. **We thank you for Caleb's family** and their love for us. We thank you for giving both of our families **two incredible sons** who are intelligent, talented, and sacrificial in their service to others. We thank you for all of our **faithful friends** who join us today. We thank you most of all for giving **your son Jesus** as a sacrifice for our sins. **May each one of us know Him more and more** as the days of our lives pass. May each one of us **discover the incredible plans and purposes You have appointed** for our lives. **Bless** David and Caleb. **Shower** them with love. **Grow** their faith. **Fill** their hearts. **Develop** your purposes in their lives. We pray in Christ's name. Amen."*

WHEN A CHILD HAS AN LGBT+ PARENT

AT LEAD THEM HOME'S FAMILY CARE SEMINAR this past season, the room was filled. In scurrying around and finalizing setup for my presentation, I failed to notice everyone in the room. As introductions began, I saw a young boy at one table. I assumed that his Mom was present because of an older LGBT+ teen sibling.

As introductions reached the table where this boy was sitting, he bravely volunteered to go first:

"My name is Danny. I am 10 years old. **I'm here because my Dad is gay.** I don't believe God wants him to be gay, but I don't know for sure. It's confusing. I came to see if it's okay for me to love my dad. I love God and want to follow God, but I also really love my dad."

Danny's mother soon added:

"I care deeply about Danny's father, my former husband. I encourage Danny to love his dad, but it has been confusing for him given our biblical beliefs. We are thankful to be here today."

Whatever message I had planned was soon abandoned: God had another plan. As introductions across the room concluded, I said a prayer of thanks for everyone present and then offered:

"No one has to give you permission to love your LGBT+ child. **Danny, you don't have to ask permission to love your father.** God made parents to love their kids and kids to love their parents. What you feel inside — that desire to love your father — well, God put that in you. He is pleased when you love your dad. You are a good son. I am so thankful that you're here today and that you love your father."

I asked Danny: "What do you love most about both of your parents?" He replied:

"My mom is a great cook and helps me with homework. She makes me special treats. She is a very loving mom. My dad plays catch with me. He is really funny. He takes me out to eat and comes to watch all my games. My parents hug me and pray with me. They love me."

I then asked Danny how he feels about his father being gay. His answer revealed the more challenging side of what kids can experience when a parent comes out. Tears started streaming down Danny's face as he said:

"I feel guilty. I feel guilty . . . because it embarrasses me. I don't want my friends to know. **I want my friends to know my dad. I just don't want them to know he is gay. I am afraid they might make fun of me or laugh at my dad.** I love my dad. I don't want to be embarrassed by him."

I asked Danny: "Have you talked to your dad about how you feel?" He replied:

"I told him I wish he would come back home and live with us. I tell him that I love him. I am afraid to tell him I'm embarrassed that he is gay. I don't want to hurt his feelings. I did tell him that God does not want him to be gay. My dad said that he understands."

I paused before responding: "Danny, it sounds like you have very loving and understanding parents."

1 It's OK to love your parent. No one has to give you permission to love your own parents. God made you to love your parents. You are following God when you love them.

2 It's OK to be embarrassed by your parent. Every child in the world has felt embarrassed by their parents. There are dozens of reasons why kids' parents embarrass them. You are not alone! In fact, your gay father or transgender mother felt embarrassed by *their* parents when they were growing up! Your parents will likely understand your feelings. It may hurt just as it could hurt the feelings of any parent, but that is alright. As parents, we love anyway! If you ever become a parent one day, *your* child will be embarrassed by *you*, too. Count on it! And guess what? It may sting a bit, but you'll smile because you love your child so much! Parents love so much that they can understand when their kids are embarrassed by them.

3 It's OK to hold to different beliefs than your parent. Do what every Christian has always been called to do: love the Lord your God with all your heart, soul, strength, and mind — and like unto it, love family, friends, and neighbors like yourself. In a family, we love no matter what. That means we love one another even when we have strong differences in belief. Your parents should support you, care for you, and respect you even when your beliefs differ from their beliefs.

4 It's OK to be sad about your parents' divorce. For some kids, having a parent come out LGBT+ may be related to your parents' divorce. Kids often experience deep sadness when their parents get a divorce because God never intended for families to break up. When divorce occurs, kids get hurt. It can be one of the most painful experiences in life! It's OK to be sad and to feel angry. God can be angry, too, when divorce tears a family apart. You are not alone in these feelings.

5 It's OK to like (or dislike) your parent's partner. Some kids have grown up with two mothers or fathers. For them, no adjustment is needed. For other kids, though, a parent's partner enters their life unexpectedly. This new person may feel like a stranger. You may be angry thinking this person caused your parents' divorce. While being respectful, it's understandable that you might be upset that your parent has a new partner. For other kids, they really like their parent's partner! Some kids might feel guilty about this — like it is a betrayal of their other parent. You should consider it a blessing if you naturally like your step-parent. It's OK to feel what you feel!

6 It's OK to talk about your feelings. Wait, it's not just OK — it's what is most needed! It is important to talk about feelings when we are celebrating life's greatest moments — and equally important when we are disappointed or angry because of life's deepest hurts. God designed us to process our emotions by talking, not by bottling them up. If you hold in your deepest feelings without outside support, it can increase how much you hurt inside. Maybe you can talk with your parents, a grandparent, an uncle or aunt, a youth pastor, or a counselor. When you're hurting, you may not want to talk, but that's when it's most important to talk to a trusted adult. Don't walk this road alone. Decide who you trust and share what you're feeling. Talking is a good thing!

7 It's OK to pray for your LGBT+ parent. Sometimes the fear or hurt that kids experience is a worry that their LGBT+ parent might not be a Christian — or might not be with them in Heaven one day. Remember that God sent Jesus to die on the Cross for all of our sins. He died for us precisely because we need a Savior. All of us need Jesus. Trust that God will be good to your family. Trust that He loves your mom and dad. Trust that Jesus died for their sins, like He died for yours. Pray to God: "Lord, let all my family be in Heaven one day. Thank you that Jesus died for us. Amen."

8 It's OK to honor your mother and father. Actually, it's one of the Ten Commandments. The best way to honor God is to love and respect your parents, even when you disagree with them. If you are sad or even angry that your mom is lesbian or your dad is transgender, God still wants you to honor your parents. That means loving them, showing respect, doing your homework, and handling your responsibilities. Try your best not to act defiantly or disrespectfully in your frustration. Your concerns will likely be heard when you follow God by honoring your parents. You'll make mistakes. It's OK.

WHEN A MINISTRY LEADER IS THE PARENT

TWO PASTOR-FATHERS SHARE ABOUT THEIR INTERNAL AND EXTERNAL CONFLICTS AS THEY WALK WITH THEIR LGBT+

CHILDREN. NEIL WRITES A LETTER TO A COLLEAGUE, AND ARTHUR WRITES DIRECTLY TO LEAD THEM HOME.

Dear Dave,

I wanted to let you know I'm doing a lot better. I mean, I am still crying several times a day, even now as I write. Even so, the Lord has been speaking to me more directly and clearly than I can ever remember (including two decades of missions work). Other similar times when I've sensed God's deep presence and guidance were also times of pain and many tears.

Since we heard the news, every class, homework assignment, meal, drive, and run has been interrupted numerous times by my sadness about Whitney. Yesterday, in my Greek class, our professor called on me. I don't remember doing the homework, honestly, but I had my notes, so I read through the verse she had asked me to do:

"Immediately after having cried out, the father of the child said, 'I believe'" (Mark 9:24).

Somehow, I made it through translating that sentence without bursting into tears. Right after my part was done, I exited the room to catch my breath.

God is gracious. In my sadness, He speaks unmistakably to reassure me that He is with our family. Other than one other classmate, no one had any idea how the Lord was speaking so clearly to me right then: *"I know. You can trust me. I am here with you. Believe that I am in control."*

The request that the father then makes to Jesus after that sentence: "Help my unbelief" — that has been my prayer since yesterday. That, and one of gratitude to the Lord for His love and presence even in the midst of this heartache.

I realized something else from that passage. Jesus is there with the Father, but He is going into agony, crying out to His Father to let the cup pass. But because the Father *doesn't* let the cup of suffering pass, we have the basis for the Good News we all know.

Today, I had a midterm in another class. But because there was much more inner peace due to God's presence and promise, I was able to focus on this work to which God has now called me, and I studied well. As I left the midterm, I walked to the car and just prayed, "Oh, God, you have heard and answered my prayers time and again. Please, if you will only answer one more, let it be this prayer." Then, as I started the car, my audiobook of *Mere Christianity* began playing.

The narrator read about the idea of a man who has been following Christ for quite a while — but who becomes disappointed when new kinds of temptation came along. Such a man figures temptation was helpful to grow him in the past, but that now, the temptation seems unnecessary. In reality, whether the man realizes it or not, God is putting him in places where he will need to be more courageous, patient, and loving than he could even imagine.

I stopped and cried out, "I know all of this, but the cost is too high, God! We're talking about my little girl!" He gently reminded me that she is not really mine. I said back, "I know. But it hurts, Lord!"

Of course, He knows what it's like. How amazing it is to know that! In the midst of all of this, He reminds me of what He did for us, for me, and for Whitney: He drank from the cup of suffering.

I am still hurting. But it is well with my soul.

Thank you for praying and caring. I appreciate you very much.

–Neil

MY NAME IS ARTHUR, AND I AM A PASTOR. **About 9 years ago, my daughter came out. A year ago, my youngest son came out to me and my wife, and we found out on Mother's Day that he had gotten married.** The sad thing is that no one came to us, wrapped their arms around us, ministered to us, or shared the love of Jesus. **I was asked to resign as Senior Pastor at a church I had been at for 20 years because my adult child claimed that she was LGBT+.** In spite of this, we love our children with Christ's love. And they know that we love them. We have a very open relationship with them and their partners and express that to them openly. Our children know our convictions on sexual morality. Our desire is to love them back into the kingdom. I John 2:6 says, 'Whoever claims to live in Him must live as Jesus did.' To live as Jesus did is to love all people, regardless of their sexual orientation. That is our calling as followers of Christ.

Lead Them Home conducted an anonymous **Survey of Pastors Who are Parents of LGBT+ Loved Ones (January 2018)** soliciting online survey responses from our email contacts. Ministry leaders — including pastors, church staff, missionaries, seminarians, full-time Christian leadership workers, and their spouses — described their experiences when a close family member (child, spouse, parent, or grandchild) came out.

DESCRIBE THE UNIQUE ASPECTS OF HAVING AN LGBT+ LOVED ONE WHILE ALSO BEING A MINISTRY LEADER.

"It is difficult to feel successful, either as a parent or as a minister. My child obviously has a different view of God and the Bible than I do. I'm still working through not carrying the weight of that on many levels."

"To a certain degree, I feel like I live with secrets, waiting for the other shoe to drop. However, this experience has also given me greater insight into the hurts that people in our congregation carry."

"It is a relief to people who are in the same situation to discover that I've been through this, that someone shares their pain. I can love someone and still not agree with what they choose to do or believe. I am all about accepting those who struggle, just as anyone struggles with any sin, and sharing the truth of God's love with them."

"Yes and no. I know I haven't done anything to disqualify myself, but I think it might be less painful if I did not have to deal with potential implications of the church because of my position."

WERE YOU EVER CONVINCED (OR TOLD) THAT YOU WERE NO LONGER QUALIFIED TO SERVE IN FULL-TIME MINISTRY?

"Yes. I wondered if I should resign or if I would be asked to. It took me a while to get to the point of believing that my daughter's choices were not based on my failure to love or teach her adequately."

"No. I never questioned being qualified to serve. I still have my beliefs that God loves me and accepts me."

HOW DID YOUR CONGREGATION OR ORGANIZATION REACT WHEN THEY FOUND OUT ABOUT YOUR FAMILY MEMBER?*

"I lost my position as Senior Pastor."

"Early on, I received wise counsel that this kind of disclosure did not need to be public. Those who need to know do. Those who don't need to know don't. We have not "outed" her. It's her story to tell. But I'm careful about who I tell. Some key leaders know. My staff knows, and they have all been very supportive."

"I had to be very careful to protect my family member. Before anyone knew, people would make comments that made me feel hurt, condemned as a bad parent, and not safe to share my struggle with many — except with a few who were safe and would pray for me. This would change over many years, but I still do not share openly, especially in condescending or condemning atmospheres."

*More than half of those surveyed have chosen not to share with their congregation or organization, reporting fear of judgment or rejection as the primary reason.

"What is hurtful to me is the underlying attitude that if someone's children don't fit the model the denomination has set, the parents must have done something wrong. While I believe in God's original design for marriage, I also realize we have all fallen short of the glory of God. The sometimes harsh attitudes and words about the LGBT+ community don't help us in our healing and dealing with the situation."

IS THERE ANYTHING PARTICULARLY HURTFUL OR HELPFUL IN HOW ANYONE IN YOUR CHURCH OR ORGANIZATION RESPONDED?

"I felt sad that no one in our community knew what to say or do. No one seemed to have imagined that a family in the church would have this 'issue.' It highlighted the fact that everyone thought gay people were 'out there' instead of right next to you in church."

"I found another pastoral staff member who was dealing with having an LGBT+ child and who opened up about it. That gave me support that I was not alone. Having Lead Them Home available was a priceless gift that helped me know it was okay to love my child and restore our relationship."

FIRST
IN OUR LIVES

BULLIED FROM AN EARLY AGE

KENNY: I started getting bullied in third grade at my Christian school. With my personality and interests, other boys did not see me as "one of them." I was quiet and sensitive, while the other boys, to me, just seemed messy and aggressive. I felt more comfortable interacting with girls. I liked the mature conversations that I could have with them.

The middle school years were the worst. Through middle school, the bullying progressively worsened. Going through puberty, I realized that I was sexually attracted to guys. Now I knew why my peers were bullying me.

In the class where the bullying was most severe, the teacher saw what was happening and never intervened, leaving me feeling helpless to find relief. I started cutting class to avoid the bullying — only to end up getting detention. At that point, I had no choice but to tell my parents. I was so embarrassed for them to know that I was being bullied.

MOM: We knew that middle school had been really tough for Kenny, but we only recently learned that the bullying had begun years before that. During middle school, Kenny wrote us a letter pleading with us to let him go to public school. Seeing his anguish, we agreed. Once he moved over to public school, Kenny was entirely free of mistreatment.

NOT MANY KIDS COME OUT THE WAY KENNY DID

KENNY: Technically, I never actually came out. My parents found out when I was 10 years old when my mom found me doodling a heart containing the name of a boy I liked in my class.

I am actually really thankful that my mom found the note. It allowed me to process this struggle with my parent's support even from an early age. My parents did not make the mistake of panicking. They acted in faith rather than fear. They trusted God, which allowed them to be patient, accept me, and nourish faith in me. I knew early on that my identity was founded on who I am in Christ. The feelings were strong, but they never defined me.

DAD: I didn't have any suspicions about Kenny's sexuality. I liked that Kenny represented males as gentle people. When we found this note, though, it hit me hard. As a pastor, I tend to take in hard news and process it right away. Pastors fall apart unless we take our lives to God and let Him walk us through it.

We could not ignore this note, so I prayed and followed my wife's lead. She opened the door to conversation, and I walked through it with her. That was when I expressed to Kenny, "I am not ashamed of you. I love you. I am so proud of you."

We wanted him to have assurance.

MOM: I had concerns well before we found the note. As a Christian parent, I didn't give those suspicions much credibility — partly as an attitude of faith, but also because I did not want it to be true.

But then I found Kenny's journal. I read the words in my boy's handwriting: "Dear Jesus, there is a boy. I think I love him. Please help me, Jesus. I don't want these feelings." Reading this, I could no longer live in denial. Kenny's struggle was real. The letter was too raw for a 10-year-old to express. I feared how my son would walk through his life this side of heaven.

FRUSTRATION MOUNTS AS SSA WON'T GO AWAY

KENNY: During high school, I kept thinking, These feelings are not going away, they're stronger than ever. So I would wake up, read my Bible, and pray. I figured that if I walked with God, maybe the attractions would go away one day.

As I entered into college, I increasingly doubted that my SSA would ever go away. Every day, I became more and more worn down. Finally, one day, I told my parents that it was too tough to walk this journey.

MOM: Kenny was calling many times a day from college having breakdowns. We thought we would have to bring him home. We worried that he might be suicidal.

DAD: I kept telling Kenny, "God wants to be first in our lives in regard to our strengths — but also in regard to our struggles." As a pastor, I walk with many families in crisis. But this time, it was my son. Knowing how depressed he was, we were worried for him 24 hours a day.

MOM: As parents, we constantly worried, *Is our son going to survive? Will He keep following Jesus? Do we have the right beliefs? Is it right for us to hold to beliefs that require Kenny to say no to experiencing love?* It was so challenging.

www.leadthemhome.org

KENNY: The summer after my sophomore year of college, I went for a run. I sat down midway and suddenly felt this peace. In that moment, I surrendered my whole life (including my struggles) to Jesus.

My focus immediately shifted to the Lord. He filled my heart and met my needs. Since that day, I have experienced purpose, satisfaction, and freedom in my life. We don't need sex to live a vibrant life. Sex is not who we are.

This thing we call "sex" is so broken. Many heterosexual people can marry, but their sexuality can be broken, too. I have a certain struggle, but so do others. Recently, I talked about my struggle with my parents and grandparents. I felt so connected to my family because they shared their struggles, too! It was a powerful time as we turned to Christ together for hope.

DAD: We had to find a creative way to build Christian support outside the church. Having extended family — and even Kenny's college coach — as part of our support was critical. With strong support surrounding us, Kenny began owning his faith, and God rebuilt his life. If only more of us had the faith that Kenny has demonstrated!

MOM: When your son who was calling 4-5 times a day for support is suddenly rising up in hope and making Jesus the Lord of his life, you know God is at work! He told us, "Mom, I might never get married. But no matter what, I choose God."

WHAT IT'S LIKE BEING A PASTOR'S KID WHO EXPERIENCES SSA

KENNY: Elementary-aged peers called me "fag" at my Christian school. No wonder I feared being outed at church! I worried about what the congregation might think about me — and about my family. From attending this Christian school, I knew full well that opinions of gay people could be ruthless. These messages were the source of so much fear within me.

Like so many PK's, I put even more pressure on myself. I figured, "I can't let anyone know because my dad is the pastor." My perceptive parents noticed this anxiety and gently assured me, "Son, it's not that big of a deal." My parents had worked with thousands of teens earlier in their ministry lives, so they knew how to engage teens like me.

DAD: As a pastor, I've always been private about our family to protect our children. With Kenny's orientation, I simply could not trust what people might say or do. Still, I declared to God that I would not worry about what people think about any of our children.

MOM: I didn't feel safe at church. I had to protect my son from gossip and further mistreatment above what had occurred at the Christian school. I didn't feel that I could talk with anyone without exposing Kenny to potential harm. Who do you trust?

KENNY: My parents have had a great influence on my life because they've modeled deep reliance on faith and prayer through our challenges. They truly and fully laid their children at the feet of God. It's that trust in God that allowed them to do such a great job parenting.

TRUSTING THAT GOD HAS A GREAT PLAN

KENNY: Today, many people who would have judged me in the past would now officially support gay marriage. Some in our congregation might say, "You are denying yourself of love." But I am not haunted by what the world thinks I'm "missing out" on. I know God so personally. There is suffering in my life, but He has blessed me beyond words.

In my job working with kids, for example, I get to be a father by speaking purpose and prayers into young lives. The joy of my calling, combined with family support, give me hope. If I can never marry a woman, it will be hard, but I have no doubt that my life will count. I will invest in, encourage, and give hope to the next generation.

GOD ESTABLISHES OUR IDENTITY

KENNY: Everyone struggles with sexual attractions. Whether we are attracted to the same sex or the opposite sex, we should not declare our identity in sexuality. We must find our identity in something perfect — or rather someone perfect: Jesus

MOM: When Kenny was a baby, a woman told me, "The Lord impressed upon me that this child will have 'the courage of a lion and the gentleness of a dove.' My prayer has always been that God would guide Kenny's steps and raise him up into a godly man. That is exactly what He did, and that is exactly who Kenny is.

DAD: When our children face battles, it teaches us a much deeper dependency upon God. I cannot fix Kenny's attractions, but the Scriptures promise that God will walk with us! Ultimately, we know that He will be good to us.

I wish that I could take on my son's struggle and carry his pain. But that is what Jesus has already done for us. Our hope is in God's faithfulness to bless our family. He loves each one of us. I try to model a dependence on God. I try to be honest with my children and my congregation that I am broken, too. I am just as deeply in need of God's grace as anyone. This is our identity: we are a people who know, love, worship, and follow Jesus Christ. Amen.

REFLECTION QUESTIONS

1. One of the most **Common Questions** people have involves the cause(s) of same-gender attraction or gender dysphoria. Why is recognition of potential inborn factors not a biblical threat or compromise? Which other answers to Common Questions did you find helpful? Do you have other questions not covered in this guide? Please discuss.

2. From **How Do I Discuss Biblical Beliefs**, how can you, as a pastor or a parent, practically express the *Six Guiding Principles* in order to foster a safe and healthy conversation?

3. After reviewing **Honoring Questions** and applying lessons from Words Matter in Part 2, how would you ask an LGBT+ loved one or friend about their beliefs? Is knowing what they believe really the most important matter at hand? Why or why not?

4. In **Cultivating A Healthy View Of Biblical Truth**, how can you equally bring your head and heart together in truth and love to develop a healthy Biblical view of sexuality? How can your church or family practically reflect the *Seven Critical Elements of Biblical Truth*? Can you think of additional elements of a healthy Biblical view? Please describe.

5. Dr. Branson Parler powerfully yet succinctly says, "Good theology plus bad timing is bad theology." What does this mean? What else does Dr. Parler say that encourages you?

6. Dr. Preston Sprinkle beautifully suggests, "Find delight in your LGBT+ child!" What is most amazing or special about your LGBT+ loved one? Pastors, what are some of the incredible gifts, talents, and character traits of LGBT+ people whom you know and love? Parents, what makes it hard to thoroughly trust God with your child's life? Please discuss.

7. In **When A Theology Question Is Not A Theology Question**, describe the typical errors that we, as Christians, tend to make when LGBT+ people ask about our beliefs. Identify three concerns with offering an abrupt doctrinal answer to every theological question.

8. If your LGBT+ loved one has a partner, describe your relationship with their partner. Are any changes needed in your engagement of your loved one's partner? What is so critical about our actions, attitudes, and words surrounding a loved one's wedding?

9. How does your church or family demonstrate care for a child who has an LGBT+ parent? With so much focus (rightly) on the care of LGBT+ youth, we can overlook youth who have gay or transgender parents. What is the chance a child in your church fears you, as their pastor, knowing about their parent? Can you think of additional "OK's" for such youth?

10. Identify unique challenges facing families in vocational ministry with an LGBT+ family member. How can your church better support them? Reading from **First In Our Life**, what is your reaction to Kenny's parents' need to protect their son from the church?

TO MORE FULLY CONSIDER THE TRADITIONAL BIBLICAL BELIEF SET WITHIN A GENEROUS POSTURE, WE

RECOMMEND DR. PRESTON SPRINKLE'S BOOK *PEOPLE TO BE LOVED* AND HIS *GRACE/TRUTH* STUDY GUIDES.

AHORA EN ESPAÑOL

POSTURE SHIFT: MANUAL DE CURSO
GUIANDO FAMILIAS DE PERSONAS LGBT+

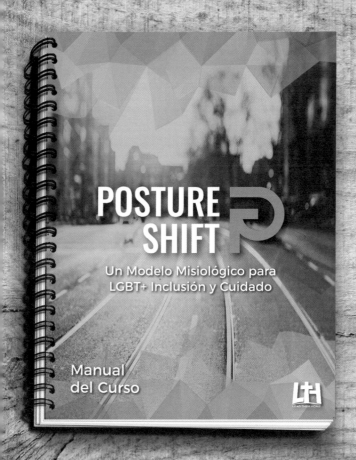

"FEAR NOT

[THERE IS NOTHING TO FEAR],

FOR I AM WITH YOU;

DO NOT LOOK AROUND YOU

IN TERROR AND BE DISMAYED,

FOR I AM YOUR GOD.

I WILL STRENGTHEN AND

HARDEN YOU TO DIFFICULTIES,

YES, I WILL HELP YOU;

YES, I WILL HOLD YOU UP

AND RETAIN YOU WITH MY

[VICTORIOUS] RIGHT HAND

OF RIGHTNESS AND JUSTICE."

– ISAIAH 41:10

PART 4:

BEYOND LESBIAN & GAY

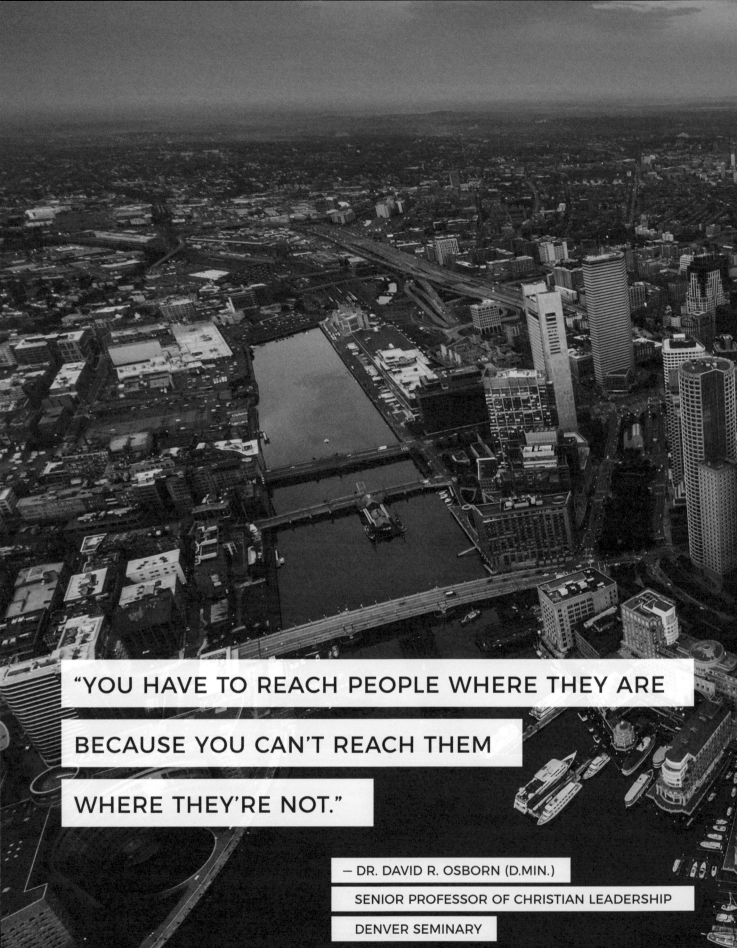

"YOU HAVE TO REACH PEOPLE WHERE THEY ARE
BECAUSE YOU CAN'T REACH THEM
WHERE THEY'RE NOT."

— DR. DAVID R. OSBORN (D.MIN.)

SENIOR PROFESSOR OF CHRISTIAN LEADERSHIP

DENVER SEMINARY

REACHING PEOPLE WHERE THEY ARE

WE WILL NOW ADDRESS GENDER IDENTITY. Admittedly, it is complex. For many, it is controversial. We have to remember that amidst complexity, our transgender and genderqueer loved ones have a difficult journey this side of Heaven. In prayer and humility, please abide in Christ as we look at how best to care for them. We need Christ's presence to remind us of the compassion that he lived out even as he died for all of us.

If you are the parent of a gay teen or a pastor seeking help engaging a lesbian or bisexual student, please do not skip this important topic. It is critical that more adults become more familiar with loving and caring for transgender and non-binary youth and young adults. Studying this section provides critical insights that will help you care for all people.

Importantly, even cisgender youth increasingly see the world through a queer or nonbinary framework. Learning how to care for transgender and genderqueer young people is necessary today — and will only become more critical in the years ahead.

From Common Questions (page 54), remember that we should not panic over a younger generation seeing gender as fluid. Among many of their peers, gender *is* fluid! But get this — 99.4% of people 25 and older settle into gender congruence (comfort with their birth gender).[1]

This fact is based on hard (secular) science that happens to reflect exactly what God said he was doing in the beginning when he made us male and female. A younger generation can create new ideas about identity (we did the same thing when we were teenagers), but it appears from the research that gender is hardwired into most of us.

For this reason, why panic and ruin our witness of Jesus Christ? He loves this next generation. He died for them just like he died for every prior generation and all the ones that will follow. Let us not think that God is shocked by this generation. Rather, let us live in confidence that the gospel has power to reach *every* generation. With that kind of faith, we don't have to resort to fearmongering. Falling into such a *posture* trap will only damage the credibility of our biblical beliefs.

Some will accuse Lead Them Home of promoting gender transition. We do not always respond to criticism perfectly, but our goal is to count it all joy. **If you get criticized, please know we're right there with you!** Let it remind all of us that most of our transgender loved ones have been threatened and harassed daily for years. We share stories in this section not to promote gender transition, but rather to comfort families who find themselves in such a situation. We are encouraging these families: *you are not alone.*

While teaching our 2-day Posture Shift Intensives course at Denver Seminary, one seasoned professor made a remarkable yet profoundly simple statement: "You have to reach people where they are because you can't reach them where they're not."

We invite you to enter Part 4 with humility and sensitivity. You never know what you might discover along the way. Learning about complex topics does not mean your position is shifting. It does mean you are growing in your understanding of vulnerable people. The more you understand, the better you can reflect Jesus Christ.

[1]Flores AR, Herman JL, Gates GJ, & Brown TNT (2016). *How Many Adults Identify as Transgender in the United States?* Los Angeles, CA: The Williams Institute.

BEYOND LESBIAN & GAY

TRANSGENDER & "PLUS" IDENTITIES

WHETHER YOUR CHILD IS...

LESBIAN
Same-gender loving females

GAY
Same-gender loving males

BISEXUAL
Attraction to both genders

TRANSGENDER
Sense of identity does not conform with birth sex

QUEER
Non-conforming orientation/identity

QUESTIONING
Uncertain orientation/identity

INTERSEX
Ambiguous/both genitalia

ASEXUAL
No/limited sexual orientation

ANDROGYNOUS
(Nonbinary or Genderqueer)
Expressing male and female traits

PANSEXUAL
Love/sex not based on gender

SSA
Unwanted same-sex attraction

+
Any other binary or non-binary identity or inclination involving sexuality or gender

...THE PROCESS OF SELF-DISCOVERY AND THE RISK

FACTORS MANY YOUTH FACE REMAIN THE SAME.

FOR THIS REASON, *OUR GUIDANCE ON HOW*

PASTORS AND PARENTS SHOULD RESPOND

REMAINS THE SAME.

For more in-depth descriptions, see Key Terms on page VI.

PRACTICAL TIPS
FOR GUIDING TRANSGENDER TEENS

Make presence and togetherness a priority. • Demonstrate high levels of acceptance, unconditional love, and affection. • Allot reasonable time for talking about life. • Set age-appropriate boundaries and flexibilities in allowing certain realms of gender expression. • **HELP BUILD AN ADEQUATE SUPPORT NETWORK FROM MULTIPLE SOURCES, INCLUDING CONSISTENT COUNSELOR CARE.** • Take your more desperate pleadings to God rather than laying impossible demands on already anxious teens. • Avoid phrases or words that trigger misunderstanding or reveal underlying bias or judgment. • Avoid us-and-them language toward LGBT+ people. • Bless your child with special treats. (ex: "Quinn, it's Friday. You did awesome in school this week. Can I treat you to your favorite drink at Starbucks?") • As your child gets older, allow them increased autonomy about "who knows." • **LOVE NO MATTER WHAT. DECIDE TO "WALK WITH" NO MATTER WHAT.** • Don't shut down their coming out or be ashamed when they come out. • If you feel embarrassment or fear, call someone in your own support network to process those feelings. • **WHEN "THE BRIDGE DOES NOT CROSS" AND DISAGREEMENTS REMAIN, PRAY.**

Realize that whatever the origin, however permanent or temporary, regardless of whether it is clinical-level dysphoria or general gender discomfort — this journey must play out organically with as much love and acceptance as possible.

For the majority of youth who eventually "outgrow" gender dysphoria (or see it lessen),[1] this process can best occur when family, home, church, and school are safe for them. This process can be delayed by actions, attitudes, and words that reject young people and deny or minimize their experience. For 0.6% of the general population, dysphoria is a lifelong experience.[2] Avoid any tempation to use a statistic relating to the majority as an unrealistic expectation for the 0.6%.

During the teenage years, we as parents cannot know which story is at play in our child's life. We can offer unconditional love, earn relational trust, help build adequate support, depend upon God in prayer, and surrender to Jesus all that we cannot fix or control. Parents, you may reach a point where it becomes necessary to establish a contract with your teen specifying age thresholds at which they can make more of their own decisions. Contact us for additional help.

[1]Yarhouse MA. (2015). *Understanding Gender Dyshporia: Navigating Transgender Issues in a Changing Culture.* InterVarsity Press.
[2]Flores AR, Herman JL, Gates GJ, & Brown TNT (2016). *How Many Adults Identify as Transgender in the United States?* Los Angeles, CA: The Williams Institute.

info@leadthemhome.org

MY CHILD IS
TRANSGENDER

One father says: **"Your child is gay. Mine is transgender. *It's not more complex, just different.* We share** in the call to love our children unconditionally."

One mother says the opposite: ***"If only my son were gay**, it would **be so much easier to understand.** But he believes he is a woman. How can this be? *What will the future look like for my son?"*

No matter what, do not lose focus on nourishing a deep sense that God will be a refuge and shelter for your family.

Walking with your child will require grace. Mistakes are inevitable. Let your child know you aren't perfect, but you are trying.

Help them feel safe to speak up if you unintentionally say something upsetting or offensive.

BECAUSE OF THE WIDE DIVERSITY IN WHAT TRANS INDIVIDUALS EXPERIENCE, WE RECOMMEND DR. MARK YARHOUSE'S BOOK UNDERSTANDING GENDER DYSPHORIA.

INSIGHTS FOR THE ROAD AHEAD

YOUR FAMILY IS NOT ALONE

New studies reveal the U.S. population of transgender people is double what researchers previously thought. **Roughly 0.6% of the general population is transgender, equating to approximately 1.4 million people.** The lowest rates are 0.3% in North Dakota, 0.31% in Iowa, and 0.32% in Wyoming. The highest rates are 0.78% in Hawaii, 0.76% in California and 0.75% in Georgia. Rates for Texas and New York are 0.66% and 0.51%, respectively.[1]

Parents, you need trusted support after disclosure. It is sad, but some people will not understand. **You need people who will walk with you and your child no matter what.**

MOVE BEYOND CAUSATION & ACCUSATION

Transgender people are not pretending or faking the pain they feel inside. Some people are born **intersex** (both genitalia or ambiguous genitalia), and similarly, **some are born with an internal psychological gender that does not match their outward anatomy.** For many others, **a conscious or subconscious wound makes it no longer safe to be their birth sex.**

Causal factors are largely unknown and likely quite diverse. Since even the greatest scientists do not fully understand causation, families, pastors, and all who care should **focus on compassion.**

FOR MORE PERSONALIZED SUPPORT, PLEASE CONTACT US.

[1]Flores AR, Herman JL, Gates GJ, & Brown TNT (2016). *How Many Adults Identify as Transgender in the United States?* Los Angeles, CA: The Williams Institute.

TRANS ≠ GAY

Refrain from equating gender identity with sexual orientation. Many transgender people are heterosexual. **Most are not looking for a sexual experience;** rather, they are seeking relief from dysphoric anxiety, anguish, and frustration. Under such heavy stress, **they are seeking internal peace (a state of being).**

UNHELPFUL COMPARISONS DAMAGE TRUST

Much focus is on talking a transgender loved one out of their experience by using sin, addiction, or mental illness comparisons. One common comparison goes like this: "She is anorexic and thinks she is overweight. I am not going to play along with a false narrative that is killing her. Likewise, my son is male. I am not going to pretend he is a woman." While the pain of anorexia indeed has similarities to the pain of dysphoria, we often use comparisons in a way that accuses, belittles, condescends, and oversimplifies. **Such an approach is unproductive, hurts our loved ones, leaves them feeling misunderstood, and severely damages trust.**

FOSTER SAFE CONVERSATIONS

We should not pretend to have power we do not have. We cannot "fix" people. We can love them. In a world that often mistreats transgender people, let's do everything possible to make home and church safe places. Safety rises when we surround transgender family members with love, include them, and allow them to share their story. How tragic if our loved one were to suffer any deep anxiety and pain, and we allowed them to remain isolated, alone, and anxious.

JOURNEY

Do not let outward appearance deny the legitimacy of a transgender person's spiritual identity. If they claim Jesus as Savior, then mutually share the Christian faith with your loved one. Rid your heart of judgment, and you just may be surprised how deep your transgender child's faith is. Go to Psalm 27, Psalm 91, or Psalm 103 where we find God as a Savior, a Refuge, a Shelter, and a Father. **No matter what, build faith identity and posture yourself to learn from your loved one's Christian faith.**

TRANSITIONING

Many transgender people do not transition. Many others transition in varying degrees. **Rather than controlling transgender loved ones, build objective education around these decisions.** It is possible that, as an adult, your transgender loved one may eventually make decisions you do not support. Some start transitioning but later stop as fear rises that they are reaching a point of no return. Not every transgender person has to transition to gain relief from dysphoria. There are non-surgical options that help *some* people. Others feel the only way to escape life-crippling pain is to fully transition. **Love. Include. Accept. No matter what.**

IDENTITY & PRONOUNS

Subject to honoring parent authority regarding minors, a transgender young adult may adopt a name matching their gender identity. Lead Them Home has determined that we will refer to adults how they self-identify as a matter of basic respect. Whether a person is male or female, every person has a soul! **We choose to reach the soul rather than trying to win a person to our idea of who they are.** Eternal salvation is of far greater importance than names and pronouns.

FOR PASTORS & CHURCH LEADERS

It is critical that our *spiritual care* of transgender people follows the model of *family care* outlined in this guide. **Parents are often isolated in finding support to help them care for their children.** We need to enter into their lives in a posture of support rather than a posture of exclusion.

PASTORAL FAITHFULNESS

GENDER CONFLICT

PASTOR STEVE FROEHLICH SHARES HIS INSIGHTS ON NAVIGATING PASTORAL AND RELATIONAL CARE FOR INDIVIDUALS WHO EXPERIENCE GENDER DYSPHORIA. EXCERPTS REPRINTED WITH PERMISSION FROM THE AUTHOR AND FROM **CRITIQUE,** *A RANSOM FELLOWSHIP PUBLICATION (MAY 2018). ACCESS THE FULL PAPER AT* **RANSOMFELLOWSHIP.ORG.**

PASTOR STEVE, YOU SHARE THE POWERFUL STORY OF ENCOUNTERING A 22-YEAR-OLD TRANSGENDER MEMBER OF YOUR CHURCH. PLEASE INTRODUCE OUR READERS TO CHRIS.

Chris is biologically female yet has never known a time, even from age three or four, in which it ever seemed normal to identify as female. My heart breaks when I think about a lifetime of pain Chris has experienced on top of fear of rejection, longing for belonging, and uncertainty about where to get help. Twice in high school, Chris attempted suicide . . . and still bears scars from many years of cutting.

WHEN CHRIS SHARED HIS DECISION TO IDENTIFY AS MALE, THAT WAS A NEW EXPERIENCE FOR YOU. TELL US ABOUT YOUR READINESS FOR CHRIS'S DISCLOSURE AND YOUR INITIAL RESPONSE.

In the spring of 2015, Chris and I had coffee to talk about the implications of living with gender dysphoria. My mind was racing as I prayerfully considered how to respond. As I pondered what to say . . . I knew (obviously) that I had much to learn and that I did not know how to evaluate the decision Chris was making to identify as male. But I replied to my friend:

*"I'm willing to know you as you want to be known. I have no doubt that you fear the possibility of rejection and even anger in response to this decision, but **I promise you that I will never shame you and I am committed to standing with you as your friend.** I'm proud of you for the courage it takes to take these steps, and for your commitment to live by faith. Is that enough for now?"*

Chris nodded gratefully, and so began my journey . . . .

YOUR LOVE FOR CHRIS LAUNCHED A PASSION INSIDE YOU TO STUDY A TOPIC YOU KNEW LITTLE ABOUT. ONE OF THE MORE STRIKING POINTS YOU MAKE IS THAT CHRIS'S EXPERIENCE IS NOT NEW TO OUR MODERN WORLD. DO YOU HAVE AN EXAMPLE FROM HISTORY?

Note what Augustine observes in *The City of God* (16:8): "As for Androgynes, also called Hermaphrodites, they are certainly very rare, and yet it is difficult to find periods where there are no examples of human beings possessing the characteristics of both sexes, in such a way that it is a matter of doubt how they should be classified."

Lead Them Home Note: *The City of God* was published in 426 A.D.

PLEASE SHARE WITH OUR READERS WHAT YOU HAVE LEARNED ABOUT GENDER DYSPHORIA.

Gender dysphoria is rare, yet I believe there are sound reasons to believe that it can be a real condition that exists apart from sexual experimentation, rebellion, or views of fluid sexuality . . . .

. . . [R]esearch gathered by Mark Yarhouse and Oliver O'Donovan strongly suggests that gender dysphoria is not delusion. According to their research, delusion usually manifests across a broad range of areas in life and personality, and usually that is not the case with gender dysphoria. Furthermore, people living with . . . dysphoria are fully aware (painfully so) of . . . biological realities and the conflicts they experience.

Gender dysphoria involves conflicted identity and . . . frequently does not involve sexual attraction. In fact, many people with gender dysphoria report greatly diminished sexual attraction.

Gender dysphoria exists when the constituent elements of a person's sex, which usually work together coherently to define a person's sex, are in conflict with one another. **I believe that . . . gender dysphoria is possibly much like an intersex condition in which elements of both sexes appear to be present in the same person.**

Lead Them Home Note: We agree that dysphoria (for some) is like a psychological intersex condition rooted partly in endocrine biochemistry.

PASTOR STEVE'S HELPFUL INSIGHTS ON COMPASSIONATE CARE

Pray for safety, peace, courage, integrity, healing, and hope.
See transgender friends and loved ones as God's gift to you and the community.
Be careful to distinguish between gender dysphoria, sexual orientation, and cross-dressing.
Practice selfless love and generosity. Do not harden your heart to others' struggles.
Be courteous and consider recognizing friends as they wish to be known.
Offer the generosity and courtesy you would like extended to you.
Repent of any anger, pride, or impatience.

SOME PEOPLE WANT TO BELIEVE THAT GOD WOULD NOT ALLOW THIS TO HAPPEN. WHAT WOULD YOU SAY TO THOSE WHO BELIEVE THAT BEING TRANSGENDER IS A CHOICE?

...[T]here is indisputably no evidence that anyone *wants* to live with gender dysphoria. To the contrary, there is consistent evidence that those who live with gender dysphoria will go to great lengths to relieve themselves of the pain and chaos that accompanies the conflict. **People who live with gender dysphoria want to be whole people and coherently sexed as male or female.**

...[T]he pain is commonly so great that 41% of people who experience ... dysphoria attempt suicide.

TRANSITIONING IS OFTEN PORTRAYED AS THE ULTIMATE RESOLUTION FOR MANY TRANSGENDER PEOPLE. HOW DO YOU SUGGEST THAT OUR READERS THINK ABOUT THE ROLE OF TRANSITION?

Even when a coherent unity of the constituent parts that work together to comprise and reveal a person's sex is absent (thereby leaving that person uncertain about his/her ontological sex), that ontological sex still exists and cannot be changed. Thus, given the role of unalterable and inaccessible characteristics, any attempt to move from an incoherent toward a coherent ontological sex will always be limited and incomplete.

Given the reliability of the body to reveal a person's sex, exceptions are rare. We should rely on the physiology as an indicator of sex unless we have significant reasons to believe otherwise.

Given that God created sex as the basis for relationship with himself and others, exceptions are to be recognized in community, not autonomously. **Exceptions require corroborating support from those in a position to speak knowledgably about a person's mind, body, spirit, affections, and chemistry.**

It is no small thing to conclude that a person's anatomy is communicating inaccurate information about that person's sex, and self-diagnosis (while important) is insufficient in itself to justify an exception.

THE "CHOICE" NARRATIVE OFTEN YIELDS DENIGRATING ATTITUDES. WHY IS THIS?

Gender coherence, or the absence of gender dysphoria, is so universally common that some people who are cynical about the existence of gender dysphoria make ungracious and demeaning quips like, "Just look down your pants — what more evidence do you need about whether you're a man or a woman?" Therefore, some people suggest either that gender dysphoria is one more kind of mental confusion or that it is cultural capitulation, a caving to social ideology.

SOME CHRISTIANS STRUGGLE TO PROCESS HOW THERE CAN BE A DISCONNECT BETWEEN MIND OR PSYCHOLOGICAL GENDER AND ANATOMICAL GENDER. CAN YOU HELP US UNDERSTAND WHY THIS HAPPENS AND HOW FAMILIES OF TRANSGENDER PEOPLE CAN FIND HOPE?

Given that sex (gender) is a complex and deeply mysterious gift from God, we must be humble about over-simplifying that complexity and speaking with improper confidence about matters we know only in part. There is no part of the universe untouched by the Fall, evil, and sin. So, we know that we will witness creational upheaval in the most profound and disorienting ways in every area of life, including sex.

One day, God will wipe away all tears, and we will stand in His presence known by name, whole, complete, without conflict, and full of glory.

HOW CAN FAMILIES AND CHURCHES FOSTER COMPASSIONATE CARE OF TRANSGENDER PEOPLE?

I'm focusing on how we love, counsel, guide, and walk with those we love within our Christian community. This is a family conversation, not an ecclesiastical statement about the transgender movement.

Even at our most glorious, we hobble and improvise. As a result, in this life our path toward resurrection is varied and incomplete — **the strong carry the weak, the courageous lead the fearful, the wise guide the foolish as together we work out our salvation with fear and trembling** (Rom 15:1; 1 Cor 12:22-26; Phil 2:12).

ABOUT THE AUTHOR

Steve Froehlich has served as senior pastor of New Life Presbyterian Church (PCA) in Ithaca, NY, since 1998. He completed graduate theological and pastoral studies at Reformed Theological Seminary (M.Div., 1991) and Gordon-Conwell Theological Seminary (D.Min., 2015). The views expressed here are his own and do not speak for any organizations with which he is associated.

info@leadthemhome.org

LIVING LIFE WITH MARK

MOLLY TELLS OF HER FAMILY'S GRIEF, GROWTH, AND HOPE THROUGH HER TEEN DAUGHTER JANA'S TRANSITION INTO HER SON MARK.

I KNEW WHAT WAS GOING ON even before confirming it. But I either wasn't sufficiently self-aware at the time, or my husband and I were just too afraid to face the reality behind all the indicators throughout our daughter's life.

When Jana was 17, I had a suspicion about her sexuality. I felt the need to know primarily because I was concerned for her safety and wanted to protect her.

One day, I was determined to get an answer and got up the nerve to ask, "Are you gay?"

I think Jana felt traumatized by my directness. She was clearly not ready to talk.

Jana was justifiably anxious: we were an Evangelical family that had fallen into a very legalistic church. I am positive that the "hellfire and damnation" tone we heard every Sunday was frightening for her.

CHURCH EXPERIENCE

When I finally confirmed her sexuality, I suddenly found myself with a need for support outside our family. Sadly, LGBT+ people were viewed by those around us as a problem to solve. Before that year, I shared this same view. But now, it was my own child. I needed real answers.

But the answers we received were tragic. Our house church leader felt ill-equipped and did not know how to help us.

MOVING AWAY

This experience broke us. In desperation, we literally moved away. We pulled Jana out of public school and into homeschool for her senior year. We justified the decision by saying she needed time to just breathe. But I will now admit that our decision was really our attempt to shield Jana from a liberal school atmosphere. As you can imagine, Jana was not happy with these decisions.

All this time, we viewed Jana as our precious child. It was out of love that we felt such passion to protect her from voices that might affirm her sexuality. At the same time, we had also made this move from a place of panic.

TRANSITION

Within a year of the incident with our house church leader, we had moved back home. Jana began dating Kendra. Soon after, though, Kendra transitioned to a boy.

That was a shock to us! What was most shocking, however, was when Jana announced that she would also be transitioning.

And so, Jana and Kendra soon became Mark and Ethan.

To have a lesbian daughter was challenging. But when we learned that Jana was transitioning, we were absolutely devastated.

> **OUR ANXIETY WAS NOT INTENDED AS REJECTION, BUT IT HAD REAL AND NEGATIVE EFFECTS ON OUR CHILD.**

GRANDPARENTS' SUPPORT

Around this time, my own parents noticed how overwhelmed my husband and I were. Our anxiety was not intended as rejection, but it had real and negative effects on our child.

So in that season, Jana, our daughter — who was now Mark, our son — moved in with my parents. Jana (Mark) continued to live with them all these years until recently when Mark and Ethan got their own place.

I am so thankful that my parents provided a loving home for Mark. As parents with our own emotions, we were exhausted. We were at a dead end. We stayed in touch regularly, but as I look back, there were times when I could not even see Mark, much less process all the changes that were underway.

She, or he, was changing at such a rapid pace. I tried to control, tried to negotiate — anything to stop the transition. While all of this was done out of sincere love for my child, I am positive that this season was very hurtful for Mark.

THE SHAPE OF GRIEF

As Jana became Mark, there were several years in which we were detached from one another. We never stopped loving our child, but she became so different so fast. In a way, we kept losing more and more of our daughter. In her place, there emerged a stranger with a new voice, a new body, new clothing, new hair, and a new scent. It was almost like a living death: our child was still alive, but everything we knew her to be — from physical appearance to dreams for my daughter — began to disappear. Yet in a way, we thought, not even death takes away your child's name and gender.

> WE NO LONGER LOOK AT OUTWARD APPEARANCES. OUR HOPE IS IN GOD AND HIS POWER TO DRAW MARK AND ETHAN TO THE CROSS.

THE CAPACITY OF GRIEF

During that season, we were vulnerable. But Jana's life was even more fragile. She was suicidal to the point of having a detailed plan to take her life.

As parents, our grief had reached past its full capacity. Our own grief so limited us that we had no capacity left to address Jana's grief. We could not protect our precious child from taking her life.

We nearly lost Jana. Thankfully, God preserved her life — and He has allowed us to play a role in helping her recover.

BIOLOGICAL FACTORS

Medically, there are unique elements to our story. I lost four pregnancies before having Jana. I had an autoimmune condition that required high doses of Prednisone. This steroid caused diabetes, which required insulin injections and progesterone to help support the pregnancy. All three medications can cause masculinization of female fetuses. But for my baby to survive, these medications were required.

As Jana matured, we were encouraged to have her checked for Polycystic Ovary Syndrome. Tests showed that her system was producing off-the-charts levels of insulin and testosterone. The doctor concluded that she had a "functionally male endocrine system." For this reason, Mark's gender falls within the classification of intersex.

I do not view Mark as disabled, but it is important for people to understand that there are factual medical reasons that play a role in Mark's gender identity. What's going on inside of him is biologically real.

Sure enough, there were signs the whole way. From pre-school through high school, Jana always wanted boys as friends. She played with the boys until it was no longer cool for them to hang out with a girl. This left Jana very isolated for many years: she simply could not relate to girls.

A CHILD I'VE ALWAYS KNOWN

Mark and Ethan are now 25 years old. All to say, we have been at this journey for many years.

Today, it deeply grieves me that I once saw Mark as a kind of death. Today, I see him as having a full soul, the very same soul of my child whom I have always known. His sense of humor. His habits. His inner strength. He is the same compassionate, loving, kind person I have always known. Other families have lost their child to suicide or violence against transgender people. By God's grace, I am so thankful that I still have my child.

Mark and Ethan bring so much joy to our lives. We no longer look at outward appearances. Our hope is in God and his power to draw Mark and Ethan to the Cross. We were put through a refining fire that has transformed us into deeply compassionate people. God's grace healed our hopelessness. Our hope is no longer based on impossible expectations for Mark and Ethan; our hope is in the power and love of Jesus Christ.

It is possible to wholly love God *and* deeply love your LGBT+ child. I am so thankful to feel deep love in my heart for Mark and Ethan. I have so much peace about placing them in God's hands and enjoying their presence in our lives. My husband and I love Mark and Ethan. We have so much fun living life with them.

A WORD FOR PARENTS

I want to caution families that there are many deadly messages out there. But for the first time ever, the church is beginning to offer life-giving help to parents like us — including the resource you hold in your hands. This guide will literally save many lives and preserve many family relationships.

At our worst point, my husband and I were in complete despair. We could not escape the depression and pain. Today, however, I am here to say that we made it through to the other side.

To parents early in a similar journey who cannot see a way forward, we want to say this: with the love of Christ, you can make it to a place of understanding. If we made it, you will make it too, because we serve the same Lord who is faithful to guide, comfort, and encourage us.

Molly is passionate about walking with parents of transgender children. Contact us if you would like to connect with Molly.

YESTERDAY, TODAY, & TOMORROW

LEAD THEM HOME HAS SERVED on the support team of Sara and Abree (previously Abe) over the last 8 years. They met with us to share their story of relating as mother and son over the most recent decade of Abree's life. Sara and Abree give us an inside look into how God has been shepherding them through a *relational* transition — and showing them the importance of love as a constant.

ABE'S STORY

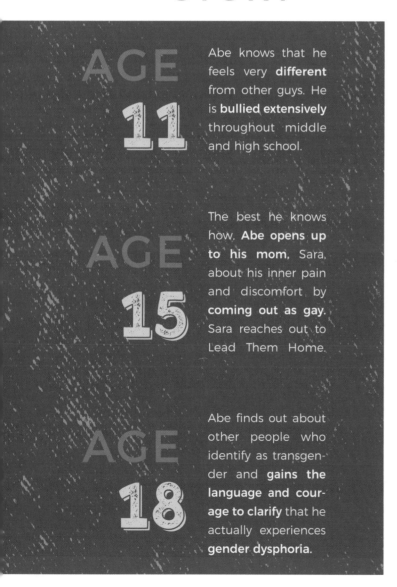

AGE 11

Abe knows that he feels very **different** from other guys. He is **bullied extensively** throughout middle and high school.

AGE 15

The best he knows how, **Abe opens up to his mom,** Sara, about his inner pain and discomfort by **coming out as gay.** Sara reaches out to Lead Them Home.

AGE 18

Abe finds out about other people who identify as transgender and **gains the language and courage to clarify** that he actually experiences **gender dysphoria.**

SARA'S STORY

"I was ignorant about what my son was experiencing. When Abe shared about dysphoria, I could not understand. I thought he was making it up. **I knew he had been in tremendous pain from the bullying he endured for many years. I knew he was depressed. Despite this, how could I make sense out of the idea that my son wants to be a girl?** Did he *want* to be a girl or did he think he *has already been* a girl? How did this happen? What did it mean?

"In the early years, I simply denied his experience. I fought to control his behavior. As Abe's appearance began changing, many people claimed to have all the answers. Their ideas were neither kind nor compassionate. To please others, though, **I found myself following the advice of these 'wise counselors' and damaging my relationship with Abe.**

"It was through the support of Lead Them Home that I first realized I was adding trauma on top of many other traumas that my son had already suffered. I just kept criticizing his choice to be a 'practicing homosexual.' I did not understand that gender identity is separate from sexual orientation. Abe was left feeling very isolated and alone. As I look back, I now see that I nearly lost my son to suicide.

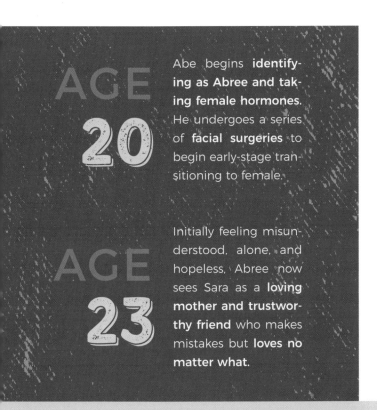

AGE 20

Abe begins **identifying as Abree and taking female hormones.** He undergoes a series of **facial surgeries** to begin early-stage transitioning to female.

AGE 23

Initially feeling misunderstood, alone, and hopeless, Abree now sees Sara as a **loving mother and trustworthy friend** who makes mistakes but **loves no matter what.**

SARA TODAY

"What I have learned above all — and what I want more than anything — is to truly love my son unconditionally. **The more I have learned to love him, the more peace I have inside my heart, the more trust I have in God, and the less anxiety Abe has felt.** He is my only child. What else can I do? As a mother, I choose to accept, care for, and love Abree."

ABREE TODAY

"I cannot speak for all transgender people. I also cannot say that all my gender dysphoria is gone. What I can say is that for some transgender people, a lack of family acceptance increases anxiety, driving many to seek peace through transition. The more my mom fought me, the more depressed I became. Feeling misunderstood, alone, and hopeless only triggered me to seek refuge through transitioning. **If you can't get relief from pain — or even positive comfort — from your family, it's only common sense to seek them elsewhere.**"

"Along the way, though, my mother changed. Instead of arguing, denying my experience, and telling me hurtful things, she suddenly just gently accepted me. She started just saying how much she loved me no matter what. **She began allowing me to talk about my gender identity without criticizing me or getting angry.** She became a great friend that I could trust.

"I was well into transitioning. I was on female hormones. I had several facial surgeries. I reached a point where it felt like I was nearing a point of no return — and it scared me. I would turn back from transitioning, but something would then compel me again to move forward. **The shifting in my confidence about what to do made me super nervous. How could I know what's right?** Even if it feels so right today, will it relieve my dysphoria over the long term? What if it doesn't help at all? How far will I go, and at what risk? It was all so confusing for me.

"During this time, my mother's love never changed. My stepfather began deepening his understanding of me as well. Suddenly, I just began to feel more comfortable in my own skin. That doesn't mean my dysphoria is gone — or that I never think about transitioning. But today, I have mostly stopped taking hormones. I don't think further surgeries are wise. I know I was born a guy. I know I am a guy. I am simply comfortable being me.

"Rather than demanding that people pass some test before I trust them, I focus on how they love me. **I also realize that if I were a parent, I would make many of the same mistakes my mother made. It is loving parents who can often make the biggest mistakes because they so want to protect their child.**

"My struggles are not entirely gone, but I am thankful to be more comfortable."

info@leadthemhome.org

WHEN LIFE IS NOT BLACK AND WHITE

WE MET UP WITH 19-YEAR-OLD LIZ AT A COFFEE SHOP IN BOSTON TO HEAR WHAT IT'S LIKE TO BE GENDER NONBINARY AND ON THE ASEXUAL SPECTRUM.

LIZ, YOU TOLD ME THAT YOU ARE ASEXUAL. CAN YOU SHARE WITH US MORE ABOUT YOU?

Sure. I identify as nonbinary/asexual spectrum. When I talk with nonbinary friends, I identify as AFAB, or "assigned female at birth." Some of my friends identify as AMAB, or "assigned male at birth."

LIZ'S EXPERIENCE OF GENDER

SO, FOR YOU, THERE ARE TWO ELEMENTS OF YOUR IDENTITY. *NONBINARY* DESCRIBES YOUR GENDER. *ASEXUAL SPECTRUM* DESCRIBES YOUR SEXUAL ORIENTATION. LET'S START WITH GENDER.

I have simply never seen a big difference between boys and girls. Emotionally, I have girlish feelings. Personality-wise, I am masculine. Since I was young, I've liked basketball, action toys, hands-on work, and anything adventurous.

People might think of me as transgender, but I just don't think of myself in terms of gender. Growing up, I was consciously aware that I was missing something that most people just "know." This can be an isolating experience that leaves you feeling very lost and kind of all on your own. Developmentally, you don't really know what's going on. My everyday life has never fit the way that this world understands gender.

I CAN SENSE THE ISOLATION THAT YOU MENTION. WHAT WAS THAT LIKE FOR YOU?

Thankfully, I was never seriously suicidal, though I did get bullied some. When schools or my parents tried to force-fit me into the "girl world," it created great anxiety for me. There were seasons in middle school when I was seriously depressed. I just didn't fit in. Moving to a technical high school helped a lot.

For me, I felt like I couldn't trust people. I began isolating myself in the online gaming world. Many of my closest friends were gamers. I would go days wearing the same baggy flannel pajama pants. I recall feeling lost, depressed, and very isolated.

WHAT'S IT LIKE WHEN PEOPLE SEE YOU AS FEMALE?

Most people understandably identify me as a female. I get that. But for people to see the feminine in me is frustrating. When people see me as masculine, it makes me feel more comfortable in my own skin.

Even as I say that, I'm not entirely settled on nonbinary. For this season of life, it's the most comfortable way to describe myself. This is the best I can understand gender for now. I'm still working it out.

WHAT SPECIFICALLY WOULD YOU LIKE PEOPLE TO UNDERSTAND ABOUT YOU?

I like it when people are genuinely curious about my identity, even if it is confusing to them. Why? It's simple. I'm human. It feels much less isolating if people know about me, rather than having to hide so much of myself alone inside.

I know people can't fully understand my experience. Statistically, there are many of *you* and few of *us*. It is lonely. So any genuine attempt to understand me is a very kind effort. I appreciate it. It makes me feel less alone.

LIZ'S EXPERIENCE OF SEXUALITY

Similar to gender, sexuality is an entirely gray area for me. When I describe myself as asexual, it means I don't feel sexual attraction towards people. In my sexuality, any kind of longing is more emotional. I don't want or even think of sex. My longing for human touch —and the meaning of it — both have more to do with feeling valued, which is more of an emotional need than a sexual need.

WHAT WAS IT LIKE GROWING UP ASEXUAL?

On the one hand, friends in high school were very loud about their interest in sex. I was curious, but any idea of actual sex was disgusting to me. My curiosity was only my attempt to get closer to understanding what my friends were talking about. It wasn't something I personally wanted.

Many assume asexual people don't want to get married. Or that our bodies don't experience arousal. Or that we don't feel romantic longings. Everyone on the asexual spectrum is different. Personally, I *do* want to get married, but I think it'll be hard to find someone who can understand my gender and asexuality. I can still feel arousal, but it only feels like a burning in my stomach, and it isn't very pleasant. And in regard to romance, some asexual people would describe themselves as "aromantic," others "gray-romantic," and still others very romantic. Personally, it's a big cloud to me. I think I am gray-romantic. It's all cloudy.

HOW WOULD YOU RECOMMEND THAT A PARENT OR PASTOR RESPOND TO AN ASEXUAL TEEN?

First, asexual people tend to come out later than most LGBT+ people because it takes so long for them to figure out what's happening inside and to understand what it all means. You think you're developing late. Then you think you're questioning. And eventually, what happened for nearly everyone else long ago just never happens for you. It can take a long time to finally understand, and it can be a really anxious road. There can be panic attacks, fear, self-hatred, depression, loneliness, and potentially even suicidal thoughts.

Second, parents and pastors need to realize that it took a lot of thought for someone to come out as asexual. Getting to that point requires a tremendous amount of processing and trying to figure out "the gray" in a world that is very "black and white" to other people. There is a stress, a weight, and an anxiety that comes with this journey.

Third, any negative response will quickly push people away from their family or church. How can anyone feel accepted if there is rejection? It takes tremendous courage for anyone to share that they're asexual.

Finally, don't tell young people, "It's just a phase." Your asexual child has likely spent thousands of hours trying to figure out what they experience on the inside and how to talk about it with others who aren't asexual. Most of those conversations haven't gone so well. I would say: don't make it about you. Just listen. Be present. Be attentive. Offer affection. And love your child well.

LIZ OFFERS AN ANALOGY

Let's say you live in a world where people love all different kinds of chocolate and talk about it every day. You know that chocolate is a huge deal — that many people like this kind or that kind of chocolate, but you yourself simply don't want it.

Being asexual is like living in a world where everyone endlessly talks about their favorite chocolate. As an asexual person, I know all about how passionate people are for "chocolate!" But, for me, it's merely an idea — not something I think about or want for myself. It can be isolating to live in a world where the biggest thing everyone talks about is unknowable or vague to me.

HOW CAN PEOPLE BEST DEMONSTRATE THAT THEY CARE ABOUT NONBINARY AND ASEXUAL PEOPLE?

First, don't say nice things to my face and then gossip or ridicule me. I would say to Christians not to make everything about you. Stop being mean to people like me. Be a listener. Be willing to learn from me as I try to find my way in the world.

You don't know what we're going through. You'll never know until we feel safe enough to share our story. If we trust you enough to share our story, you will actually find out just how vulnerable we really are — vulnerable in terms of willingness to share, but also vulnerable to mistreatment and condemnation.

NOTE: Individuals who identify as nonbinary (NB) may also describe themselves as androgyne, genderqueer, or androgynous.

Lead Them Home's Social Media Director Josh Proctor addresses stereotypes across the gender and sexual identity spectrum. On every point of this spectrum, there is a valuable person with a real-life story — someone who must daily navigate their life while often facing misunderstanding and mistreatment. Here is just a glimpse into some of their experiences.

BISEXUAL

Many falsely assume that bisexual people can simply direct their desires toward a certain gender. While some bisexual people are highly attracted to both genders, others are primarily attracted to a certain gender. For some, attraction is predictable. For others, a cyclical swing occurs — often at unpredictable intervals.

When 23-year-old Brandon is attracted to the opposite gender, all his emotional, romantic, and physical attractions are geared toward girls. He has initiated dating relationships with girls during this phase. In one case, he and his girlfriend fell in love. He hoped she'd be "the one." Privately, he thought, *Maybe the cycling has stopped. I pray so.*

But one day, the cycle in Brandon's attractions shifted — yet again! He suddenly felt resistant to his girlfriend wanting to hold hands. Should he wait it out until the cycle shifts again? In this case, he disclosed this challenge to his girlfriend to limit the hurt she'd feel. After they broke up, Brandon said, "I hate my life! I can't help what I experience, but I hate it!"

As pastors and parents, it would be a mistake to assume that being bisexual is easy. Bisexual people can actually face as many difficulties as lesbian and gay people do. In fact, they often experience bullying, exclusion, and rejection at similar levels to gay and transgender youth.

PANSEXUAL

Catelyn, a 21-year-old college student, shared, "I used to identify as bisexual, but my problem is that I don't really see people for their gender. I just see the person." While a bisexual person is attracted to someone for reasons including those *linked to their gender*, a pansexual person experiences attraction *apart from or regardless of gender.*

A lack of information and education on pansexuality can make for a longer process of self-discovery for pansexual people. Many initially come out as bisexual only to later realize their attraction does not fit well in that category. Additionally, the lack of information brings about mistreatment, sometimes even from other LGBT+ people. They may be accused of "wanting attention," "going through a phase," or even being promiscuous.

We have to recognize that there are many factors impacting how a person experiences attraction. This varies widely from person to person. As pastors and parents, we can't assume we understand how someone experiences their attractions — much less the degree of difficulty they face in their daily lives. More than anything, we need to listen compassionately and openly, realizing that every individual is unique.

QUESTIONING

With the complexity of gender, sexuality, and romantic attraction, it should not surprise us that many people need time and space to truly understand the nature of their experience. This is true especially when considering that gender and attraction can be in flux for some young people.

When teens or even young adults identify as questioning, they are attempting to find positive value and reduce the confusion or uncertainty they experience inside.

When a loved one is questioning their sexuality or gender identity, the last thing they need is pressure from those around them to decide *who they are* or *what they want.* What young people need most from pastors and parents is patience, compassion, and a safe place to be heard.

INTERSEX

Intersex occurs when a person is born with variation in external sex characteristics that do not clearly fit the categories of male or female. Figuring out one's gender identity as an intersex person can be confusing and play out into young adulthood.

Early surgical intervention is unreliable as a predictor of adult gender identity. For this reason, many intersex people advocate for delaying surgical intervention until gender identity is firmly established.

Our faith communities must support parents of intersex children in order to lower the anxiety they carry about their child's future. We must give intersex children and their parents complete assurance of God's love for them — and our commitment to walk with them no matter what!

I FORGIVE YOU

MARK (FROM "LIVING LIFE WITH MARK" ON PAGE 86) WRITES A FORGIVENESS LETTER HE SENT TO HIS PARENTS. MARK HAS SHOWN PROFOUND GRACE TO HIS FAMILY. AMIDST BELIEF GAPS AND RELATIONAL MISTAKES, HE TREASURES HIS RELATIONSHIP WITH THEM.

I never thought it could be like this: my parents, my boyfriend, and me — all together, happy, and smiling, while I am in my full manly and bearded glory and unashamed. But that is finally what I am.

I was born female into a very religious family, and I thought that my gender and sexuality issues were just a test from God to make me stronger in my faith.

When I finally "failed" that test and realized who I always was underneath that very shallow facade, both my and my parents' world was turned upside down. First coming out as a lesbian, and then a transgender man — and then by falling in love with another trans man and coming out again as a gay man. It's a lot for anyone to undertake.

And although there were many years of screaming matches and slamming doors and eventually me moving out when I was 17, I knew that my parents still loved me even if they didn't accept me. And I knew that they only wanted what's best for me in their own way.

Mom and Dad, I forgive you for not knowing what to do. I forgive you for doing and saying hurtful things at the time. I forgive you for sending me to reparative therapy. I forgive you for taking me out of public school and moving me far away from my friends. I forgive you for panicking.

And I thank you for sticking around, for not giving up, and for trying. It's taken 8 years, but I am happy to call myself your son, even if those words are still hard for you to say. I am proud of how far you've come. I'm proud that you want to help other Christian parents of LGBT+ kids and let them know that they can still love God and love their kids, no matter what journey they are on.

And I will always know that you love me, even if the concept of who I am has been hard to grasp. I wouldn't trade you for the world. You've made me the man I am today.

— Mark

"ABOVE ALL, KEEP LOVING ONE ANOTHER EARNESTLY, SINCE LOVE COVERS A MULTITUDE OF SINS." – 1 PETER 4:8 (ESV)

info@leadthemhome.org

REFLECTION QUESTIONS

1. In **Reaching People Where They Are**, Dr. David Osborn says, "You have to reach people where they are because you can't reach them where they're not." This statement is true for all people, but what does it imply for how we care for transgender and nonbinary people?

2. What is gender dysphoria? Imagine and describe what it would be like to live with it. What are some popular misconceptions about gender dysphoria?

3. In **Practical Tips**, how might our care for teens with a transgender or "plus" identity differ from our care for LGB teens? How might it be similar? How can pastors (and the rest of us) support transgender, nonbinary, and other "plus" identified young people and their families?

4. What are some of the unique challenges parents and families face as they seek to build acceptance and support for trangender and "plus" identified loved ones?

5. What is it that frees us from fixating on causation in regard to the origin of gender dysphoria? Why is it necessary to move beyond trying to solve the causation question?

6. Dr. Yarhouse notes that the majority of youth eventually outgrow gender dysphoria (or see it lessen). How do we care for transgender loved ones with hope even while understanding that we can't predict the trajectory of their dysphoria? How can such statistics be misused against transgender youth in ways that damage their sense of acceptance from their family?

7. What are a few practical ways you can care for transgender and "plus" loved ones in a way that is appropriate both to their vulnerabilities and their age? (It may be helpful to revisit **Risks LGBT+ Teens Face** and **Navigating Relational Gaps**.)

8. Does using a transgender or nonbinary person's preferred name and pronouns necessarily indicate approval of gender transition? Why or why not? What is the relational benefit of using a loved one's preferred language? Are these benefits worth it?

9. In **Pastoral Faithfulness & Gender Conflict**, identify some of the key points Pastor Steve Froehlich makes about gender dysphoria. (For more insights, link to his full article.)

10. Describe how each **Real Life Profile** increased your understanding. What did you learn about those who identify as asexual? In **Overview of Other "Plus" Identities**, what unique insights did you gain regarding bisexual, pansexual, questioning, and intersex persons? As pastors, how can we make church safe for all transgender and "plus" loved ones?

"ABOVE ALL THINGS HAVE INTENSE AND UNFAILING LOVE FOR ONE ANOTHER, FOR LOVE COVERS A

MULTITUDE OF SINS [FORGIVES AND DISREGARDS THE OFFENSES OF OTHERS]."

– 1 PETER 4:8

94

Family Care Seminar

Family Care Seminar is a workshop designed to equip, comfort, and encourage Christian families of LGBT+ loved ones.

This confidential setting allows families to come together and care for one another while getting equipped with a biblical mandate to love and extend Christ to LGBT+ family members. Families who attend our seminar are radically transformed by the experience and spiritually equipped to walk with their loved ones no matter what.

Purchase an individual-user download of a prior Family Care Seminar:

LEADTHEMHOME.ORG/RESOURCES

Contact us to learn more about hosting Family Care Seminar at your church:

INFO@LEADTHEMHOME.ORG

"I WAITED PATIENTLY AND EXPECTANTLY FOR THE LORD; AND HE INCLINED TO ME AND HEARD MY CRY.

HE DREW ME UP OUT OF A HORRIBLE PIT [A PIT OF TUMULT AND OF DESTRUCTION], OUT OF THE MIRY CLAY (FROTH AND SLIME), AND SET MY FEET UPON A ROCK, STEADYING MY STEPS AND ESTABLISHING MY GOINGS.

AND HE HAS PUT A NEW SONG IN MY MOUTH, A SONG OF PRAISE TO OUR GOD. MANY SHALL SEE AND FEAR (REVERE AND WORSHIP) AND PUT THEIR TRUST AND CONFIDENT RELIANCE IN THE LORD."

– PSALM 40:1-3

PART 5: »

PRAYING IN FAITH & TRUSTING IN GOD

FOR TRUSTFULNESS

O Heavenly Father,
thou understandest all thy children;
through thy gift of faith
we bring our perplexities
to the light of thy wisdom,
and receive the blessed
encouragement of thy sympathy,
and a clearer knowledge of thy will.
Glory be to thee
for all thy gracious gifts.
Amen.[1]

FOR QUIET CONFIDENCE

O GOD of peace,
who hast taught us
that in returning and rest
we shall be saved,
in quietness and in confidence
shall be our strength;
By the might of thy Spirit
lift us, we pray thee,
to thy presence,
where we may be still and know
that thou art God;
through Jesus Christ our Lord.
Amen.[1]

[1]Church of England. (1960). *The Book of common prayer
with the additions and deviations proposed in 1928.*
Cambridge: University Press.

SHINING LOVE

by Roberta C. Raftery

Believer, what do you express
As you look at another?
Do your eyes show love
To your sister and brother?

Or do they show disdain
For the one you see
For they are not at all
What you want them to be?

For you measure a man
Only by what you see
And not by what God
Can cause him to be.

Yet Jesus desires
To give you
His loving heart
And His eternal view;

For He looks at men
As those for whom He died
For He had seen their needs
And heard how they had cried;

And He desires today
That others may see
His love shining forth
Through you and through me,

That men might know
That they have worth
And how God longs to give them
A spiritual new birth.

SPECIAL WORD
FOR LGBT+ LOVED ONES

I N MENTIONING PRAYER, there is a risk that some LGBT+ readers may interpret Lead Them Home as encouraging parents to "pray away" a child's sexual orientation or gender identity. If you have read the first four parts of *Guiding Families*, it is my prayer that you know this is not our intention.

By suggesting prayer, our purpose is to invite *all of us* to bring our greatest challenges, fears, doubts, worries, anxieties, and questions into the presence of God. In Matthew 11:28-30, Jesus invites each one of us:

> "Come to Me, all who are weary and heavily burdened [by religious rituals that provide no peace], and I will give you rest [refreshing your souls with salvation]. Take My yoke upon you and learn from Me [following Me as My disciple], for I am gentle and humble in heart, and you will find rest (renewal, blessed quiet) for your souls. For My yoke is easy [to bear] and My burden is light."

You might be an LGBT+ teen with a history of bullying. For you, Jesus might be inviting you to bring your trauma to Him and receive His healing touch and comfort. You are made in His image. He is your Heavenly Father. He never intended for you to experience mistreatment. He deeply loves you.

Or maybe you are an LGBT+ adult whose parents or extended family reject your partner. *Anyone* (gay, straight, or transgender) who deeply loves their partner or spouse would be hurt by conditional acceptance — or even worse, overt exclusion. Maybe Jesus is inviting you to bring your hurt into His presence — or even to offer forgiveness for wrongs done to you.

100

For a parent who has made mistakes, maybe you already offered an apology and sought your child's forgiveness. Your child, though, may not be ready to let go of the hurt they have experienced. Maybe Jesus is inviting you to keep the faith and cast your dependence upon Him to help you restore the relationship with your child.

Or possibly you have been loving and accepting throughout your child's journey, but your child is demanding that you shift your beliefs before they will have any meaningful relationship with you. Maybe Jesus is inviting you to bring your hurt and surrender it fully at the Cross.

We all need God. We find Him most deeply when we bring *our everything* to Him. Whatever our need, we experience peace when we surrender our lives into His presence. In 1 Peter 5:6-7, His Spirit invites us:

> *"Therefore humble yourselves under the mighty hand of God [set aside self-righteous pride], so that He may exalt you [to a place of honor in His service] at the appropriate time, casting all your cares [all your anxieties, all your worries, and all your concerns, once and for all] on Him, for He cares about you [with deepest affection, and watches over you very carefully]."*

But can God be trusted? *Only if we trust Him.* He desires relationship with us. He hungers to be *our everything.* For our ultimate security and rest, God promises refuge in Psalm 91:1-2:

> *"He who dwells in the shelter of the Most High will remain secure and rest in the shadow of the Almighty [whose power no enemy can withstand]. I will say of the Lord, "He is my refuge and my fortress, My God, in whom I trust [with great confidence, and on whom I rely]!"*

Prayer is not about an attempt to *fix* or *change* or *judge* or *dismiss* any reader of *Guiding Families.* To the contrary: you are a prized possession. You are a child of the King of Kings who says:

> *"[I have] plans to prosper you and not to harm you, plans to give you hope and a future. Then you will call on me and come and pray to me, and I will listen to you. You will seek me and find me when you seek me with all your heart. I will be found by you" (Jeremiah 29:11-14).*

God promises that as we seek Him, we *will* find Him.

On the following pages, may you find encouragement, comfort, protection, or whatever you most need.

THE GOD OF ALL COMFORT

The following is a part of a letter the apostle Paul wrote to Christians in Corinth to bring them to the one he calls "the God of all comfort" (2 Corinthians 1:3-11, International Standard Version).

³Praise be to the God and Father of our Lord Jesus Christ, the Father of compassion and the God of all comfort,

God's compassion and comfort are readily available during our most troubling times. Jesus invites us: "Come to Me all who are weary and burdened. I will give you rest for your soul" (Matthew 11:28). He knows every way that we may hurt over our family and friends. He offers us His presence and desires to comfort us.

⁴who comforts us in all our troubles, so that we can comfort those in any trouble with the comfort we ourselves receive from God.

No situation is beyond the reach of God's comfort. David writes: "The one who lives in the shelter of the Most High, who rests in the shadow of the Almighty, will say to the Lord, 'You are my refuge, my fortress, and my God in whom I trust'" (Psalm 91:1-2)! Some of us have faced impossible situations and experienced God's faithfulness. He walked with us every step of the way. We have been comforted by God, and now we can encourage others to fully place their trust in God. If you are in an early stage of grief — or are continuing to hurt from family rejection — this promise may seem far away. In due time, God will prove faithful: you will be comforted. One day, you will be the comforter of others. God rebuilds our hope even when we have lost all hope.

⁵For just as we share abundantly in the sufferings of Christ, so also our comfort abounds through Christ.

⁶If we are distressed, it is for your comfort and salvation; if we are comforted, it is for your comfort, which produces in you patient endurance of the same sufferings we suffer.

⁷And our hope for you is firm, because we know that just as you share in our sufferings, so also you share in our comfort.

⁸We do not want you to be uninformed, brothers and sisters, about the troubles we experienced in the province of Asia. We were under great pressure, far beyond our ability to endure, so that we despaired of life itself.

⁹Indeed, we felt we had received the sentence of death. But this happened that we might not rely on ourselves but on God, who raises the dead.

¹⁰He has delivered us from such a deadly peril, and he will deliver us again. On him we have set our hope that he will continue to deliver us,

¹¹as you help us by your prayers. Then many will give thanks on our behalf for the gracious favor granted us in answer to the prayers of many.

From the sufferings of Christ, our comfort is secured. This comfort, though, came at a great cost to God. As a Father, He endured the excruciating loss of his only Son. In a similar way, we suffer when it feels like we are losing — or being forsaken by — those we love. To begin the process of receiving God's comfort, we first have to sacrifice our attempts to change reality or control our loved ones. We must let go and place our trust in God. Trusting God, though, requires that we act in faith. In the words of St. Francis of Assisi, we can pray, "O Divine Master, grant that I may not so much seek to be consoled as to console."

As we accept reality and surrender control, we lose everything! At this point of surrender, we likely will feel utter despair — a helplessness that leaves us no other option but to cry out to God. In crying out to God, we can be filled with His presence and gain the comfort of Christ. Abiding in Jesus, we can then practice the patient endurance needed for the journey ahead. Our goal is not to escape suffering, but to suffer well — to suffer in the comforting presence of God. It is in this secret place that our hope in God's power can be firm and secure: fears turned into hope; doubts transformed into faith; anxieties replaced with peace; and depression lifted into joy. He will do this for us. Believe.

When the sufferings set before you seem like "deadly peril," it is critical to redirect your thinking to the power of God. Most of us have previously faced threatening situations. God has previously been faithful to rescue, deliver, help, recover, and protect. For our loved ones, God will be equally faithful. We must surround our family with supportive prayer from trusted Christians who are committed to walk with us no matter what. Through prayer, God's "gracious favor" will shower over your life.

DECLARING A DECREE
OF GOD'S PROTECTION

When God's people need guidance and rescue, we can personalize the promises of His Word, confess them aloud, and trust His desire to help our family.

WE HIDE IN THE LORD AND DECLARE OUR RELIANCE UPON HIS LOVE AND POWER:

The Lord will defend us and even fight for our family as we hold our peace and remain at rest. (Ex. 14:14*)

Resting in God, **the Lord will save us**: a quiet, trusting confidence in Him shall be our strength. (Is. 30:15)

The Lord will ordain peace for our family. He keeps us every moment, lest anyone harm us. (Is. 26:12, 27:3)

He is our hiding place; **The Lord will protect us** from trouble and surround us with songs of deliverance. (Ps. 32:7)

The Lord will keep and save our family from harm. We can trust Him to hide us. He is our refuge. (Ps. 16:1-2)

WE RENOUNCE SELF-SUFFICIENCY AND LEAN SOLELY UPON GOD FOR RESCUE AND HELP:

We have no power to face this trial. We do not know what to do! We have no choice but to fix our eyes on God. Listen! **The Lord will uphold us** as we place all our faith in Him. (2 Ch. 20:12, 20:20)

The Lord will preserve us even when we are the utter contempt of neighbors. We are strong and courageous as we wait for, hope for, expect the Lord! (Ps. 31:11,24)

Enemies too strong for us may hate us, but **the Lord will be our stay and our support**. (Ps. 18:17-18)

The Lord will battle for us against strong enemies: with Him on our side, we shall do valiantly! (Ps. 108:12-13)

Let us boldly approach the throne of God's unmerited favor to us sinners — to receive mercy and find grace! **The Lord will guide us** in good time. (Heb. 4:16)

Our hope and expectation are only and earnestly in God! **The Lord will deliver us** from all our transgressions and protect us from becoming the scorn of others. Let those who seek our life be confounded. The Lord is our help! (Ps. 38:15, 39:7-8, 40:14,17)

The Lord will revoke sentence for His people and relent for our sake when He sees that our power is gone and none remains. Let us surrender what we cannot control and not pretend to have false power over others' lives. (Dt. 32:36)

WE DECLARE THAT GOD IS MERCIFUL REGARDING OUR SINS AND MISTAKES:

We have become a reproach to everyone around us. **The Lord will listen to our prayer**: let each member of our family pray to Him because He is merciful, not because we have done right. (Dan. 9:1-18)

The Lord will give mercy and loving-kindness when we cry out to Him. He can even cause us to find sympathy among those who harass and ostracize us. (Ps. 106:43-48)

We feel sorrow and confess our sins. Our enemies and those who wrongfully hate us are multiplied, but **the Lord will not forsake our family**. (Ps. 38:16-22)

The Lord will blot out our transgressions according to the multitude of His tender mercy and loving-kindness, He will wash us and give us a clean heart. (Ps. 51)

God forgives iniquity and passes over our transgressions. He subdues and treads underfoot our iniquities. **The Lord will cast our sins away** into the deep sea. (Mic. 7:18-19)

Let us rend our hearts and return to God who is merciful, slow to get angry and filled with unfailing love. **The Lord will revoke our sentence.** (Joel 2)

The Lord will wipe away our transgressions for His sake. He will not remember our sins. (Is. 43:25)

God is gracious, slow to anger and full of mercy and loving-kindness. **The Lord will not always accuse us,** neither will He keep His anger forever. He will not treat us as our sins deserve. As a father has compassion for his children, so the Lord loves and pities those who fear him. For He knows our frame; He remembers that we are but dust. (Ps. 103)

> "THE LORD IS CLOSE TO THOSE WHO ARE OF A BROKEN HEART AND SAVES SUCH AS ARE CRUSHED WITH SORROW FOR SIN AND ARE HUMBLY AND THOROUGHLY PENITENT."
>
> – PSALM 34:18

*Scripture paraphrases and personalized statements regarding God's promises are based on the AMPC Version.

WE DECLARE OUR TRUST THAT THE LORD LISTENS TO US AND PROVIDES FOR US:

No matter what we face, God expectantly waits and earnestly longs to be gracious to our family. **The Lord will surely be gracious to us** at the sound of our cry; when He hears it, He will answer us. (Is. 30:18-19)

The Lord will guard our family and give each one of us perfect peace as we lean on and confidently hope in Him. (Is. 26:3)

In our most hopeless moments, **the Lord will hear our desperate cries** for His help! Our protection will be found in His presence. (Ps. 17:1-2)

The Lord will move mountains to answer our prayers when we ask in faith for His help. (Mt. 21:18-22)

"Lord, we believe! Help us with our unbelief!" **The Lord will help us believe** when when we struggle with doubt and fear. (See Mk. 9:17-29)

WE DECLARE THAT THE LORD'S HELP IS HERE:

According to God's abundant mercy, **the Lord will send rescuers** to save us from our enemies. (Neh. 9:26)

When we cry out to the Lord, He will bring us out of our deepest darkness and break our bonds. Even in trouble, give thanks to God for His lovingkindness for **the Lord will rescue us**! He can break gates of bronze and cut bars of iron. (See Ps. 107)

Many question whether God will save our family, but He is our shield, the lifter of our head and hope. We will sleep in peace trusting God, for **the Lord will sustain us**. (Ps. 3:2-5)

Will not God defend and protect our family when we cry out to Him day and night? Will He defer and delay helping us? We believe **the Lord will defend and protect us** speedily. (Lk 18:7-8)

God is our helper, ally, and upholder. He is also with others whom He uses to protect us. We can thank God right now because **the Lord will help us through every troubling situation**. (Ps. 54)

Our hope in God's promise for salvation is based entirely upon faith alone. We do not deserve it. We can never earn it. **The Lord will give and secure salvation** to all who believe. He is our God, who gives life to the dead and speaks of nonexistent things that as if they already exist. (Rom. 4:16-17)

Elijah prayed and trusted God for rain. His servant reported that there was no rain, but Elijah told him seven times, "Go and look again." When his servant spotted a cloud as small as a fist, Elijah took radical action believing with certainty that God was bringing rain. We believe that **the Lord will 'rain' blessings upon our family**. (See 1 Kgs. 18)

WE DECLARE THAT GOD WILL PROTECT US:

The Lord will remember our family in times of distress and need. He will not wipe out our good deeds and kindnesses done for Him. He will spare us according to His great mercy and lovingkindness. (Neh. 13:14,22)

While people (even some friends) may gossip and imagine the worst for us, we trust that God favors and delights in us. Enemies will not harm us, because **the Lord will preserve our integrity** and set us in His presence forever. (Ps. 41)

If we are destroyed, will our dust praise God? Will our destruction proclaim His faithfulness? For this reason, in faith, we trust God to help us! **The Lord will turn our wailing into dancing**. He will remove our shame and clothe us with joy. Our hearts will sing thanks to Him forever! (See Ps. 30)

God will never let us be put to shame or let our hope be disappointed. **The Lord will keep us from harm**. (Ps. 25:1-2)

The Lord will be faithful. He says there is no condemnation for those who are in Christ Jesus. (Rom. 8:1)

No weapon shall prosper against us. Every tongue that speaks against us in judgment shall be cut down. **The Lord will give us peace** (righteousness, security, and triumph over opposition) as part of our heritage in Him. (Is. 54:17)

Faith is the assurance of requests we ask of God, the hope for answers we cannot yet see, and the conviction that **the Lord will answer our prayers**. (Heb. 11:1)

For every member of our family, God invites us to "come to Him." When we are exhausted and beaten down, **the Lord will give us rest for our soul**. (See Mt. 11:28-30)

May our family dwell in the shelter of the Most High. In doing so, we will find protection, provision, and rest. **The Lord will be our refuge and fortress!** On Him we lean, rely, and confidently trust! God will command His angels to guard and preserve us in all our ways. (See Ps. 91)

On the day God delivers us, **the Lord will be proven faithful.** We shall say: "Behold our God, upon whom we waited and hoped expectantly that He might save us! We waited for Him; we will be glad and rejoice in His salvation." (Is. 25:9)

"FOR I CONSIDER [FROM THE STANDPOINT OF FAITH] THAT THE SUFFERINGS OF THE PRESENT LIFE ARE NOT WORTHY TO BE COMPARED WITH THE GLORY THAT IS ABOUT TO BE REVEALED TO US AND IN US!"

– ROMANS 8:18

YOU DON'T NEED TO PRAY
THAT GOD MAKES ME
STRAIGHT

BY GREGORY COLES

T IS A TRUTH UNIVERSALLY ACKNOWLEDGED that a good conservative Christian boy who realizes he's gay will spend years in agonized and fervent prayer asking God to make him straight.

At least, that's what I did.

Beginning at the age of 12, I measured my spiritual life according to my progress toward heterosexuality. I tried to notice girls. I tried not to notice guys. I invented "crushes" and told people about romantic desires I didn't actually have for my female friends. I even tried to lust after a picture of a scantily clad woman once, just to see if I could do it. (In retrospect, not my best idea. Cut me a break. I was 12.) But by the grace of God, I never did manage any lust over that picture. I might as well have been staring at an office supplies poster.

I tried and prayed and tried and prayed, and I failed on all counts. **If loving Jesus was supposed to be turning me straight, I obviously didn't love Jesus very much.** But I was determined to keep trying.

It seemed impossible, at the time, to imagine that I had any other options *besides* praying to be straight. I'd heard about gay people who rejected God altogether — but I refused to become one of those. I'd heard about gay people who believed the Bible left room for same-sex marriage, and I was sympathetic to their arguments — but no matter how much I wanted to agree, I wasn't quite persuaded. And I'd heard about the people who told stories of becoming straight, the "ex-gays."

If I wasn't part of the first camp or the second camp, I reasoned, surely I would be part of the third camp. Surely I would be healed. And surely, even if I never quite arrived in that Promised Land of Straightness, it was my responsibility as a Christian to keep praying for it, to keep wanting it. (God loves persistence, right?)

> IT'S POSSIBLE TO BE HETEROSEXUAL WITHOUT HONORING GOD, AND IT'S ALSO POSSIBLE TO HONOR GOD WITHOUT BEING HETEROSEXUAL.

Fifteen years later, I still hold a lot of theology in common with my 12-year-old self. I still believe that same-sex marriage isn't an option for me as a follower of Jesus. I still believe that following Jesus is absolutely worth it. I still believe that God can do anything, and that we're called to pray persistently for his will to be done.

But I've stopped praying to be straight. In fact, most of the time, I've stopped wanting to be straight. **If you offered me a choice today between a Wonder-Pill-that-Makes-Gay-People-Straight and a Tylenol, I'd take the Tylenol.**

What changed, exactly?

There are plenty of ways I could answer this question.

But for now, I'll focus on just one of the reasons I've stopped praying to be straight:

It's possible to be heterosexual without honoring God, and it's also possible to honor God without being heterosexual.

Christians who object to my decision to call myself "gay" are often quick to remind me that sexual orientation isn't a biblical category. And they're quite right. Jesus and the Apostle Paul didn't have 21st-century notions of sexual orientation, in the same way that they didn't have Twitter accounts or favorite NFL teams. Instead, they talked in terms of three basic sexual categories:

1. **Sinful sexual behavior** (most often the Greek noun *porneia* and its cognate verb *porneuo*, as in Matt. 15:19 and 1 Cor. 6:18).

2. **Sinful sexual lust** (most often the Greek noun *epithymia* and its cognate verb *epithymeo*, as in Matt. 5:28 and 1 Thess. 4:5).

3. **Holy stewardship of sexual desire in opposite-sex marriage or singleness** (as in Jesus' commentary on marriage and singleness in Matt. 19, and Paul's commentary in 1 Cor. 7).

Here's the remarkable thing about these three categories: all three of them are available to both gay people and straight people. Gay or straight, we are all drawn to sinful lusts and behaviors, though the particular sins that appeal to us will differ depending on our orientation. Gay or straight, the Bible offers us vocations within which we can choose to steward our sexuality, even if we continue wrestling against our sinful predispositions for as long as we live. After the Fall of Adam and Eve, we all bear the marks of indwelling sin, and we all bear the image of a God who fashioned us and gleefully declared, "It is very good!"

A few weeks ago, I went to a barbecue at the house of my dear friends Dan and Nicole. Nicole and I got to talking about her new workout routine, which she assured me was going to make her look much more beach-ready. "You're already beautiful," I said, because it was true.

Another friend overheard us and yelled to Dan, who was out on the patio: "Greg's flirting with your wife!"

I poked my slightly chagrined head out the patio door.

"Coles," Dan told me magnanimously, "I'm not worried about you stealing my wife. For... a variety of reasons."

He was wise not to be worried. I'm about as likely to have an affair with his wife as I am to develop a craving for haggis. It's not that Nicole isn't beautiful, or that I don't love her dearly. It's just that I'm incapable of lusting after women. (And like I said, I even tried it once.) I'm not drawn towards sinful behaviors or lusts involving women, just like I'm not drawn to the same kind of holy sexual stewardship through marriage that many straight guys are.

GAY OR STRAIGHT, THE BIBLE OFFERS US VOCATIONS WITHIN WHICH WE CAN CHOOSE TO STEWARD OUR SEXUALITY, EVEN IF WE CONTINUE WRESTLING AGAINST OUR SINFUL PREDISPOSITIONS FOR AS LONG AS WE LIVE.

There is a form of sexual holiness that comes easy to me in ways it doesn't come easy for my straight brothers in Christ. And by the same token, their journeys toward holiness will be easy in ways mine may never be. **Being gay doesn't make me uniquely broken, as if I'm some slip of the divine chisel. It makes me just plain broken, like everybody else. I'm exactly unremarkable enough to be a recipient of grace.**

God is still welcome to make me straight if he wants to, just like he's welcome to turn water to wine or transform the entire cast of *Hamilton* into giant ferrets. But he doesn't seem too interested in doing any of those things at the moment.

So these days, I don't pray to be straight. I pray that I'll fall more deeply in love with Jesus, that I'll be drawn deeper into holiness. If you want to pray something for me, I hope you'll join me in that prayer.

ABOUT THE AUTHOR

Gregory Coles is the author of Single, Gay, Christian *(InterVarsity Press, 2017). In addition to writing about his obsession with Jesus on* **gregorycoles.com**, *Greg is also a Ph.D. candidate in English and a worship leader in his church. This essay was originally posted on the blog of The Center for Faith, Sexuality & Gender at* **centerforfaith.com**.

TAKE HEART

BY MITCHELL YAKSH

I WANT TO ENCOURAGE YOU. After everything you have been reading and learning, I think you might need it. If you're anything like me, you might be remembering every past mistake you have made or every interaction that did not end well.

Take heart: you are not out of opportunities to care for those around you. There are still so many more chances to show authentic care and love for those in the LGBT+ community who have been hurt and rejected by others. As you do so, I want to give you four encouraging reminders.

1. YOUR WORDS HAVE POWER

You have already seen countless Scriptures about what words can do when misused. Yet words can do incredible work in uplifting and encouraging others. Proverbs 25:11 (NASB) says, "Like apples of gold in settings of silver is a word spoken in right circumstances."

This "word spoken in right circumstances" might be using your loved one's preferred pronouns. Or maybe it's using your nephew's new last name following his marriage to his husband. You can use your words to uplift your LGBT+ loved one, giving them a priceless gift. This demonstrates that you care enough to listen to them. And this will create the opportunity for you to speak into their lives in many other ways in the future.

2. YOUR RELATIONSHIP HAS MEANING

It is easy to believe that your LGBT+ family member would rather have life without you. They may have even said that to you at some point. However, there is not a person out there who does not want a fulfilling relationship with their family. Look no further than mainstream television.

Most TV shows are driven by a group of people who, in some way or another, represent a family unit. Maybe it's an actual family that always finds a way to be there for each other. Or maybe it's a group of strangers thrown together by random circumstances, forced to come together to support each other. These shows represent something every person desires: a loving, supportive family unit.

A relationship with you has meaning to them. And that is something to celebrate! Yes, there are many aspects of relationships that make this complicated and difficult at times. Nevertheless, your existing and future relationship with your LGBT+ loved one is an encouragement because they ultimately desire it. It means they care about you, too.

3. YOUR LOVE HAS INFLUENCE

Your love is not something that is just flippantly added to someone's life like a patch on a vest. Love is active. It is transforming. It is powerful. No wonder Peter told early Christians, "Above all, keep loving one another earnestly, since love covers a multitude of sins." (1 Pt. 4:8, ESV) Even Solomon, with God's divine wisdom, saw this fact, saying, "By steadfast love and faithfulness, iniquity is atoned for." (Pr. 16:6, ESV)

Your love will not just be another part of your relationship with your LGBT+ loved one. It will be an active and transformative power in their lives. Your love can inspire them to live better lives, be genuine in their other relationships, and serve as an example of authentic love and care. Most importantly, it can demonstrate what the love of Christ is really like.

4. YOUR FAITH HAS VALUE

Few things are more inspiring than seeing a strong faith foundation in someone's life. However, this is only possible if your LGBT+ loved ones are close enough to get a view of it. Because the Christian faith is about a personal relationship with Jesus Christ, the only real way another person can see your faith is if you are deeply and intimately involved in their life.

You have the opportunity to be a blazing-bright light of the Gospel to the LGBT+ community. If you have strong convictions for the Scripture and a passionate desire to see others follow Jesus Christ, you are doing a disservice to keep anyone from being up close to witness it. This means removing whatever obstacles might be in the way. Jesus says, "Nor do people light a lamp and put it under a basket, but on a stand, and it gives light to all in the house" (Mt. 5:15, ESV). Don't hide your lamp from your LGBT+ loved ones.

Brothers and sisters in Christ, I want to encourage you. You have a ministry opportunity that not many people get. You have someone close to you in your life with whom you get to share the love of Jesus. Take heart and know that God will prepare you for this. He will equip you with everything you need. And I know that He will do an incredible work in you and through you as His love is shared with your LGBT+ loved ones.

ABOUT THE AUTHOR

Mitchell Yaksh is the ministry resident at First Christian Church in Decatur, IL. He serves on staff coordinating education for LGBTQ+ outreach. Mitchell also writes under a pseudonym for the *Your Other Brothers* blog at **yourotherbrothers.com**.

AIMING HIGHER / BURDENS LIGHTER

BY MEG BAATZ

MANY OF MY PREDECESSORS AND PEERS HAVE walked away from the traditional biblical sexual ethic. And I don't blame them.

Largely, we have only known traditional theology as a package deal with the "rocks" of trauma, pain, and rejection. This weight can literally be deadly. Even if we could lift off every burden of injustice, I must admit that the theology in itself can, at times, feel like a divine disappointment.

That disappointment is fueled by a world living like romance is the highest form of love, and sex the highest form of intimacy. Even churches take more cues from culture than from Scripture on what "finding love" and building a family ought to look like.

No wonder many believers are asking, "Is our theology itself just another rock blocking LGBT+ people's path to flourishing?"

BOTH "SIDES" FALLING SHORT

In a practical *and* theological sense, both "sides" (traditional and affirming) fall short of God's design for family. Christians on both sides look to romance and sex as the hope for LGBT+ people. We still essentially tell LGBT+ people (and heterosexual people too!) that getting married will meet all their relational needs.

Meanwhile, our Heavenly Father calls us as siblings in Christ to an even bigger, more fulfilling experience of family. His vision for family transcends any of our ideas founded upon human promise, biology, or fleshly need.

So what *is* God's design for family? Our answer needs to be bigger than "straight marriage" or "gay marriage." Our answer is nothing less than spiritual family as God intended.

ONE SMALL EXAMPLE

What might this spiritual family look like in practice? I can start by showing you what it has meant for me.

I share a household with a Christian married couple who has caught a glimpse of God's design for spiritual family. In addition to raising two baby boys, they have opened their lives to domestic community with myself and two other single people. We all belong to the same small group and local church. We share meals, parties, prayers, tears, and a dedication to resolving conflicts as they arise (and they do!). My pastors know about my sexuality, and they even invite me to sit in on staff meetings when they're preparing sermons that require sensitivity in this area of life. I can talk to my housemates about gender, sexuality,

dating, friendship, marriage, and the like. They listen and share their own experiences and hardships in these areas. The single folks can sometimes stay home with the babies while the married ones go out on a date. The rent we pay allows the wife to stay home with her kids most days. But my favorite part is simple: at the end of the day, I have a beautiful family to come home to.

Since entering into this domestic Christian community, burdens like loneliness, finances, temptation, an uncertain future, and even the Great Commission have become a lot lighter — and not just for me.

AIMING HIGHER

We tend to think a biblical view of family primarily involves marriage, sex, and bearing children. But God's design for family is much more vibrant than our limited ideas. In His Word, we read that a celibate man can leave a legacy more enduring than sons (Is. 51:5). An unmarried woman can raise up strong believers that outnumber the children of a married woman (Is. 54:1). The poor, the foreigner, the homeless, the fatherless, the rejected, those with disabilities, the sick and dying — all can belong in this family (Lv. 19:34, Zec. 7:10, Lk. 4:18-19, Jas. 5:14-16). The widow and orphan can be brought into households, imbued with dignity and provided for relationally and practically (Jas. 1:27). A girl of any age or marital status can find authentic, non-competitive friendship with other sisters in Christ (Lk. 1). A guy of any age can access spiritual fathers and vulnerable, life-giving friendships (Col. 4). A non-family member can receive the full inheritance of a biological child (Gal. 3:29). And a man who already has a family can look at anyone who does God's will and say, "here are my mother and my brothers!" (Mk. 3:34-35).

Brothers and sisters, is this not our Father's design for family?

BURDENS LIGHTER

Dare we depart from His design? Will we settle for less than His best? We have a glorious privilege to boldly become this kind of family to one another. If we're planning on holding to what the Word says about family, we had better hold *completely* to what the Word says about family. What an opportunity we have to pray for and live into God's design! Let's keep imagining with Him all the possibilities for life-giving spiritual family. If we do, we will set a sustainable course to preserving a historic view of sexuality. And *when* we do, I'm convinced all of us will have higher hopes and lighter burdens, allowing us to stay holy and blameless to the very end.

ABOUT THE AUTHOR

Meg Baatz is the creative director at Lead Them Home. She lives in Denver, CO, and is passionate about helping people find and be family in Christ. She is planning to start writing a book on spiritual kinship and celibacy.

PRAYING THROUGH THE STAGES

Many families ask how they can preserve their biblical beliefs in the midst of circumstances that are challenging to their beliefs. One way is to remember that **there is power in prayer.** In other words, keep your prayer closet! This is the shelter where you can honor God with your beliefs, place your petitions before him, and seek His comfort for any pain, sadness, or anger that you feel.

7

"My son, Matthew, is just 7 years old but already very effeminate. I just don't understand why my son is not masculine. I love him, yet I have two concerns. First, I am worried that his effeminacy might make him gay. Second, **I am ashamed to admit this, but I find myself feeling a bit of disgust** at how girlish he can act."

Lord, you have given me Matthew. I surrender what I can't control or fix. I don't know that my son will be gay. Regardless, Matthew is my son. Help me to offer him unconditional love. Help Matthew to feel completely loved and secure in my arms. **Protect him from being teased and bullied. Help him to always know that I have his back. I pray that Matthew will be confident as a young man.** Thank you, Lord, for such a special boy. Forgive me when I feel disgusted by his mannerisms. I ask you, Lord, to heal me, so that I can always see my son through Your eyes. I love him so much.

10

"**Our daughter, Jordan, has never been comfortable in her own skin.** Since she was young, she has gravitated toward boys' clothing, toys, and activities. I was a tomboy growing up, but this goes way beyond that. She is 10 years old now. Since age 5, she has routinely declared that she wants to be a boy."

Lord, help us honor our vibrant and unique Jordan. Thank you for her many gifts and talents. I worry about her anxiety. My little girl has so much stress about her gender. I worry about her hobbies and preferences. I worry that I will mess up no matter what I do. All our redirecting has only caused Jordan to distrust us. I surrender every thought that tempts me to over-control my little girl. **Help me to celebrate her life, appreciate her personality, shower her with love, surround her with affection, and build her up with accepting words.** Please help her to trust us. I pray that You will increase Jordan's comfort with being a girl. Prepare us for the road ahead, and help us to radically love our Jordan.

"Daniel, our 13-year-old son, has been bullied throughout elementary and middle school. He is very withdrawn and depressed. **He just told us he is pansexual. I had to look the word up, and I still don't understand!** He likes a guy at school. This culture is convincing kids that sexuality is whoever you're attracted to. I am in shock. I am angry. We have been loving Christian parents. Why is he doing this to us?"

*Lord, my emotions are all over the map. I hug Daniel one moment, and the next moment, I am so angry. Help me to accept and understand rather than lecture and shame. **I cannot change the ideas of this world, so help me stay focused on what's most helpful for Daniel.** He has suffered greatly. He is depressed — even suicidal! Lord, preserve my son's life! Help us get the support network we need. **Help us as parents to grieve well so that we can focus on helping Daniel.** Protect our son. Surround him with good friends. I pray that our youth leaders will help our family. Help Daniel to trust how deeply we love him. Help him to have hope. Educate us so that we do not add to Daniel's trauma. Let our every word and every hug bring the love that he most needs right now.*

"Kaleigh is 16 years old and increasingly has a mind of her own. After coming out at age 14, everything was smooth. She easily deferred to our biblical beliefs, even claiming our beliefs as her own. **Lately, though, she is less interested in faith, more irritated by church, and less willing to share with us.** We are tempted to control her every step, yet we realize that gaining influence and trust may be the bigger win for us as parents. We've made big mistakes, but also have learned from and apologized for our many mistakes. We have a limited time to rebuild her trust in us and preserve her faith in God. At times, we just feel helpless."

*Lord, our little girl is not so little anymore. She has become a beautiful young woman with her own ideas in a world that will soon become bigger than our family and the small town we call home. We thank you for Kaleigh. We trust that you are bigger than the challenges that we are facing. We pray that you will keep your Light shining in her heart. Keep Christ living in her heart. Draw her close to you. Help us to let go and trust God. It is not easy, but we must trust our little girl into your hands. **This is so scary, but Lord, we are reminded of your faithfulness!** You will complete the work you started. We pray that Kaleigh will find her own personal relationship with you, Jesus. Let her hear your voice saying, "Come to me, all who are weary and burdened" (Mt. 11:29). May our daughter find rest for her soul in you alone. Be her refuge. Be her shelter. Help her come to you.*

"Ben is away at college. He had been on a solid path, holding to a biblical view of marriage and sexuality, experiencing fellowship among other like-minded Christians who are same-gender attracted. Then, he met David. They've fallen in love. **His beliefs have changed, but he is also holding on to his Christian identity.** Thankfully, he trusts us. I don't think he realizes all the anguish we often feel. We largely sheltered him from any of our reactions that might hurt him. Today, Ben asked to bring David home for Thanksgiving."

*Our Father in Heaven, please deepen Ben's faith in and reliance upon Jesus. Holy Spirit, keep a hold on Ben's heart. **We pray against attitudes and forces that could damage Ben's faith.** We pray against believers' judgment of him. We pray against unbiblical ideas. Help him to discern truth from error. Help us to keep loving Ben well. As we venture into this unexpected phase, help us to also see David as a child of God. May our family generously welcome David. Let us never fall into the trap of criticizing David — and losing our son's allegiance. Please navigate our Thanksgiving holiday because this is all new. Ben is on a different path. We are determined to walk with him on this path. Anoint us with Your presence as we engage Ben — and David.*

22

"We prayed that Troy would outgrow his discomfort with his gender. It started at age 13. Today, though, he announced on Instagram that he is now Troye. He — or she — is on hormone replacement therapy (HRT). Everything we're facing is so complex and impossible to imagine. All that we thought we knew about our child is gone. **What do you do when the son you've known for 22 years is no longer your son?** It seems like the whole world is celebrating. We're grieving. We love Troye. Troye is always welcome home. But what do we say to our 8-year-old daughter? What do we say to my 86-year-old father? Where is hope in this situation?"

*When all hope fades and the world turns upside down, "our eyes are fixed on you," Lord (2 Ch. 20:12). We have no power to fix our son. We have no power to make his gender dysphoria go away. We have no power to convince him that remaining a man will become more comfortable over time. We have no power to confront all the options for transition. We have no power, so we desperately "cast all our cares and concerns" on you, Jesus (1 Pt. 5:7). You will be our hope, our refuge, our strength, and our guide. You will be Troye's Savior. Help us to share Your presence with Troye. Help us to accept, relate well, and welcome Troye home with loving arms. We choose to follow you, Jesus, and lay down our lives for Troye. You will be good to our family. **Surround us with people who can helpfully support us.***

25

"Our story is not so simple. Sara, our 25-year-old daughter, hired Michelle to be her diet mentor. The next thing we know, 42-year-old Michelle is leaving her 15-year marriage to her husband — for our daughter! Sara just told us that she and Michelle are madly in love. **Why did she choose a woman who could be her mother?** It's so unsettling. I am 45 years old! People say I should just love my daughter's partner 'like your own child!' I am not a cruel person, but I cannot accept this. It just makes me nauseated."

*Lord Jesus, how I need you! I want to be happy, but I am angry. I want to have order, but I am out of control. I want to be optimistic, but I feel hopeless. I want to feel confident, but I feel so unsure. **I strive to live in faith, but I wonder where You are.** In my troubles, I cry out: "You will guard and keep in perfect and constant peace those whose mind in both inclination and character is stayed on you, because he commits himself to You, leans on you, and hopes confidently in You." For this reason, I choose to "trust in the Lord… and confidently hope in Him forever; for the Lord God is the everlasting rock of all ages" (Is. 26:3-4). With the peace and security of your promises, I will find strength and wisdom to walk this journey.*

28

"The big day is here. **Our son Thomas is getting married today.** It's not what we expected. He is marrying his fiancé Mac. We love Mac (he has become family to us), but we have also feared this day for years. For months, we have wrestled over what our role can be in a marriage ceremony that we do not find to be biblically permissible. We never questioned whether or not to attend. Many fellow believers warned us not to go — otherwise, we would be 'condoning and enabling a sinful lifestyle.' Thankfully, our pastor believed that being present is an opportunity to have a strong relationship with Thomas and Mac in the years ahead. Beyond attending, though, it is confusing. I mean, I will be smiling, hugging, feasting, and dancing — but inside, I also will be sad."

*Lord Jesus, I am reminded that you are a God of holiness and grace. Without the sacrifice of your only son Jesus, who could have a chance at standing before God in all your glory? As I face impossible questions for which it seems there are no easy and comfortable answers, I am reminded that I need your grace in my own life. Father, "We are praying to you because you are merciful, not because we have done right" (Dn. 9:18, GNT). **With humble knowledge of our own sinfulness, give us the grace to be fully present with your love among Thomas, Mac, and his family, and the many relatives and friends who join us today.** In the midst of our personal grief, we count our blessings. One blessing is that we really do love Mac. Thank you that we have a son-in-law whom we really find easy to love. Since the day he was born, Thomas has given us so much joy. We are so proud of our son. Father, you will give us everything we need for this season. Thank you.*

PARENTS SHARE ABOUT THE SCOPE OF THEIR JOURNEY, HOW THEIR FAITH WAS CHALLENGED OR STRENGTHENED, AND HOW GOD PROVED FAITHFUL.*

The Lord has been so faithful! He has provided sweet prayer partners. He has given me words of hope and encouragement from his word at just the right time. He has provided resources at times when I asked for help and direction. **When I was nervous about sharing with our church leaders, the Lord went before us,** prepared their hearts, and gave us such support and love.

Like many of the longsuffering parents I know, we wouldn't have chosen this path by any means. **But we actually shudder to think of how much growth in the Lord we would have missed without this path!**

God has a spotless track record with us through many difficulties and trials over the years. We had no doubt he'd be with us every step of the way through this one, too — and he has. God has helped me be slow to speak when I wanted to make some snarky remark. He has helped me pray for her partner and her husband (yes, it's complicated). **He has helped me accept that this is a decision she made and not some fault of my poor parenting.**

We know that God loves our daughter and have tried to release her to His good care. **He has given us peace, removed our parental guilt, and to this day, he remains our hope.**

He has guided us to resources like LTH for encouragement, understanding, and direction. He has exposed our own sinful hearts and is at work in them for our good and his glory. **He comforts us in our sorrow and brings peace in the midst of this storm. We trust him beyond what we can see.** We love our daughter more unconditionally than ever before, and we thank God for this hard journey.

God has humbled us, stripped us of our prideful, arrogant hearts (still more work to be done), and brought us to our knees! It has been an extremely difficult journey, but God has proven himself faithful and ever-present through times of joy and times of utter despair. He has deepened our trust in him as we've witnessed time and again his all-sufficiency at work in our lives when we felt too weak to move forward. **My husband and I are now actively helping other families currently treading these new, uncharted waters.**

He spared our son's life when he attempted suicide. He has given me hope that there can be healing in our relationship. He has shown me how judgmental I can be and is working in my life to change that.

I have learned so much. I have healed enough to admit to others that I have a gay daughter. In fact, **I would like to help others who are dealing with this or even those who don't understand LGBT+ people.** It truly has been a journey and process, one that I believe God is using in my life to grow me in ways I wouldn't have otherwise known.

God has demonstrated unfailing, never-changing love for us. He is showing us how love truly covers all things. While we may not understand all of this, God does. **It has been a lesson in how much we can trust God with our children's hearts and release them to him — a true act of surrender.** He is not surprised by any of this, and we have the faith that God will use all of this for his glory. It just may look different than what we think it should look like. We don't begin to understand the ways of God, but he proves himself faithful, so we must trust. In the meantime, we try to love how Jesus loves. It's only by God's grace that we can do any of these things correctly.

When our child came out to us, the bottom fell out for our family. With each turn in the story, God was there at the bottom with us. **We cry out for our own healing** and intimacy with God and with our child. Jesus has been incredibly faithful to hold our family together through the hardest moments and to draw our child to himself.

*Lead Them Home Survey of Parent Engagement of LGBT+ Children (October 2017)

God has been with us and guiding us through this process from the beginning. When she first came out, we had no friends or support system who were in any way familiar with how to deal with our situation. **We are grateful that we had a pastor who was willing to admit he didn't know the answers but still stood with and supported us as we prayed our way through each challenge.** Encountering Lead Them Home many years into our journey was very helpful; they confirmed the soundness of the guidance we had received from God. The children our daughter and her partner have are among the greatest blessings in our lives. Both of their children have already opened their hearts to Jesus, and we can see evidence of the Spirit in their lives. We don't know what the future holds, but we are confident that God loves our daughter and her partner dearly — and that he will lead them someday into a relationship with him.

I'm still on the journey. I worry about my child but realize that so much is out of my hands now. **My child is healthy, safe, and able to support himself. All of these are blessings. I'm just not sure what will come in the future.**

I see God's faithfulness in *all* ways — the strength to look at my own brokenness; the desire to love more like Jesus; freedom from feeling at fault for my son's sexuality; courage to talk to other Christians who have distorted views or treat LGBT+ people as lepers; boldness to ask for prayer in my Christian community; and the ability to feel compassion for LGBT+ people and not "other" them any longer.

It's very early in this walk, and I have yet to see God really working. But I do believe he prepared me beforehand by placing into my circle of influence podcasts, articles, and other resources that I was able to tap into before my child came out. So my heart was already prepared in a small way to receive the news. I believe God had a hand in that. **I'm waiting with as much patience as I can muster right now to see God's hand move more powerfully in this walk.** I'm still in a state of grief and sadness most of the time — and I feel a huge lack of hope in this world in general and in our lives specifically. Most days, that's where I am.

God has strengthened our trust in this classroom of suffering. He has never left us and has even given us a sense of calm when we most needed it. He has broadened our understanding of the LGBT+ community and grown our compassion for them. **We've been humbled as a family because of previous judgments we had placed on "homosexuals" and their parents. God has shown us the pain and suffering of the LGBT+ community in ways we never even considered.** We now look through a clearer lens of how God sees people. I still don't believe gay marriage is God's best plan for his children, but I also recognize how judgmental I was. God is teaching our family that we need to change our approach in the church by not shaming and condemning people.

We realize now that this journey isn't just about our son; it's about God changing us! We've changed so much. **We haven't compromised our Biblical stance on homosexuality, but we're no longer so quick to make a judgment on people.** We're more willing to reach out to the gay community and demonstrate that Christians aren't the stereotypical gay bashers they believe us to be.

God has given us hope. **We've chosen to trust God and play the long game with our son.** We're convinced God put him in our family (he's adopted), and that gives us peace to know that this hasn't taken our heavenly Father by surprise.

God has shown me, my husband, and our three children that his plans for *all* of his children require sacrifice, obedience, and loss of dreams — all to teach us humility and grace. **Walking into this world has shattered a self-righteousness we weren't even aware of, teaching us just how much mercy and grace it took for God to love and forgive *us*. It has changed our entire ministry and how we relate to others.** We're trying to view everyone we encounter in the light of "one beggar telling another beggar where to find bread." God has grown within our son a depth of wisdom, love, and understanding. His character has been an amazing encouragement to us, his siblings, those he counsels, and the church he attends. We've watched him blossom as he teaches others how community offers us love, accountability, and obedience to God and his commands. Now, we feel in ourselves a healing and passion to love and come alongside others. We now model a more authentic gospel of grace than we knew before. This gospel reaches into every fiber of our being as we honor and glorify God, the one who has given us all things!

REFLECTION QUESTIONS

1. Before reading *Guiding Families*, what did you see as your biggest prayer request? Have your requests or needs changed since you began reading this guide? If so, how?

2. In **The God Of All Comfort**, the apostle Paul brings us into the very presence of God and the deep comfort he offers us. How does this passage impact you? Please describe.

3. What promises of God seem far away to you? What are the barriers to you seeing God as one who wants to comfort you and your family right where you are?

4. What are some areas in your life where you feel God's comfort, and what are some areas where you're still waiting to feel his comfort?

5. Under **Declaring A Decree Of God's Protection**, which promises seem most important for your family to cling to right now? How are you counting on God to be faithful to you and your family? What can you do to cast all your dependence upon the Lord?

6. In **Take Heart**, Mitchell Yaksh encourages parents who may be feeling regret and uncertainty about their relationship with LGBT+ children. Meg Baatz, in **Aiming Higher, Burdens Lighter,** paints a picture of belonging in the spiritual family of God. As pastors and parents, how can we pray and act in faith toward creating homes and churches that are safe for LGBT+ loved ones?

7. Greg Coles asks that you not pray that God makes him straight. He is not rejecting any prayers you might petition to God on his behalf, so what is the important point he makes? How does this shape your focus when praying for your LGBT+ loved one?

8. In **Praying Through The Stages**, we capture the importance of dependence upon and trust in God for every season of life. What stage of life is your loved one currently in? What is your current "Praying Through the Stages" prayer for your LGBT+ loved one? Pastors (and all who care), how can we surround families of LGBT+ loved ones through every stage?

9. The parent survey responses in **God's Faithfulness** prove that God is at work in the lives of parents, families, and loved ones! Life is a long journey, but how has God been faithful thus far?

10. When we feel desperate, we tend to focus on stress or unmet needs instead of actually *being with God.* Jesus says, "Come to me all who are weary." He wants to lighten our burdens and give us rest for our souls. What can you do to bring your whole self to Jesus?

"HOW LONG, O LORD? WILL YOU FORGET ME FOREVER? HOW LONG WILL YOU HIDE YOUR FACE FROM ME? ... MY ADVERSARIES WILL REJOICE WHEN I AM SHAKEN. BUT I HAVE TRUSTED AND RELIED ON AND BEEN CONFIDENT IN YOUR LOVINGKINDNESS AND FAITHFULNESS; ... I WILL SING TO THE LORD, BECAUSE HE HAS DEALT BOUNTIFULLY WITH ME." – PSALM 13:1, 4B, 5A-6

info@leadthemhome.org

"WHERE NO WISE GUIDANCE IS, THE PEOPLE FALL,

BUT IN THE MULTITUDE OF COUNSELORS

THERE IS SAFETY."

– PROVERBS 11:14

PART 6:

GUIDANCE FOR ALL WHO CARE

32 TIPS
FOR
RELATIONAL EFFECTIVENESS

1. Be a Missionary. Understand that hurt and judged people easily anticipate condemnation.

2. Five Minute Rule. There is a brief initial window to prove that I am safe and comfortable to be with.

3. Build Trust. Develop relationship in order to cultivate and nurture spiritual (interest) growth.

4. No Agendas. Never bait and switch the purpose (and related content) of getting together.

5. No Biases. Engage others as whole persons: never deconstruct a person to one dimension of their life.

6. No Triggers. Avoid words or phrases (clichés) that stereotype or reflect judgmental attitudes.

7. No Hammers. Resist any temptation to use doctrine to position God against others.

8. No Hang-Ups. Let go of any hang-ups that hold me back ("What if my friend becomes attracted to me?").

9. Surrender Disgust. If people disgust me, I have the real problem (low missional effectiveness).

10. Listen Well. Make direct eye contact, smile warmly, and genuinely listen to what others share.

11. Answer by Asking. I do not have to carry the weight of every question. I can ask a question back.

12. Engage Like Jesus. Look. Smile. Love. Pause. Ask. Listen. Pause. Ask. Listen. Pause. Love.

13. Be Curious. Be sincere and curious enough to draw out their story in their own words.

14. Offer Safe Space. People given space to self-reveal can more freely discover God's will for their life.

15. Honor Their Partner. I best honor my friend by asking about those who are important to them.

16. Lose False Power. I lack the power to condone or enable sin by asking about my friend's life.

17. Be Authentic. Avoid attempting to appear relatable by front-lining all the gay people I know.

18. Walk Humbly. Weep with those who are sad (grieving); laugh with those who are happy (funny).

19. Do Justice. If any protection is needed, be the first person to defend against harm.

20. Love Mercy. See beyond sin to express acceptance, love, and compassion.

21. Level Playing Field. If the topic of repentance surfaces, share about it in first person (i.e. my own life).

22. No Sin Comparisons. Sin comparisons ultimately break down. It may be tempting, but it doesn't work.

23. Recognize Gifting. Be perceptive and generous in identifying positive qualities, traits, gifts, and talents.

24. Nourish Faith. Commit to nourishing rather than chopping at the roots of a person's faith identity.

25. Refuse to Judge. Jesus reminds us that there is absolutely no room for judgment (see Mt. 7:2).

26. Practice Patience. Who am I to determine the Spirit's next step for someone's journey of repentance?

27. Remember Salvation. Did I earn it? No! Without the Holy Spirit invading my life, I could *never* repent.

28. Be Invitational. Invite them to share a meal or coffee — specifically, invite them to be "with me."

29. Include Them. The gospel of exclusion has *no* power to reach already banished persons.

30. Reveal Jesus. Always reveal the presence of Jesus within me and extend His amazing invitations.

31. Share Scripture. Consider it missional success even if I only read through the Psalms with my friend.

32. Show Affection. Respecting others' comfort and safety, appropriately offer physical and verbal affection.

NO AGENDAS

BY TY WYSS

*Ty Wyss has written one blog post for each of the 32 Tips. Here, he expands on Tip #4. Read them all at **wallsdown.org/blog**. Reprinted with permission.*

 "BAIT AND SWITCH" IS DEFINED AS "offering something desirable to gain favor, then thwarting expectations with something less desirable." In the advertising world, a bait and switch is done intentionally. But in the church world, it's done unknowingly. Most Christians I know wouldn't intentionally be deceptive, but their actions produce the same consequence as a bait and switch: a feeling of being duped.

In relationships with LGBT+ people, many resort to a bait and switch method because they're not sure how the truth will be received. What does this actually look like?

- "Let's go out to lunch! I'd love to get to know you!" Then, during lunch, telling them what the Bible says about homosexuality, rather than actually getting to know them.

- "Hey, you should come to my church, we love gay people and so does God!" Then, once the LGBT+ person feels like part of the community, we tell them that, in order to remain part of this community, repentance in their sexuality on our timetable is a must.

Repentance is important, but it's not a qualifier for whether I love you or include you in my life. If so, I've just given you something attractive (relationship and community) and then put a higher price tag in order to keep it. *Bait and switch.*

I've heard many gay people tell the story of the Christian who pursued them (supposedly) for friendship, but after some time had passed and the person didn't change their mind about homosexuality, the friendship tapered off. Was the interest in their life based only on their eventual repentance?

It makes me wonder how many people, straight and gay alike, the Christian community has approached like this. We are commissioned by our Lord to win souls, to proclaim the kingdom of God, to show that Jesus is the way to true life. But we receive it as yet another task on the religious list of "thou shalts." So when someone isn't "getting it," we feel like we're failing — and we move on to someone else so we can feel "successful."

This tendency exposes that we've missed the heart of God towards others (and likely towards ourselves as well). **Jesus didn't spend time with people to "get them saved." He spent time with people to show the heart of the Father towards them.**

Jesus was the image of the invisible God: he told people that if you've seen him, you've also seen the Father. He demonstrated the Father's mercy, kindness, and compassion towards them. What people *did* with his mercy, kindness, and compassion was entirely on them. Christ wasn't concerned with the number of followers he had. He was concerned with doing the Father's will — which ultimately was to accurately relay the Father's heart of lovingkindness toward those who were doubting it. His *accurate reflection of God* was his success (rather than *people's response* to his reflection).

This understanding frees me to love without an agenda. It takes the pressure off of me to get someone to feel conviction, turn from sin, or change behavior. It also frees me up not to have to sell Jesus to anyone.

It's important to check our motives before we pursue relationship. **A good question I ask myself is, "If this person were to never change their mind or behavior, or were to never accept Jesus — would I still pursue them?"** Will I still see the point in loving a fellow fallen image-bearer? Will I still see the value of loving others simply for the reward of knowing I loved another person? These questions force me to surrender my own goals for someone's life, to step out of the seat of God, and instead to be used as a conduit for love and accurate reflection of Jesus.

A gay friend of mine once said, "I just need to know: if I never see things your way regarding my sexuality, will you still be here?" It was pointed and deliberate. I checked my heart and thoughtfully considered his statement. "Yes," I said. "How you identify, who you date, or who you have sex with will never change the fact that I enjoy our friendship and genuinely appreciate you as a person. I love you. And I'm here to stay." It reminded me that God doesn't want to spend time with us with the sole intent to change us. He delights in us. And it's his delight that makes me feel so valued that I want to follow and obey him.

So how are your relationships with others? Do you pursue people with the goal of changing them — or with the goal of simply loving, delighting in, and enjoying them? What I think we'll find is that those we have sought to change, God will use to change us as well.

ABOUT THE AUTHOR

*Ty Wyss is the Founder of Walls Down Ministry, an organization that equips the church to reach out in their daily lives to LGBT+ neighbors and loved ones. Learn more at **wallsdown.org**.*

THE FIFTH CALL

RILEY, A 21-YEAR-OLD COLLEGE STUDENT IN THE WESTERN U.S., SHARES ABOUT THE EFFECTS ISOLATION — AND, EVENTUALLY, LOVING SUPPORT — HAD ON HIS LIFE.

I WAS IN A VERY ISOLATED, LONELY PLACE. I HADN'T TOLD MY parents — and with the stress of school and life, I was so full of emotions that I didn't even know how to control them. It seemed like I could barely do anything but cry.

One day, it was so bad that I actually wrote a suicidal letter.

In my letter, I wrote to my parents. I told them that I love them and that I experience same-gender attraction. I also wrote to my brother and sister-in-law, whom I had just found out were going to be having a kid. I told them to tell my future nephew or niece that I love them. That was the most piercing part of the letter.

Before I did anything else, I tried calling five people. One by one, each call ended with no answer.

Finally, on the fifth call, I got an answer. It was Mike, my campus ministry leader.

When I told Mike about my letter, he told me to rip the thing up and throw it in the trash. So that's what I did. Then he told me that he wanted to meet up with me.

I remember walking up to Mike's door — shaky, hesitant, and unsure what to expect. It may have been God's power telling me to keep going, but I just took a step of faith and walked in. Sitting there with Mike, it took me a while to even talk. Finally, what I had been keeping inside for 10 years came pouring out.

During that meeting, Mike told me that if I'm going to get through this part of my life, I really need hope. He said, "You just need a little bit of hope. Even a tiny bit will work."

So as the night went by and the next day came, I gained a little more hope. Mike got me connected with Lead Them Home, and they connected me with a couple in town that they knew would be safe. I had also found out about another guy in my campus ministry who experienced same-gender attraction and could relate to what I was going through.

Even today, I go through tremendous ups and downs. But with a support team at my back, I know that in the future, I can keep going, spreading the word of God, and growing closer to Him.

WHAT HAS BEEN THE IMPACT OF A SUPPORT NETWORK ON YOUR LIFE?

I have a lot more comfort and a lot less anxiousness. Having that kind of a secret can be a really exhausting thing. I had turned to pornography, I had turned to alcohol — it was all because I kept on just stuffing the feelings down. Having someone I could talk to about it really helped a lot.

WHAT DO YOU WANT PARENTS TO KNOW IF THEIR CHILD WERE EVER TO COME OUT?

First, know they didn't choose this. I cannot tell you how many times I've asked God, "If I could have any other problem, why this?" Second, know it's just as hard for your kid to tell you as it is for you to hear. I had kept everything in for 10 years. My parents would always ask me, "Why don't you tell us anything?" It's not so much that I didn't want to communicate with them, it's just that I'm so used to keeping everything in.

WHAT WOULD YOU TELL A TEEN WHO IS LGBT+ AND NOBODY KNOWS?

Go to a youth pastor or another adult whom you know is a safe person. See if they can give you any advice or connect you with safe people. Get a support team that will have your back, and *then* tell your parents. For me, that's what really gave me the courage and strength — along with the power of God — to tell my parents about what was going on.

In only a few short days, Riley's decade of isolation turned into one point of support. That quickly multiplied into eight points of support — including Riley's parents, who responded with acceptance.

Just a few months later, Riley got to hold his newborn nephew in his arms.

ADAPTED WITH PERMISSION FROM
STRUGGLE CENTRAL: QUARTER-LIFE
CONFESSIONS OF A MESSED UP CHRISTIAN.

DEEP DARK SECRETS

BY THOMAS MARK ZUNIGA

LATE INTO THE UNTHINKABLE NIGHT, I picked up a pen. With tears splattering the pages of my journal, I wrote. Held nothing back as I confessed deep dark secrets stretching back nineteen years. Struggles that went far beyond isolation and bullying and shame among the other boys.

Struggles like lust. Years of lustful thoughts and glances which had escalated in recent weeks to pornography. Excessive amounts of pornography.

Twisted pornography.

Beyond my already candid confessions, my struggles with lust delved into the complex and convoluted. They were messier and far *worse* than any "normal" person with "normal" lust and "normal" battles with pornography.

For the first time in nineteen years, I confessed. Confessed to myself and confessed before God what I'd known my entire life but never actually admitted — like a shadow in my heart that never dissipated, day or night. After dancing around the issue in twelve journals, stretching back to my very first journal as a 7-year-old, I penned the words plainly on crinkled, tear-strewn pages.

Openly admitted my life-long struggle with homosexuality.

I wept and wrote about everything — my recently kept secret of gay pornography and the even longer kept secret of my sexuality. Emotional and physical attractions to other boys from as early as first and second grade.

For the first time in my life, I held nothing back as I wrote page after sulfuric page.

The next day, I grabbed my journal, noting the added weight of its confession-laden pages, and stepped downstairs. I approached my parents in the living room, their eyebrows crinkling in perplexed acceptance as my dad took the blackened book. I just couldn't bear breathing audible life into the blood-stained words still wet upon the pages, so I let my written words do all the initial talking.

But it was finally *talking* nonetheless.

A heart-pounding, face-to-face-to-face conversation later followed in my parents' bedroom. Gallons of tears and snot were deposited onto their bed that day.

But the storm would calm. Waves would cease. Light would break the thunderclouds — even shine.

My parents accepted me. Supported me. They affirmed my decision to "come out" to them before I tested chasms far deeper than mere pornography.

Three years later, I told my younger brother and sister in the living room. My siblings were just as supportive as my parents. My sister affirmed that my reveal didn't change anything; my brother claimed it changed everything. She still loved me regardless, and he felt honored to be brought into this new, inner realm of my life.

I felt so loved. Loved by siblings who still stood behind their older brother, still believed in him despite his brokenness. This brokenness that I never chose.

I'd never been prouder to be their older brother.

Despite my waterfalls of tears in bedrooms and living rooms, I've almost masochistically enjoyed this process — opening up my soul to trusted others. The night after coming out to my siblings, I went to bed freer than the night I'd confessed to my parents. I felt unbelievably relieved that my entire family now *knew* me. Truly knew.

Four precious people could now share the load of my deep dark secrets when for nineteen years I'd honestly assumed zero ever would. I guess I'd have to find another secret to carry with me to my grave.

ABOUT THE AUTHOR

Thomas Mark Zuniga is the cofounder and editor of **yourotherbrothers.com,** a community navigating faith, homosexuality, and masculinity. He's written two books — *Struggle Central* and *Running To: In Search of Home on the Open Road.* He lives in Asheville, NC, and is passionate about brotherhood and the intersection of struggle and redemption.

info@leadthemhome.org

WHEN A LOVED ONE COMES OUT:
SEVEN TRUTHS TO CONSIDER
BY HAYLEY MULLINS

SELECTIONS FROM AN ARTICLE FROM REVIVE OUR HEARTS, USED WITH PERMISSION. ACCESS THE FULL ARTICLE AT **REVIVEOURHEARTS.COM.**

PERHAPS YOU JUST RECEIVED some surprising news. You may be feeling confused, guilty, betrayed, or even angry with God. Amid your emotions and uncertainty, God's Word offers hope-filled answers for you today.

1. BEING "QUICK TO LISTEN, SLOW TO SPEAK, SLOW TO BECOME ANGRY" IS ALWAYS A WISE REACTION.

It's easy, when emotions are high, to lash out in anger or (in the name of love) start throwing out Scriptures toward your loved one. **Though sharing truth is right at its proper time, consider that it may not be the first thing God is asking you to do.** The Bible gives us the way of wisdom: "...[L]et every person be quick to hear, slow to speak, slow to anger; for the anger of man does not produce the righteousness of God" (Jas. 1:19–20).

Their decision to tell you probably wasn't made overnight. It's more possible that they've been wrestling for a while — and have been experiencing some deep pain. They may even be expecting you to reject them. Letting them share honestly lets them know they are heard and loved — and will actually help you minister to them better. Their situation may not actually be what you assume. Are you willing to wisely *listen* before you speak?

2. REGARDLESS OF THEIR CHOICES, YOUR LOVED ONE IS MADE IN GOD'S IMAGE AND HAS VALUE AND WORTH.

Here's some deep, beautiful doctrine: God has graciously placed the *imago Dei* (image of God) in every person (Gen. 1:27). From the Garden of Eden, each man and woman has been given the privilege of reflecting God and His glory in Creation. Yes, sin — including sexual sin — has caused that image to be displayed imperfectly. But every human being is endowed with the gift of dignity, value, and worth in the eyes of their Creator.

Your son changing his name or your cousin coming to Christmas dinner with a same-sex partner doesn't mean their value before God has diminished. **His Creation ordinance still stands — and with it, our need to show all people respect as bearers of God's image.** Recognizing this does not mean approving of all your loved one's choices, but it does mean approaching them with an attitude of respect.

3. YOUR AND MY SIN (AND NEED FOR THE GOSPEL) IS THE SAME, NO MATTER OUR TEMPTATIONS.

We will never fully value and demonstrate the beauty of the gospel until we recognize our own neediness before God. Paul writes about this in Romans. After explaining that God has given His people spiritual advantages, he writes this:

*"But now the righteousness of God has been manifested . . . the righteousness of God through faith in Jesus Christ for all who believe. **For there is no distinction: for all have sinned and fall short of the glory of God,** and are justified **by his grace as a gift** through the redemption that is in Christ Jesus"* (Rom. 3:21–24, emphasis added).

If you hold to biblical teaching on sexuality, it can be tempting to look at your friend or relative with disgust. But do you look at your own sin and feel as repulsed? **God has offered you grace in Christ because you needed it and couldn't earn it.**

If you're thinking, *I do recognize my neediness, and it's overwhelming!*, here's hope: your neediness is exactly what qualifies you to help others.

4. ACCORDING TO SCRIPTURE, SAME-SEX SEXUAL EXPRESSION ISN'T GOD'S BEST . . .

This is one of the hardest truths of Scripture: God is not honored by sexual relationships between people of the same gender. You may already embrace this truth (or you're wrestling with it). You know verses where same-sex sexual acts are described as "dishonorable," "contrary to nature," "unrighteous," and "contrary to sound doctrine" (Rom. 1:26–27, 1 Cor. 6:9, 1 Tim. 1:10).

Yes, homosexual acts are sinful. This statement is true, but it's very tempting to just stop here. **There's more to the story — and it requires more than simply throwing out Bible verses without love as grenades.** (Do you see the ellipsis on the header above? Let the next truth finish the thought.)

5. ... BUT OBEDIENCE TO GOD'S COMMANDS AND DESIGN CAN BE A VERY HARD ROAD.

Consider the implications for your loved one to follow Jesus in their sexuality. They may:

- have to give up someone they're deeply connected to.
- have to give up their community and identity.
- face deep loneliness.
- have seasons of depression and feeling unloved.
- face misunderstanding in the Church and outside.
- battle desires that cannot be fulfilled obediently.
- never have a family or children of their own.
- not be able to enjoy the physical intimacy of sex.

Jesus said following Him would be difficult and full of self-denial (Matt. 16:24). You probably feel some of that "cross of discipleship" each day—praying for a prodigal, feeling rejected by friends who want to gossip, submitting to an unwise decision of someone in authority. Let your own experiences give you compassion toward your loved one. If they're struggling against their desires, look at that list and be willing to ask questions about their fears and pain. And if they are pursuing a same-sex relationship, consider that those may be some of the reasons. Can you enter into the difficulty with them? **Is there a way, as their mom or sister or friend, that you can help provide for some of those needs?**

6. GOD DESIRES AND IS ABLE TO RESTORE WHAT IS BROKEN BY SIN'S CURSE, BUT IT MAY NOT HAPPEN IN THIS LIFE.

After that last point, you may be feeling heavy-hearted. But there is hope. God "is able to do far more abundantly than all that we ask or think" (Eph. 3:20). With this truth in your pocket, you can look at your loved one and think, *If Jesus is their Savior, He can change them*.

That said, while praying and hoping, we have to avoid creating an idol called "completely free from temptation." God's plan for your loved one, even if He draws them to Himself, may not mean they'll experience automatic transformation. They will still struggle with temptation (probably even same-sex attraction). God may have marriage in mind for them; He may not. They could be on a long road of both victories and failings. But the goal is the same for all who follow Christ, whether they experience homosexual feelings or not. **God's purpose for His children is always their sanctification and His glory — not attraction to the opposite gender.**

The redemption of our bodies (and your loved one's sexuality) will not be complete until the day Christ returns. But take heart: In that day, there will be no sin, no temptation, no sorrow, no loneliness, and no pain for all who belong to Him. So as you trust the Lord with your loved one's situation, remember that He is able to turn it to good, and for His people, He will.

7. CHRIST-LIKE LOVE MEANS SACRIFICIALLY SEEKING OTHERS' WELFARE WHILE PURSUING GOD'S GLORY.

When the Pharisees questioned Jesus on the company He kept, He was bold and unashamed: "Go and learn what this means: 'I desire mercy, and not sacrifice.' For I came not to call the righteous, but sinners" (Mt. 9:13). This is where it gets practical and personal. **Your loved one (like all of us) needs community, a family, and hope. Where better to experience these things than around your table, in your church, and in the everyday stuff of life?**

As you show love and share your table with your loved one, **you may face the same rejection as Christ did** from the Pharisees. But remember, our Lord says, "I came for the ones (including us!) who need my friendship and salvation." By sacrificing your comfort in this way, you can be God's means of showing Christ's grace in the world.

Also know that **loving and welcoming does not negate any of the other truths above.** We must seek God's best for our loved ones, which always means honoring Him first. We are never to sacrifice truth, but we also are not to sacrifice love. First John 3:18 says it best: "Little children, let us not love in word or talk but in deed and in truth."

As you work through your own emotions and choose to show Christ's love, rest in the comforting truths above. And consider . . . our sovereign God is working behind your friend or relative's confession. They're sitting next to you for a reason; perhaps you are in their life "for such a time as this" (Est. 4:14).

ABOUT THE AUTHOR

Hayley Mullins is a musician by training, a writer by calling, and a child of God by grace. Her passion is helping people find abundant life in Christ through life-on-life discipleship and the written word. She serves with the Revive Our Hearts team in editorial services. When she's not writing, you can find Hayley chasing adventures in libraries, on hiking trails, and through deep conversations. Read more of her work at reviveourhearts.com.

ANY CHRISTIAN PARENTS CONTACT LEAD THEM HOME to ask how they can relate to their children's LGBT+ friends from school or youth group. In the past, many were concerned about rapid changes in our culture or felt anxious about the influence of LGBT+ peers on their children. Today, most Christian parents who contact us are genuinely wondering, *What can we do to help?*

With more Christian parents asking how they can positively engage their children's LGBT+ friends, this is evidence that the Church is ready to live out the Gospel in ways that look more like Jesus. **There is reason to have hope: churches are beginning to create a new history of radically loving LGBT+ people.** While all this is at an infancy stage, the willing heart that for so long was missing is now here — and ready to love!

WELCOMING YOUR CHILD'S LGBT+ FRIENDS

10 GUIDING INSIGHTS

FOR PARENTS WHO AIM TO EXPRESS ACCEPTANCE FOR LGBT+ YOUTH

1 **Assure your children that all their friends — gay, straight, questioning, or transgender — are welcome in your family's home.** Many Christian youth quietly assume that their parents don't want LGBT+ friends in their home. Always be specific in extending the welcome to your children's LGBT+ friends.

2 **Assess how LGBT+ people have been discussed in your home over the years.** Have your children heard statements that honor and respect LGBT+ relatives and friends — or have they heard gay jokes and denigrating statements? As parents, has your rhetoric reflected views that demonstrate love for LGBT+ people — or have people been treated as a political issue or threat to your family and faith?

3 **Reach out to the parents of your children's LGBT+ friends.** Do not patronize people as if they need your pity (no one likes to be treated this way), but invite their family into your home for dinner. This family may be surrounded by neighbors who support LGBT+ causes, yet never actually act so neighborly. There is opportunity for Christians to be uniquely hospitable — even in today's affirming world.

4 **Avoid guessing that your child's friend must be gay due to external appearance (dress, stature, mannerisms, features, talents, or interests).** Some less "feminine" girls are lesbian, but many lesbian girls are actually quite feminine. Operating in stereotypes is ultimately a form of discrimination. It can be too easy to fall into this kind of thinking without knowing it, but your children will likely notice it every time.

5 **Do not shy away from engaging an LGBT+ youth after they disclose their sexual orientation or gender identity.** If they open up, make sure you don't shut down. Ask basic questions like, "Could you tell me more about your story?" to convey that your family is safe. Silence after disclosure is commonly interpreted as rejection. Silence can leave a young person feeling exposed, misunderstood, and judged.

6 **Recognize that Christians are viewed as hateful toward LGBT+ people.*** This reputation precedes any interaction you have with your children's friends. Before you even get to establish your heart's integrity, youth may already anticipate that you are a right-wing hatemonger. Every action, attitude, and word must be genuine and thoughtful. Welcoming eye contact and a genuine smile will help.

*A 2007 Barna Group study found that 9 of 10 outsiders found Christians anti-homosexual.

Let's spend the coming years learning how to keep LGBT+ youth in our churches and growing in their faith. When we lose one along the way, let's make a concerted effort to contact them and learn what happened. Based on what you discover, make amends for any mistakes and warmly invite this young person back to church. As a parent, you may see or hear things that a busy youth leader might miss. Let staff know but also step in the gap. **On our watch, let's do what's possible to ensure that we don't lose even one LGBT+ teen.**

7 **Remember from "Words Matter" (Page 38) that *every word counts*.** You can smile, cook a steak dinner, and bake cookies, but all these efforts may count for nothing if unnatural words spill out of your mouth. Usually, the most honoring language is the simplest to say. If you try too hard to think of a unique way to talk with LGBT+ people, there is a greater chance of offending someone. Be natural. Keep it simple.

8 **Reject the notion or fear that your older children's LGBT+ friends might be a negative influence on your younger kids.** Many younger children will not even know about sexual orientation. An LGBT+ friend will not make your younger children gay. If any of your children do one day realize they are gay or transgender, it will be helpful that you have already demonstrated acceptance of LGBT+ people.

9 **Exchange talking for listening.** The more we talk, the greater risk that we unintentionally put our foot in our mouth. You can learn a lot by listening. Lead Them Home used to *tell* pastors our biblical apologetic for generously loving LGBT+ people. When we switched to *asking* leaders for their apologetic ideas, ownership of our Posture Shift teaching dramatically increased among ministry teams. By asking honoring questions, you plant seeds of trust that can blossom into the fruit of influence.

10 **Be a safe parent or lay leader for LGBT+ youth at your church.** In Evangelical church settings, youth likely still hear unthoughtful statements about gay and transgender people. Build such safe rapport with LGBT+ youth that they know you are always available to protect them. Do not place the entire burden upon church staff. As a parent or lay leader, *you* can offer youth safety and inclusion.

THE BEST QUESTIONS YOU COULD EVER ASK YOUR CHILDREN'S GAY AND TRANSGENDER FRIENDS

1. "Matthew, **how was your week?** What topic did you select for your history project?"
2. "Nina, does your family have any fun **summer vacation plans?**"
3. "Jacob, what have you been doing to prepare for the **upcoming SAT exam?**"
4. "Dana, I will contact your mom about dinner at our place. **Is your family in town next weekend?**"
5. "Myca, thank you so much for honoring us with your story. **What is it like to identify as genderqueer?**"
6. "Greg, I am so sorry that you experienced bullying. **What can parents like us do to protect LGBT+ kids?**"
7. "Kate, **can you make it to youth group if you have a ride home?** We're always available to drive you."
8. "Sammy, we are so grateful to have you on this mission team. **How is the mission trip going for you so far?**"
9. "John, thanks for joining our family night. **What board games do you and your family most enjoy?**"
10. "Thomas, you said you identify as pansexual. **Tell me more.** I am curious what that's like for you."

Every question is simple, yet every question reflects an authentic relationship that is under construction or even deeply established. Good questions reveal that a young person is experiencing invitation, hospitality, conversation, community, laughter, fun, significance, safety, and belonging. Good questions demonstrate that a young person is known by a Christian family. Good questions show that Christian parents are making a concerted and sincere effort to invite, include, and get to know their children's LGBT+ friends.

info@leadthemhome.org

8 THINGS I WISH EVERY CHRISTIAN LEADER KNEW ABOUT GAY TEENS IN THEIR CHURCH

BY LAURIE KRIEG

The following includes selections from a pastoral paper used with permission from The Center for Faith, Sexuality & Gender. Access the full resource at **centerforfaith.com/resources** under Pastoral Papers.

THOSE GAY TEENS IN YOUR CHURCH? I WAS ONE OF THEM. I didn't really know it yet — I didn't identify as gay — but I was attracted to women. Nobody suspected me. I hardly suspected myself. Whenever I felt the draw towards women, I squashed it down. *That's a sin. Not just a sin, but the worst-worst sin,* I believed.

When I share my testimony, I usually fast-forward to my secret same-sex relationship in college while attending a Christian university, facilitating small groups, and leading worship at the same church where my dad was a pastor. I often continue the story to a scene post-college where I wrestled between two choices: kill myself or come out as a lesbian atheist. A wise person showed me another way — to sink my whole self into the truth of the gospel.

But today, I want to push pause right at the moment I was first wrestling with my sexuality and ask High School Laurie: *What do you wish your church knew about you? What do you wish they would do for you?*

This paper does not speak for every LGBT+ person who walks boldly or secretly through your church doors, but I hope it speaks for some. Here are eight things I wish my church had known about me:

1. I HAVE NO IDEA WHO I AM.

Sexuality aside, I hardly knew who I was in high school. Some of this was because the human brain is not fully developed until we are 25 years old, but some of it was because I was a chameleon. I am not the first or last chameleon to walk through high school.

I wish I had been taught back then how to get to know the real me. God was calling her forth, but I didn't know how to answer him. I didn't know what tools to use to bring the real me before a real God in a real world.

2. I NEED A GOSPEL-CENTERED IDENTITY.

I didn't need self-help books; I needed an identity that was unwavering. The only unchangeable identity out there is found in the God of the Bible. I needed to learn how to read the Bible and let it read me. To express my pain through lament like the Psalmists. To learn how the gospel fuels the joy that equips me to die a thousand deaths every day. To know how to listen to God, to fast, to celebrate, to meditate on the word, and to let him into the secret places of my heart.

Had I known an identity based not on my goodness or failings but on God's grace, I might have been spared the hours I spent begging a God I thought hated me: "Please, squash me and start over."

3. I AM A PRODIGAL, TOO.

Because I was such a good kid, people assumed nothing painful or messy could be hiding behind my smiling face and shiny blonde hair. We say in sermons that the older brother is just as much a prodigal as the younger. But let's be honest: The older brother doesn't cause as many problems. The parent or pastor can take a mental break knowing the hardworking firstborn is getting stuff done. We don't have to have a sit-down, "How's your heart?" chat with them because their heart seems good.

We need to have those heart-to-heart talks with the good kids and the bad kids alike. We need to recognize that a well-behaved faith is not always a sign of a healthy heart; sometimes, it's the mark of a heart running from a terrifying reality within.

Some parents of LGBT-identifying or questioning teens are shocked because their "good" kid is suddenly a prodigal whom they feel has "turned" on them. These parents forget that we are all prodigals — gay, straight, genderqueer, valedictorians, New York Times bestsellers, older sisters, or pig-slopping younger brothers.

4. I NEED ROOM TO BE MESSY.

A teen may have already come out, but parents often don't hear the secret question mark at the end of the sentence: "I am gay...?" A teen may be wrestling primarily with what to do about their attractions. (Do I want to be a celibate gay Christian? A same-sex attracted Christian? Someone who is open to dating the opposite sex?) Statements like, "No, this is not who you are" (which a teen interprets as, "You're not actually attracted to the same sex"), will isolate a teen from parents at the very moment parental support is most important.

That isolation can become a Grand Canyon of misunderstanding. The child may then choose an easier emotion like anger to cover their pain, and double down: "Yes, I am this person, and I'm going to go live it out right now," or turn their anger inward towards suicidal ideation and self-harm.

We need to let our teens have room to be messy while we instill a gospel-centered identity. You, the parent, need to grieve — just not on your child.

5. KNOW THAT IN PLACES OF PAIN, YOU CAN SPEAK JESUS TO ME.

When I was in a secret same-sex relationship, I remember staring at certain people and wishing they would ask me how my relationship was going. If someone I hardly knew had asked me, "Why are you doing that!? Don't you know it's sin?" I would have answered with a giant wall: "I'm fine! You just hate who I am!" But if someone had come alongside me with genuine curiosity, I could have opened up about secret pain inside.

In the end, this is what happened to me. "It's so hard," I wept to my pastor-father. Instead of rebuking my same-sex behavior, he grieved with me and pierced my heart with the love of Christ. It opened up my heart to my dad while simultaneously showing me Jesus's love — something I felt for only seconds per week in that season.

In the compassionate mentoring ministry I direct, young clients come prepared to lob verbal grenades, rejecting us before we reject them. But we startle them with empathy. "You want to talk about it? How's it going with her?" When we courageously, tenderly engage mess (even sin-laden mess), we begin to hear the truth behind the walls: "I hate myself. I hate my life. I actually don't know who I am. Is there something better than this?"

Right there is where Jesus offers living water. Right there is where the gospel is preached: We see you. We love you. We have experienced a better way — not of straightness, but of walking alongside one another through sexual brokenness, looking to Jesus as all of our hope and wholeness.

6. FROM LEADERS, I NEED BOTH BIBLICAL THEOLOGY AND PROTECTION.

In my teens, I needed wise, tender, courageous guidance to teach me what the church believed about sexuality. Otherwise, I was going to pick the easiest theology I could find and go with it. By default, we slide into sin, not holiness. We need to be taught what is holy — not only by our youth pastors, but by our senior pastors. Love me and people like me enough to preach — with empathy and compassion — the truth about sexuality.

When you speak about same-sex sexual ethics, you must also keep in mind that you are speaking to a highly vulnerable population. This is why a pastor must speak truth only alongside empathy ("I can understand sexual brokenness") and compassion ("I see your specific brokenness, and I can never 'get it' enough").

When pastors take this heart posture, speaking out in specific protection for vulnerable populations from the main stage, it could sound something like this: "Everyone in this room is loved uniquely and individually. We want to care well for all of you. Your physical, emotional, and spiritual safety is our top priority. We do not tolerate bullying, unkindness, or rudeness towards anyone based on race, gender, religion, or sexual orientation. If we hear about it or see it happening online or in person, we will take it very seriously."

7. I NEED A MENTOR (OR FIVE).

Chances were high that I would end up leaving the church completely. Chances are even higher for kids in youth group today: 40-50% of high schoolers connected to a youth group will drop out in college, and 59% of Millennials have stopped attending church completely.

What's the solution? According to longitudinal research from the Fuller Youth Institute, "More than any single program or event, kids were far more likely to feel like a significant part of their local churches when adults made the effort to get to know them." They recommend a 5:1 ratio, or five significant adult relationships per teen. Young people are far more likely to experience increased support, less shame, and a submission of brokenness to the Lord when they see how truth embodies itself in people.

8. REMOVE THE ASSUMPTION THAT EVERYONE IS ONLY ATTRACTED TO THE OPPOSITE SEX.

Don't assume every young woman is attracted to guys and every guy is attracted to young women. Practically, this means making subtle shifts in the ways we talk about sex and attraction. "Guys, I know you want to hang with the girls (wink wink)..." becomes, "Okay, I know you all want to chat..." Rooming may need to be reconfigured at overnight events to ensure everyone feels comfortable (this is a big conversation that must be handled delicately). Additionally, rethinking gender stereotyping at events would be kind to the silent LGBT+ kid who often feels incredibly "other." Perhaps even once per year the guys' day out could include painting pottery along with paintballing. The young women's day could include grilling meat as well as a day of pedicures.

CONCLUSION

You won't get this right every time. If you haven't done it already, you *will* fail your LGBT+ kids — and your straight kids — many times. When stepping into any conversation concerning the above 8 ideas with an LGBT+ student, it would be wise to begin with, "Hey, I want to understand and to care well for you. But I don't know what I don't know. If I offend you, will you please tell me? I don't want to hurt you."

Humility draws hearts together no matter our differences in theology or life experience. Humility is unquestionably the reason I stayed in the church, even while I lived a double life. The churches I attended and the people in them were imperfect, but they were humble. They wanted to grow and to learn. It gave me hope that perhaps one day I would be free to share all of my struggles with them, knowing they would learn to receive me and my story as another amazing but ordinary example of the gospel: I am more sinful than I believe, and I am more loved than I can imagine.

ABOUT THE AUTHOR

Laurie Krieg is Executive Director of Hole in My Heart Ministries, a teaching, writing, and mentoring ministry for those wrestling with issues related to sexuality. Laurie writes and speaks nationally. Learn more at himhministries.com.

BEING A GREAT FRIEND TO PARENTS OF LGBT+ CHILDREN

CHRISTIAN PARENTS OF LGBT+ CHILDREN often face tremendous pressure. As many parents attempt to nourish a vibrant faith life in their child, some parents are simply trying to keep their child alive (literally).

They have witnessed their son suffer through bullying. They have seen their little girl get pummeled by peer rejection. Some parents have watched helplessly as a depressed child sank into suicidality. More than a few have had to hug and kiss their dying child goodbye after a fatal suicide attempt.

Tragically, at the same time parents are aiming to honor God and love their LGBT+ child, they can be *ruthlessly criticized* by other Christians when their child comes out (or is outed) within their church community.

Here are just a few recent stories reported to us:

> *"A woman in my church whom I barely know told me,* **'You shouldn't have gotten that divorce. No wonder your son's now a homosexual.'"**

> *"Our family friend made sure to let me know that* **I caused my daughter's lesbianism.** *He indicated that I let her choose this lifestyle — that I lacked the wisdom to set godly boundaries."*

> *"I was told that* **I better tell my trans-whatever son that effeminate men go straight to hell."**

One mother recently called on her last shred of hope:

> *"I just wrote my goodbye letters. I am done with this life. When my husband died, my daughter was young. My church has been our refuge all these years. Now that people are finding out that my adult daughter is transgender, they have turned against us. They blame me for my daughter's decision to transition.* **I have not felt this abandoned since my husband's death."**

After reading portions of *Guiding Families* to this mother over the phone, the Holy Spirit filled her with hope! She tore up the suicide notes. She sensed the Holy Spirit confirming that she must decide to live in order to love her only child.

Realizing the injustice, this mother declared: "I gotta go fire some friends!" How sad — with that kind of "support," who needs friends?

"...BUT THERE IS A FRIEND WHO STICKS CLOSER THAN A BROTHER." – PROVERBS 18:24

However, parents of LGBT+ children *do* need friends — faithful friends! Friends who listen, support, pray, and believe in their character as Christ-followers. Being the parent of a LGBT+ child neither negates nor diminishes one's Christian faith. Having a gay or transgender child does not make someone an ungodly parent!

No parent owes anyone a justification for loving their LGBT+ child. In doing so, though, others may accuse them of condoning sin.

One brave mother of an 8-year-old son, who has been insisting he is a girl since age 3, reported:

*"My husband and I tuck our son into bed every night, hold him, and silently pray that God will help him be comfortable in his own skin. We're not in denial — it may get more complex as he grows up, but we're committed to loving him! I will not entrust our story to our church. I've heard what people say about transgender people. They have no idea what it's like to walk this path. **We'll never trust our son's well-being to even Christian friends. We're building support outside our church — where confidentiality is assured.** We will do whatever is necessary to protect our son. Later on, he will need to look back and know that we've always been here for him."*

These stories should be a wake-up call for the rest of us. Parents of LGBT+ children have been crying out for trustworthy support and asking, "Where are our faithful friends when we need them most?"

FAITHFUL FRIEND FUNDAMENTALS
COMPASSIONATE CARE FOR CHRISTIAN PARENTS OF AN LGBT+ CHILD

1. **REDUCE ISOLATION** by offering safe space for confidential conversation and support. Isolated parents of LGBT+ children experience higher anxiety, depression, and loneliness.

2. **REJECT BIAS** by learning what your friends and their child are experiencing. Avoid books and resources that denigrate LGBT+ people as such ideas neither honor nor help people.

3. **REFINE LANGUAGE** by listening first and speaking words that encourage, uplift, foster hope, prove love, and built trust. Every word counts! (See "Words Matter" on page 38)

4. **REACH GENTLY** by inviting a family with an LGBT+ child into your home for dinner. Demonstrate that safe community, acceptance, and warm hospitality are available to them.

5. **REFLECT CHRIST** by modeling to your children generous care for hurting people. This can empower your children to become trustworthy friends who include LGBT+ peers.

GUIDELINES FOR YOUTH, STUDENT, AND CAMPUS MINISTRIES

1. INCLUDE

John the Baptist never took an "inventory" of sins or "weeded out" certain people. He baptized anyone who came in sincere humility.

Jesus invited everyone: "Come to me all who are weary. I will give you rest for your soul" (Mt. 11:30).

Some youth may identify as Christian, but they are not yet born again. We would never try to convince a teen that he or she is not really a Christian. Be careful not to target LGBT+ youth in this way. **Nourish their faith identity where they are!**

2. LISTEN

It takes courage for LGBT+ teens to come out. They risk potential rejection or judgment. Your first reaction is critical. **Maintain eye contact and thank them for trusting you with their story.**

Tell them, "I really want to hear your whole story." Pastors are busy, but following this kind of disclosure, it is important to **make time immediately to listen.**

Ask honoring questions that demonstrate understanding and sensitivity. This will allow you to learn about potentially harmful risk factors (bullying, teasing, exclusion, or family rejection).

3. PROTECT

NO gay jokes. Some jokes may be funny even to LGBT+ people, but why risk deeply hurting one vulnerable teen who needs Christ's love? Some jokes are funny only when told by LGBT+ people, but the humor is lost when the same joke is told by a Christian leader.

NO bullying. Teasing, name-calling, anti-gay rhetoric, outing someone, social media harassment, threatening words, and hitting or pushing are all acts of bullying. **Bullying is not acceptable under any circumstance.** It can even be a crime. **Safety first:** Bullying hurts and kills gay and straight teens. Protection of LGBT+ youth must be a top priority. Creating safe space requires advance planning and standard protocols.

Report immediately. Educate and empower staff, lay leaders, and student leaders to protect youth and report bullying when LGBT+ youth are being mistreated. What would Jesus do?

4. INVEST

Words are important, but **justice requires action steps. Offer to join students in anti-gay bullying prevention programs.** Include in your teachings the stories of teens who lost their lives due to bullying. For young adults 18 and older, **offer panel discussions** where LGBT+ youth (including those with unwanted same-gender attraction) can share their story.

Encourage student leaders to be attentive to include *any* **teen** who appears isolated or subject to mistreatment and exclusion. Advise them: "Do more than just invite a vulnerable student into your social group. *Discover* what he or she likes to do — and *join in* that activity or interest together."

Identify gifts and utilize God-given talents in Kingdom endeavors. **Connect a student's gifts and talents to God's calling upon his or her life** (mission trips, worship team, service project, etc.).

www.leadthemhome.org

FOR ALL WHO CARE
INSIGHTS FOR RELATIVES, FRIENDS, AND NEIGHBORS

"ONE OF MY FRIENDS CAME TO ME SEEKING HELP IN CARING FOR AN LGBT+ LOVED ONE. WE ARE GOING TO MEET LATER THIS WEEK TO TALK. WHAT APPROACH WOULD YOU RECOMMEND FOR OUR CONVERSATION?"

1. Encourage them toward *acceptance*; explain why it does not equate with *approval*.

2. Educate them on specific vulnerabilities LGBT+ young people face.

3. Expand their "lens" to understand that **posture** is part of a godly **position:**

   Orthodoxy = Right Beliefs + Right Life Practices + Right Treatment of Others

4. Equip them with additional resources such as *Guiding Families*.

"HOW SHOULD I PREPARE FOR THIS KIND OF MEETING?"

ASK — "Did I earn, achieve or deserve my salvation? **How did I receive salvation?"**

READ — Romans 1, but don't stop there! Continue to Romans 2:1-4 and Matthew 7:1-3.

PRAY — "Lord, **live out Your presence through me** as I reach out with Your love."

ADJUST — Set your posture to **be a listener** (avoid knowing all the answers).

GO — Offer a **shepherd's heart** rather than a Pharisee's hammer.

LISTEN — **Just sit with** families in their grief and uncertainty.

INVITE — "Come to Me all who are weary and burdened. **I will give you rest"** (Mt. 11:30).

info@leadthemhome.org

POSTURING THE CHURCH FOR CORPORATE RECONCILIATION

BY NATE COLLINS

*DR. NATE COLLINS DISCUSSES HOW THREE COMMUNAL HABITS CAN HELP LOCAL CHURCHES TO BE MINISTERS OF RECONCILIATION TOWARD LGBT+ PEOPLE ON A CORPORATE LEVEL. ADAPTED FROM **ALL BUT INVISIBLE** (ZONDERVAN, 2017) WITH PERMISSION. PURCHASE THE BOOK AT **ZONDERVAN.COM**.*

GENERATION AFTER GENERATION OF MARGINALIZING gay and lesbian men and women has produced a church culture that is simply not equipped to cast a compelling vision for what gospel flourishing could look like for a nonstraight person.

It takes a lifetime of learning to know how to live out gospel obedience in the day-to-day messiness of our lives. As the context within which we learn this obedience, the body of Christ bears a unique responsibility to use its corporate imagination to cast a vision for what this gospel obedience looks like for gay people.

To do so, the church must embody communal habits that will, over time, put the hearts and minds of Christians into a humble, loving posture that can foster reconciliation. Our calling is to enculturate the habits of confession, repentance, and love both at the individual and corporate level of the local church.

CONFESSION

The first reason for confessing our sins is that only God can provide the forgiveness we need (1 Jn. 1:9). But the Bible gives another reason: "so that you may be healed" (Jas. 5:16). This social element of confession is different from the vertical element of confessing one's sins to God. While forgiveness comes from God, by confessing our sins to one another, we receive healing.

It's also possible to distinguish between individual and corporate confession. Corporate confession can be unpopular, even destabilizing, but it is necessary. The question facing us today is whether individual groups or tribes of Christians have made particular, identifiable mistakes in their interactions with gay people. If so, then these would seem to be occasions for Christians to corporately assume a posture of regret, contrition, and humility.

> IT IS A BEAUTIFUL THING TO OBSERVE THE IMPACT HUMBLE REPENTANCE CAN HAVE ON A MARGINALIZED POPULATION.

REPENTANCE

Although repentance begins with confession, believers must follow up with actions. If a group of Christians confesses as a corporate body that their faith tradition has portrayed gay people merely as enemies, repentance must entail acts that remedy this. Confession and repentance can be a compelling witness to the transforming power of the gospel, but they can also be a witness to spiritual beauty. It is, quite simply, a beautiful thing to observe the impact that humble repentance can have on a marginalized population as it is reconciled to a group that has contributed to the marginalization.

LOVE

The apostle John writes, "By this everyone will know that you are my disciples, if you love one another" (Jn. 13:35). Love undergirds confession and repentance and is the seal of their authenticity. If someone confesses harboring hateful feelings toward gay people, then acts of love toward gay people are an appropriate course of action to pursue as an act of repentance.

> CHRISTIANS MUST ACT TOGETHER IN LOVE WHEN THEY CONFESS THE WAYS THEY HAVE FAILED TO TREAT GAY PEOPLE WITH DIGNITY, AND THEIR CONFESSION MUST BE FOLLOWED BY SINCERE ACTS OF REPENTANCE.

If Christians act together in love when they confess the ways they have failed to treat gay people with dignity, and if their confession is followed by sincere acts of repentance, then it is because they have been carried along by God's love for those who bear his image. Love is the beginning, the middle, and the end of reconciliation.

ABOUT THE AUTHOR

Dr. Nate Collins is the author of *All But Invisible: Exploring Identity Questions At The Intersection Of Faith, Gender, And Sexuality* (Zondervan, 2017). He has a PhD in New Testament from the Southern Baptist Theological Seminary. Nate is the president and founder of Revoice, an organization that supports, encourages, and empowers gender and sexual minorities so they can experience the life-giving character of the historic Christian tradition. Nate has been married to his wife, Sara, for 14 years, and they have three children.

LEAD WITH JUSTICE

BY RAY LOW

JESUS LEADS WITH JUSTICE. Throughout the gospels, Jesus is constantly reaching out to both the people regarded as immoral (such as the tax collectors and "sinners"), or the people simply regarded as unclean (the leper, the blind, the poor). In each story, we see only a brief snapshot of the ministry of Jesus as He demonstrates a radical kind of love towards people who have been discarded by society.

While not compromising on issues of righteousness, Jesus allows compassion and relationship to take precedence in His interactions with those on the economic and moral fringes of society. **And from this, we can learn two things about leading with justice.**

HAS NO ONE RETURNED TO GIVE PRAISE?

The first is that **Jesus reached out to people regardless of whether they ended up following Him.** Think about how Jesus compassionately healed ten men with leprosy even though only one came back in faith to give praise to God (Lk. 17:11-19). Jesus imposed no belief or faith requirements for His mercy on those who needed mercy.

> ## JESUS IMPOSED NO BELIEF OR FAITH REQUIREMENTS FOR HIS MERCY ON THOSE WHO NEEDED MERCY.

I wonder if we could do the same for the LGBT+ community. With LGBT+ teen suicide rates up to 8 times that of the general population of youth in America, I wonder what it would look like to combat bullying in our schools, homophobia and transphobia in our culture, and workplace discrimination against LGBT+ people. With 20-40% of homeless youth identifying as LGBT+, I wonder what it would look like to provide homes and shelter for those who are in need.

Justice is about leveling the playing field for all to come and meet Jesus. It's about upholding the inherent dignity and worth of every person, as well as every person's basic right to food, health, and shelter. It is

> ## WHAT A BEAUTIFUL PICTURE IT WOULD BE IF WE ABANDONED OUR IMAGE AND OUR NEED TO BE "RIGHT" ALL THE TIME — AND INSTEAD SHOWED COMPASSION TO THOSE WHO NEED IT.

only within that context of radical love that we can begin to see hearts transformed by the power of the gospel.

WHY DOES HE EAT WITH TAX COLLECTORS AND SINNERS?

Another radical aspect of leading with justice is its determination to operate outside the obstacles of public scrutiny. Jesus surprises the Pharisees and the teachers of the law when He chooses to invite a tax collector to follow Him and winds up hanging out with an entire community of people regarded as morally corrupt and deficient (Mt. 9:9-13).

Naturally the religious leaders begin to question Jesus' behavior, going as far as to challenge Jesus' own integrity (Lk. 15:2). Still, Jesus continues to minister all the more faithfully, despite what it might make others think about His moral beliefs — because **Jesus knew that having a relationship with those who needed mercy and love was far more important than His personal right to defend His behavior.**

What a beautiful picture it would be for churches to do the same in reaching out to the LGBT+ community, being unhindered by the fear of judgment from other religious communities and leaders. What a beautiful picture it would be if we abandoned our image and our need to be "right" all the time, and instead showed compassion to those who need it. We might be called apostate, wayward, or heretical. Jesus was called far worse things.

LEAD WITH JUSTICE

Jesus reaches out to people regardless of whether or not they turn and follow Him. Jesus also reaches out to people regardless of His own theological reputation. Justice is about creating spaces in our churches that are free from homophobia or transphobia, where all can come and experience the redeeming love of Christ.

ABOUT THE AUTHOR

Ray Low is currently serving as a pastor in New York City after having been fired by his previous church for his sexual orientation despite his commitment to obedience and celibacy. He has a passion for discipleship, evangelism, and social justice issues, and his dream is to see reconciliation between the Church and the LGBT+ community. Follow his writing at **leadwithjustice.com.**

THE JUSTICE GENERATION
WRITING A NEW CHURCH HISTORY

Victimization of gay and transgender people still happens today. We read earlier about 22-year-old Crystal, our young transgender friend who is homeless on the streets of Indianapolis due to family rejection.

We also read of 20-year-old Liam's commitment to celibacy, yet he was called a "fag" and removed from working with children in his church. There are countless similar stories.

We need to build a new Church history. With dedication, we can eliminate family rejection of LGBT+ loved ones in this generation. Along the way, though, expect resistance from fellow Christians. Prepare to be called a heretic. When you lay down your life for marginalized people, you may just get trampled along with them.

But count it all joy! Know that you are taking Jesus in you to people where they are — and experiencing only a fraction of the mistreatment that LGBT+ people have suffered for decades. Missionaries never ask for trouble, but they are willing to pay a price to lift up the brokenhearted.

Some of us simply want to blame the media. We are angry that cultural icons and liberal politicians are robbing us of a biblical sexual ethic. We fear that any kindnesses shown to LGBT+ people will slip into biblical compromise.

Meanwhile, one of the great compromises of our day is the pornography epidemic plaguing the Church. It has already robbed us of God's anointing to renew our hearts — and to heal our land.

If we — the majority — will not repent, we don't offer much of a biblical path for others to follow. Failing to repent, it is too easy to slip into substitutes — like sitting on the sidelines waiting for LGBT+ people to repent. We denigrate them and consider them to be a threat to our religious liberty.

We have all the liberty needed to cry out to God and repent. Politicians and entertainers don't control our hearts. *We* are responsible for our lives. *We* are accountable for our sins.

We **must repent.**

Repentance is needed because pornography poisons our souls and strips us of the power of God's Living Word. If we want to see a biblical sexual ethic thrive again in the Church, we must live it out — and treat LGBT+ people kindly along the way.

Kindness is key.

LEAD THEM HOME HAS A VISION TO CREATE a *new* Church history — one where Christians honor God and radically love LGBT+ people.

This will not cost us our biblical position on marriage and sexuality, but it does require a *posture shift.* We must adjust our actions, attitudes, and words to more humbly follow and reflect Jesus.

To build a new church history, we must first come to terms with our past. For decades, we were complicit in mistreating LGBT+ people. At times, we participated in condemning gay and transgender people. More often, we failed to protect them from bullying, condemnation, discrimination, family rejection, suicidality, and homelessness.

Our majority status with its incumbent power kept us from seeing how we failed to protect LGBT+ people.

LET'S WORK TOGETHER ACROSS THE

GENERATIONS TO OFFER OUR WORLD

A NEW CHURCH HISTORY.

Using majority power to posture God against vulnerable people is not only unkind, but it also destroys the reliability of biblical truth. No wonder even many Evangelicals are moving away from a biblical ethic on marriage and sexuality.

Consider this. We used Scripture to mistreat people of color — and we were wrong. We used Scripture to mistreat women — and we were wrong. Some today use Scripture to mistreat LGBT+ people, so the presumption among many Christians is that surely we must be wrong — again.

If you allow a marginalized people group to be mistreated for decades, eventually a new generation will rise up and call it injustice. And if that new generation cannot get us to see what they see, ultimately, they will abandon what they see as an unreliable truth in order to accomplish justice (kind treatment of people).

When this happens, they are not far off the mark! While Scripture holds truth and grace together as two equally tethered strands reflecting the full character of our Heavenly Father, the Bible continually defaults to love.

Consider 1 Corinthians 13:13, which states:

> *"And so faith, hope, love abide [faith — conviction and belief respecting man's relation to God and divine things; hope — joyful and confident expectation of eternal salvation; love — true affection for God and man, growing out of God's love for and in us], these three; but the greatest of these is love."*

Do you know what happens when a new generation rises up and begins to call out our blind spots? The *opportunity* is that we listen to them, learn from them, recognize our sins, repent, confess, and begin to build a new Church history addressing their insights and concerns.

The *risk*, however, is that we mock them from a position of generational power. We minimize their gifts and talents. We become suspicious of their focus on justice. We accuse them of biblical compromise and consider them a grave threat to the church. We write off their concerns simply because we can. We refuse to see.

We need to build a new Church history.

It is time to honor the passing of the gospel torch to the next generation. We must do so because, ultimately, we will age out. Even if we happen to be one of the fortunate few aging leaders who still possesses authority to speak to millions, we all eventually die.

There *will* be a next generation. Considering our mortality — and recognizing that a next generation must assume its place in history — is a healthy exercise. It reminds us to genuinely look for the spark of the gospel in next-generation Christians.

What is there to see in the justice generation? *Nothing short of exactly what God has planned.*

The Lord is shaping this next generation with gifts, talents, insights, and missional skills necessary for such a time as this. The very thing that we, the Church, must do is exactly what they, the next generation, are equipped to do.

The justice generation has grown up with LGBT+ people. They genuinely love gay and transgender family members. They listen to and respect their queer friends. They don't hesitate to invite nonstraight neighbors over for dinner. They understand the importance of belonging for marginalized people. They know that discovering Christ can often be a long journey that begins with acceptance.

This next generation is not a mistake. They are exactly what we need to build a new Church history.

Our generation has made mistakes. Instead of helping hurting people, we crushed their spirits. We owe apologies for countless mistakes. We need an infinite amount of forgiveness.

We failed to love LGBT+ people. We slipped into an ungodly posture and mistreated people. The fruit of our errors is that many, even in the church today, now consider a biblically sound sexual ethic to be a very unreliable truth.

If you deeply care about a biblical ethic for marriage and sexuality, you might be tempted to double-down on condemning LGBT+ people and battling culture. This approach will only further erode the reliability of our truth. Preserving biblical truth begins with repenting of mistakes and committing to radically loving people whom we have wounded and ostracized.

To the justice generation: if you react to our mistakes, you risk getting the gospel just as wrong — but in an opposite way. If our generation had a truth-centric gospel that offered little *love*, there is a risk that you may over-correct and abandon God's *holiness* in an attempt to love well.

For the sake of a God-honoring expression of the gospel of Jesus Christ, let's work together across the generations to offer our world a new Church history: one that honors God and radically loves LGBT+ people.

Amen.

> "AND HIS MERCY (HIS COMPASSION AND KINDNESS TOWARD THE MISERABLE AND AFFLICTED) IS ON THOSE WHO FEAR HIM WITH GODLY REVERENCE, FROM GENERATION TO GENERATION AND FROM AGE TO AGE."
>
> – LUKE 1:50

THE PULSE
OF THE GOSPEL

LEAD THEM HOME CAPTURES THE STORY OF PULSE

SURVIVOR AND OUR NEW FRIEND, **LUIS JAVIER RUIZ.**

BORN INTO A MILITARY FAMILY, WE LIVED IN CITIES across Europe and the United States. During my high school years in El Paso, Texas, my father left the military and both of my parents became pastors.

Growing up, I heard horrible messages about gay people. Even at church, pastors made effeminate gestures as they belittled LGBT+ people. At school, I loved athletics but avoided playing because boys routinely called me "fag."

As a teen, realizing I was attracted to guys, surviving meant hiding. As a Latino first-born son in an ultra-conservative family, I was expected to honorably carry on our family name.

At age 18, exhausted from repression, I came out to my parents. It crushed them.

My parents would never disown me. They loved me. But I soon learned that an unspoken prohibition against sharing real life creates relational distance yielding a sort of disownment. With no permission to share about my life, I unknowingly closed off my life to my parents.

As our church found out, I became viewed as a rapist. Christians gossiped about my parents. In college, I met a friend who helped me to accept my sexuality — but this only made it more difficult for my family to relate to me.

I felt so much anxiety about my parents' pain that I joined the military. On duty in Iraq, I was bullied extensively. Some of these men who watched me get bullied by day would show up in my bed at night seeking sexual favors.

Life as a gay man disconnected me from God, my family, and the church. I eventually left the military and moved to Orlando. Many friends had been disowned by families and kicked out of churches. Others, like me, just felt unaccepted by our parents. We became a close-knit family for one another. We protected one another.

In 2015, I felt a nudging to return to Jesus. For nearly a year, I separated myself from gay friends. I resisted sexual temptation. It was like losing my family all over again.

No wonder I said "yes" when friends asked me to celebrate my birthday with them. It was one night later — the evening of June 11, 2016 — that we debated whether to celebrate at one of our homes or go to Latin Night at the Pulse nightclub.

One week earlier, my Mom had called and told me: "Son, I had a dream that your friends were dying. There was blood everywhere. You were yelling, 'Mom, help me!' It was just a nightmare, but God wanted me to share this with you."

We ended up at Pulse. Latin Nights were always jam-packed. Everyone was dancing. In the early hours of June 12, 2016, as bartenders issued the last call for drinks, we heard what sounded like fireworks. Someone yelled: "Run for your life!"

Suddenly, the killer appeared in front of us. The room filled with the smell of gunpowder as he unloaded a spray of bullets into the scattering crowd. An eerie pause followed as he reloaded. In only seconds, he was firing away again. We could see the flare of his gun with every shot.

Too many people were trying to escape through the narrow doorways. We were stuck and people were stampeding over one another. As the killer fired away, friends fell to the floor dying. Victims cried out, "Jesus, save me!"

Endless shots. Pauses. More shots. This was no nightmare.

Once outside the building, we faced another jog-jam at the fence. People began trying to climb over it. We decided to kick it down. As the fence fell, my leg got stuck in it. As I fell, people trampled over me.

Thinking I would surely die, I dialed my Mom to tell my parents that I am so sorry. As they answered, gunfire rang out just as my phone battery died. In El Paso, my parents soon heard the news and were so afraid that I had been killed.

A friend helped me hobble to a nearby 7-11. Gunshots thundered as people screamed and died. A woman appeared from nowhere and told me: "Son, you're not supposed to be here." She raised her hands to heaven for God to stop the shooting and disappeared as quickly as she had appeared.

The 7-11 store manager, a hero, invited endless people inside the store and gave us shelter and water. In shock but feeling a strange peace, I sensed the Holy Spirit say: *Don't you know I saved you because you are called to share the Gospel?*

Many of us were wounded but afraid to go to the hospital. As the shooter saw wounded people escape, he yelled that he would be "going to the hospital to finish the job."

While waiting for the FBI to release everyone at the scene, I got enough of a charge on my phone to call my parents. I was desperate to tell them how sorry I was. As they answered, they were weeping and said: "Son, we are so sorry!

"We love you!"

www.leadthemhome.org

The FBI finally released everyone at 6:00 am. Hours later, the pain and swelling in my leg forced me to go to the hospital.

As I waited for treatment, a nearby TV airing live Pulse coverage slowly displayed the pictures of victims. I feverishly texted close friends to check on them, but there was no reply. I watched as my friends' pictures appeared on the TV.

Of the 49 people brutally murdered, 35 were my friends.

No, they were *my family*!

Unwanted by our families and churches, many LGBT+ Latinos became one big family. Everyone knew everyone. In one night, so many family members killed. Gone forever.

My parents were desperate to fly to Orlando to see me, but they could not afford it. Local churches raised money for my entire family to come. When they arrived, my parents were different. They loved me — and they loved on all my friends!

Their love led many to Christ.

On national TV, my Dad said words that I will never forget:

"I almost lost my son. Many parents did lose their children. As a pastor, I want to say on behalf of the church that we're so sorry to the LGBT+ Community. Many kids who died were from our families and congregations. We have made too many mistakes. We have to love our children."

Through this trauma, my parents' love, and the work of the Spirit, I had a Road to Damascus conversion. As scales fell off my eyes, I gave my life to Jesus, realizing He had been trying to love me all these years. He had never stopped loving me!

It wasn't a gay-to-straight thing, it was a lost-to-saved thing.

Orlando House of Prayer took me in, made me a son, bound up my wounds, encouraged me in the Word, and prayed for me when I was hurting. Some churches feed the homeless, but my church became my home and fed my soul.

I finally experienced the Gospel. I knew that I was forgiven, that I would be in Heaven, and that God had a plan for my life. The chains of bondage began breaking off my heart. The struggle of being attracted to men was no longer something I *needed* to do. Faith was no longer a performance I had to achieve — or fake. I finally found freedom in the love of Jesus.

All people, gay and straight, and transgender, need to be saved! Jesus is enough to meet all of our needs. The Bible says that we never know when we might face our last moment in this life. It is urgent: *we need to accept Jesus.*

> "BLESSED BE THE LORD, WHO BEARS OUR
> BURDENS AND CARRIES US DAY BY DAY,
> EVEN THE GOD WHO IS OUR SALVATION!
> SELAH [PAUSE, AND CALMLY THINK OF THAT]!
> GOD IS TO US A GOD OF DELIVERANCES AND
> SALVATION; AND TO GOD THE LORD BELONGS
> ESCAPE FROM DEATH [SETTING US FREE]."
>
> – PSALM 68:19-20

No matter what it costs, we must give our lives to Jesus and no longer live according to the flesh, the world, and our limited understanding. *You can come to Jesus right now.*

I was delivered from the jaws of death, saved by the Gospel of Christ, and now I'm called to bring the invitations of Jesus to LGBT+ people. People say that it took one of America's worst mass killings to bring me to Christ. No, it took a mass killing to awaken the church of Jesus Christ to love LGBT+ people.

I recently found out that I am HIV positive. I have a deathly disease, but I am alive in Christ. Inside the Pulse club that night, a mother had just learned that she was cancer free. She met her gay son to dance and celebrate this wonderful news. As the killer pointed his gun at her son, she dove in front of him taking the bullet. She died for her beloved son.

This is what Jesus Christ has done for you — and for me.

Come to Jesus now. He loves you! He always has loved you.

Growing up, my father was first sergeant and pastor when I needed him to be my dad. Recently, after my HIV diagnosis, he flew to Orlando. We both wept as he held me in his arms for a long time. He asked forgiveness for his mistakes. For years, I wanted nothing to do with my father. Now, I was experiencing the dad I needed as a teenager.

I learned that it's never too late to have my father be my Dad.

And for the sake of the gospel, *it is never too late for the church to be the Church.*

TO HONOR PULSE VICTIMS, BULLYING VICTIMS, AND HOMELESS LGBT+ YOUTH,

LET US ELIMINATE FAMILY REJECTION IN THIS GENERATION.

REFLECTION QUESTIONS

1. Which of the **32 Tips** do you find the easiest to live out? Which is hardest for you? Ty Wyss in **No Agendas** writes, "Repentance is important, but it's not a qualifier for whether I love you or include you in my life." How does the life of Jesus reflect this statement?

2. **The Fifth Call** and **Deep Dark Secrets** capture the devastating impact that isolation and loneliness can have on LGBT+ hearts and minds. How can pastors and parents work together to make churches and homes safer for LGBT+ loved ones?

3. In **When A Loved One Comes Out** and **8 Things I Wish Every Christian Leader Knew**, Haley Mullins and Laurie Krieg offer 15 combined insights to help create safer homes, families, and churches. Discuss which of their points are most important to you.

4. **Welcoming Your Child's LGBT+ Friends** offers *10 Guiding Insights* to ensure that every Christian home is a refuge, shelter, and place of belonging and acceptance for LGBT+ youth. Which of the 10 insights is most compelling to you? Please discuss.

5. For all who care, **Being a Great Friend to Parents of LGBT+ Children** captures the isolation parents often feel. Refer to the five *Faithful Friend Fundamentals*. How can you live out each fundamental to be a true friend to parents of LGBT+ children?

6. Nate Collins casts a beautiful vision of **Posturing the Church for Corporate Reconciliation**. What are ways that your faith community might take action steps toward reconciliation with LGBT+ people?

7. In addition to Ray Low's ideas in **Lead With Justice**, what other areas of injustice need to be addressed before we can build trusting relationships with LGBT+ people?

8. **The Justice Generation** captures a vision of God raising up and equipping the next generation to help the Church repair decades of relational mistakes in engaging (or failing to engage) LGBT+ people. As pastors and parents, how can we harness and shepherd this next generation for the sake of the Gospel reaching LGBT+ people?

9. **The Pulse of the Gospel** powerfully captures the survival and salvation story of Luis. In his story, Luis says, "People say it took one of America's worst mass killings to bring me to Christ. No, it took a mass killing to awaken the church of Jesus Christ to love LGBT+ people." How can our Christian families and churches expand upon what Orlando churches did in the aftermath of the Pulse shooting?

10. As you finish *Guiding Families*, what are your thoughts? Your hopes? Your concerns?

"HE HAS TOLD YOU, O MAN, WHAT IS GOOD; AND WHAT DOES THE LORD REQUIRE OF YOU EXCEPT TO BE JUST, AND TO LOVE [AND TO DILIGENTLY PRACTICE] KINDNESS (COMPASSION), AND TO WALK HUMBLY WITH YOUR GOD [SETTING ASIDE ANY OVERBLOWN SENSE OF IMPORTANCE OR SELF-RIGHTEOUSNESS]?"

– MICAH 6:8

JUSTICE INITIATIVE

Lead Them Home is focused on constructing **justice bridges** from the church of Jesus Christ to LGBT+ communities across North America and beyond. Our objective is to eliminate family rejection of LGBT+ loved ones in *this generation*.

We join LGBT+ people with one voice standing against all forms of victimization including bullying, exclusion, and family rejection. Our Justice Initiative will work toward eliminating mistreatment of LGBT+ people. Such trauma can lead to isolation, depression, suicidal ideation, or homelessness.

On the preventative front, we will continue to reach Evangelical leaders and faith communities with our highly credentialed and time-tested Posture Shift Seminar. We will publish resources that launch Posture Shift teaching points into practical application in churches, ministries, families, and homes.

Guiding Families is preserving family relationships and preventing suicides. Posture Shift is making churches more inclusive and safe for LGBT+ people interested in growing in their faith in Christ. These efforts lower family rejection, church exclusion, and mistreatment of LGBT+ people.

Despite these efforts, bullying, teen suicide, and youth homelessness remain victimizing factors impacting LGBT+ people. For this reason, we will work to help hurting people recover from the impact of bullying, depression, suicidality, and homelessness.

One such justice bridge is our construction of an online database of drop-in centers and shelters serving LGBT+ youth. Our website now allows Christians across North America to locate a shelter in their city or within their region. We aim to mobilize free services and supplies for these drop-in centers and shelters.

Christians can cook meals, clean facilities, or volunteer their services, including job placement mentoring; skill development; and assistance with employment, educational, or job training applications. Christians can also assemble and donate survival packs that help homeless LGBT+ youth disguise themselves from predators when stuck on the streets.

Over time, there will emerge many other ideas for serving LGBT+ and Christian organizations positioned to reach vulnerable youth. Such ideas include scholarships that help homeless LGBT+ youth advance toward a college degree and seek a job to pursue personal independence.

We have worked for over a decade to prevent family rejection. We have taught on the statistics of gay youth homelessness and the factors that lead to it. Now, through justice bridges from the church to LGBT+ communities, we will know the young people behind the statistics by name — young people like Crystal, whose story was featured in *Guiding Families* on page 18. We will love them, care for them, pray for them, and lay down our lives helping them recover — all in the name of Jesus Christ.

GET INVOLVED: LEADTHEMHOME.ORG/JUSTICE

info@leadthemhome.org

FROM OUR CHAIRMAN

THERE ARE MANY WAYS TO RESPOND TO LIFE'S MOST challenging events. One of the most difficult issues for parents, relatives, and caregivers is when an individual discloses for the first time that they are gay. The response of parents, relatives, and caregivers is of critical importance.

Knowing how to respond makes an enormous difference to the person who has taken the risk to disclose.

This publication gives clear and thoughtful ways to consider how best to respond. You will read the responses of parents and others who discuss their own reactions to disclosure.

This is an essential publication for everyone who works with individuals and families who are dealing with their own reactions to the discovery that someone they know and love is gay.

Bill Henson and his staff have put together this useful and powerful publication as a tool for parents and professional caregivers.

As a psychologist and a pastor, I find this publication an essential tool for helping families and caregivers respond in a way that will be most helpful. The message of love and care in the context of Christian truth is powerful in maintaining truly redemptive relationships.

The Rev. Dr. Ray Pendleton
Sr. Professor of Counseling, Gordon-Conwell Theological Seminary
Asst. Rector for Pastoral Care, Christ the Redeemer Anglican Church

MISSION

Our mission is to love LGBT+ people in the church.

VISION

Our vision is to increase family acceptance, enhance church inclusion, and nourish faith identity in LGBT+ people.

APPROACH

We train church leaders, guide families, provide care to LGBT+ people, and build justice bridges to serve LGBT+ communities.

JOIN US

Have you or your family, church, or ministry benefited from *Guiding Families?*

Please consider helping us advance gospel work by becoming a financial partner. Give as an individual, business, or organization via check, debit or credit card, or electronic check (ACH) — or consider us for a mutual fund or stock investment.

Start your recurring or one-time gift at **leadthemhome.org/give.**